BBC RADIO 3

The BBC presents the 120th season of Henry Wood Promenade Concerts, broadcasting every Prom live on BBC Radio 3

CW00344484

Clockwise from top left: Henry Wood surveys the bomb damage after an air raid destroys the Queen's Hall in 1941; Marin Alsop conducts at the Last Night of the Proms 2013; Promenaders queue outside the Royal Albert Hall in 1945; a Dalek invades the stage at the Doctor Who Prom 2013

THE PROMS
1895–2014

The Proms brings the best of classical music to a wide audience in an informal and welcoming atmosphere. From the very outset, part of the audience has stood in the central 'promenade' arena. Prom places originally cost just a shilling – similar to today's price of only £5.00. The concerts have always mixed the great classics with what Henry Wood, founder-conductor of the Proms, called his 'novelties' – in other words, rare works and premieres.

1895
The 26-year-old Henry Wood launches the Promenade Concerts with Robert Newman, manager at the newly opened Queen's Hall; Wood conducts the Proms throughout its first 50 years

1914
The 20th season of the Proms opens 11 days after Britain declares war on Germany. In a show of patriotism, a bust of King George V is displayed by Wood's conductor's rostrum and Elgar's 'Land of Hope and Glory' ends the First Night

1927
The BBC takes over the running of the Proms

1930
The new BBC Symphony Orchestra becomes the orchestra of the Proms, later joined by other London orchestras

1939
Proms season abandoned after only three weeks following the declaration of war

1941
The Proms moves to the Royal Albert Hall when the Queen's Hall is gutted by fire after being bombed in an air raid

1947
First televised Last Night of the Proms; first year every concert is broadcast on radio, on the BBC Third Programme

1966
First non-British orchestra at the Proms: the Moscow Radio Orchestra, under Gennady Rozhdestvensky

1971
Three Proms take place away from the Royal Albert Hall: *Boris Godunov* at the Royal Opera House; Beethoven's *Missa solemnis* at Westminster Cathedral; and a concert of contemporary works conducted by Pierre Boulez at the Roundhouse

1996
First Proms Chamber Music series; first Prom in the Park

1998
First Blue Peter Family Prom, signalling a new commitment to events for families

2002
The Proms goes digital on BBC Four; on-demand listening begins online

2003
Proms in the Park reaches out to all four nations of the UK with the unique festival atmosphere of the Last Night

2008
Proms Plus expands to precede every main evening Proms concert; the first Doctor Who Prom brings Daleks to the Royal Albert Hall; the opening weekend includes the first free Prom

2013
Marin Alsop is the first woman to conduct the Last Night of the Proms

BBC PROMS GUIDE 2014 CONTENTS

16

24

32

CONCERT LISTINGS

BOOKING

VENUE INFORMATION

86

STAY INFORMED

Join us on Facebook:
facebook.com/theproms

Follow us on Twitter:
@bbcproms (#bbcproms)

Sign up for our newsletter:
bbc.co.uk/proms

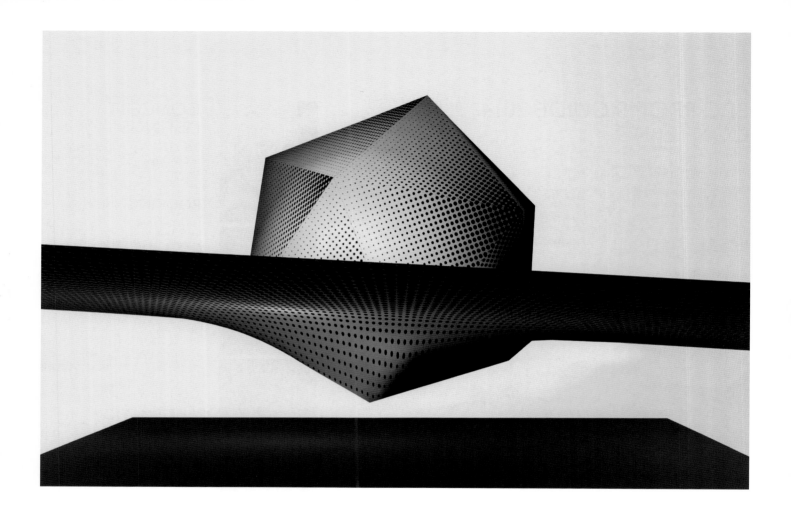

Edge of Sound:

*Dare to take the step with
BBC Concert Orchestra in 2014–15*

BBC Proms – Visions of the New –
Friday Night is Music Night – Edge of Sound

bbc.co.uk/concertorchestra to find out
what's on and sign up to our e-newsletter

BBC National Orchestra & Chorus of Wales

At the BBC Proms 2014

First Night of the Proms: BBC National Chorus of Wales with Sir Andrew Davis **18 July**

Duruflé Requiem with Thierry Fischer **27 July**

Elgar Symphony No 1 with Mark Wigglesworth **6 August**

Nielsen Symphony No 5 with Thomas Søndergård **11 August**

Sibelius Symphony No 5 with Thomas Søndergård **12 August**

"The marvel of this performance – stillness and atmospherics apart – was undoubtedly the fierceness and trenchancy of its rhythmic impulse"
The Arts Desk

0800 052 1812 bbc.co.uk/now @bbcnow

BBC RADIO 3 · BBC cymru wales · Cyngor Celfyddydau Cymru Arts Council of Wales · Noddir gan Lywodraeth Cymru Sponsored by Welsh Government

BRECON · BRISTOL · CARDIFF · MA...
...UDNO · LLANGOLLEN · LONDON · ...
ST DAVIDS · SWANSEA · WORCESTE...

17 JUL – 23 AUG

THE GERSHWINS' PORGY AND BESS

The Gershwins' Porgy and Bess by George Gershwin, DuBose and Dorothy Heyward, and Ira Gershwin Book Adapted by Suzan-Lori Parks Musical Score Adapted by Diedre L. Murray

Photos: Pride and Prejudice 2013 David Jensen

2014 SEASON ALSO INCLUDES:

15 May – 07 Jun
ALL MY SONS
By Arthur Miller

12 Jun – 12 Jul
HOBSON'S CHOICE
By Harold Brighouse

21 Jun – 12 Jul
TWELFTH NIGHT
RE-IMAGINED FOR EVERYONE AGED SIX AND OVER

By William Shakespeare

28 Aug – 13 Sep
TO KILL A MOCKINGBIRD
Adapted for the stage by Christopher Sergel

Based on the novel by Harper Lee

Backing our most precious resources.

The arts.

The arts are something our nation does brilliantly. No wonder millions of visitors fill UK art galleries, theatres and concert halls. It's an integral part of our culture that helps promote us to the rest of the world. That's why we've been helping to support institutions such as the Royal Opera House, Tate Britain, the National Portrait Gallery and the British Museum for more than 35 years. Over the past 5 years, nearly 10 million people have experienced a BP supported event and we will continue to help bring what the UK does so well to a wider audience.

Find out more at facebook.com/bp

Inspiration with Every Note

WELCOME TO THE
2014 BBC PROMS

It's a great pleasure to welcome you to the 2014 BBC Proms. Though this year marks our 120th season, the vision of the festival has remained the same since its inception – namely, to bring the best classical music to the largest possible audience. The Proms has always sought to build new audiences. This can be clearly seen in our ticket prices, not least our Promming (standing) tickets, which this year are held at £5 for the ninth year running. Without the support of the BBC – through you, the licence-fee payers – this extraordinary value for money would not be possible. Our mission to create the widest access to classical music has also been helped enormously by the growth of technology since the BBC took over the running of the Proms in 1927. The audience for the Proms is now genuinely international and it is the global classical music world that we celebrate in welcoming more international orchestras than ever before to the Proms (and indeed to the UK) this summer.

We have begun to understand the increasingly important role that classical music is playing in countries such as Brazil and Venezuela, and orchestras from these countries have made exciting appearances at the Proms in recent years. We also recognise the power of music to bring nations and people together and this year's appearance by the West–Eastern Divan Orchestra under Daniel Barenboim will be another reminder of the unique possibilities that music brings to promote understanding across traditional borders.

So I am delighted that, alongside our more regular orchestral visitors from across Europe and the USA, we are able to welcome ensembles from Australia, China, Greece, Iceland, Lapland, Qatar, South Korea, Singapore and Turkey. Many of these groups will be bringing repertoire from their

Clockwise from top left: John Wilson returns with his orchestra to perform Cole Porter's *Kiss Me, Kate* (Prom 21); singer-songwriter Paloma Faith makes her Proms debut, alongside the Guy Barker Orchestra (Prom 65); Han-Na Chang, cellist and conductor, directs the Qatar Philharmonic Orchestra's Proms debut (Prom 67)

nations and it is a pleasure to introduce them and their international soloists, often with new works, to the Proms. The range of what orchestras offer is remarkable and their artistic health is testimony to their determination to produce high-quality performances, not least within often trying circumstances, both social and financial. There is huge excitement among these orchestras around their visits and I know that they will receive a warm welcome from our audiences.

Almost half of the Proms in the Royal Albert Hall are given by our BBC orchestras and I cannot remember a time when such flourishing and exciting partnerships have existed in these groups. Without these orchestras, the BBC Singers and the two BBC choruses, planning the Proms on this scale would not be as creative and distinctive. It would also be impossible to keep exploring new programming ideas without the dedication and hard work of the Proms team.

In addition to the feast of music from abroad, we have in recent years celebrated British music. We continue that momentum not least by honouring two fine living composers both celebrating their 80th birthdays this year. The music of Sir Harrison Birtwistle and Sir Peter Maxwell Davies is featured this summer as is that by Walton, another knighted Lancastrian!

We also mark the 150th anniversary of the birth of Richard Strauss. After the success of our big operatic projects last summer – not least Wagner's complete *Ring* cycle – it is exciting to present three of Strauss's operatic masterpieces: *Elektra*, *Der Rosenkavalier* and *Salome*. There is also the staging of a non-operatic work when Sir Simon Rattle and the Berlin Philharmonic are among the musicians to present Peter Sellars's realisation of Bach's *St Matthew Passion*.

Bach's other great Passion setting, the *St John*, is conducted by Sir Roger Norrington, one of our British conductors celebrating significant birthdays this year. Sir Roger (80) will, like Sir Andrew Davis (70), conduct two Proms, while Donald Runnicles (60) conducts three, and it is a thrill to welcome back Sir Neville Marriner in his 90th-birthday year, with the orchestra he founded, the Academy of St Martin in the Fields, alongside its new Music Director, Joshua Bell.

Sakari Oramo, Chief Conductor of the BBC Symphony Orchestra, will be in charge of the Last Night for the first time (in addition to conducting three other Proms and making his Proms debut as violinist during our lunchtime Proms Chamber Music series), and there are two Proms each conducted by Jiří Bělohlávek, Semyon Bychkov, Riccardo Chailly and Valery

Clockwise from above left: The Proms' 150th-anniversary celebrations of Richard Strauss's birth includes three complete operas; *War Horse* puppets from the National Theatre's award-winning production mark 100 years since the start of the 1914–18 conflict; Riccardo Chailly conducts two Proms with the Leipzig Gewandhaus Orchestra

Gergiev. On the penultimate night, Chailly leads his orchestra and choir from Leipzig in the annual Proms performance of Beethoven's 'Choral' Symphony; Gergiev brings the World Orchestra of Peace, helping to mark the centenary of the start of the First World War. Among the other concerts honouring that anniversary are the War Horse Prom, in which the extraordinary puppets from the National Theatre's acclaimed production make an appearance alongside the Proms debut of Gareth Malone and the Proms Military Wives Choir.

There are more debuts too. Look out for the first ever CBeebies and BBC Sport Proms, and first appearances at the Proms by Paloma Faith, the Pet Shop Boys and Rufus Wainwright, as well as other special Late Night Proms including Laura Mvula hosting her first solo appearance.

Look out for the first ever CBeebies and BBC Sport Proms, and first appearances by Paloma Faith, the Pet Shop Boys and Rufus Wainwright.

All this and Cole Porter's take on *The Taming of the Shrew* in *Kiss Me, Kate*, the now eagerly awaited annual appearance of John Wilson and his orchestra; the wide-ranging and attractive Proms Chamber Music and Proms Saturday Matinee series at Cadogan Hall; an array of commissions and premieres, including two of the last works by the late John Tavener; and star soloists such as Janine Jansen and Roderick Williams on the Last Night.

As ever, all the Proms are broadcast live on BBC Radio 3 and our selected broadcasts on other BBC networks continue this year, as Radio 1, Radio 2 and Radio 5 live join in the mix. There are 28 televised Proms, a remarkable commitment from our TV colleagues to bring the Proms to an ever expanding audience. This summer will see the Proms available on more digital platforms than ever before, offering audiences new ways to consume the range of Proms content. So, wherever you are and however you choose to listen and watch, I hope you enjoy the 2014 BBC Proms. •

Roger Wright

Roger Wright
Director, BBC Proms

BBC
SCOTTISH SYMPHONY ORCHESTRA

Chief Conductor: Donald Runnicles
Principal Guest Conductor: Ilan Volkov
Associate Guest Conductor: Andrew Manze
Artist-In-Association: Matthias Pintscher

DISCOVER:
the 2014/15 Season at Glasgow City Halls

Shostakovich Symphonies 5,10,15

Sweet Harmony: Shakespeare and Music

Donald Runnicles's 60th Birthday Concert

James MacMillan Piano Concerto Cycle with Peter Donohoe

Wozzeck in Concert

Plus concerts in Aberdeen, Ayr, Edinburgh, Inverness and Perth, and on BBC Radio 3.

BBC SSO at the BBC Proms :

Prom 23: Mozart's Requiem
Prom 24: Mahler 9
Prom 39: Ein Heldenleben
Prom 42: Vaughan Williams' 'Pastoral' Symphony

bbc.co.uk/bbcsso

David Hill

James MacMillan

Join the BBC Singers as they celebrate their 90th anniversary with a stunning series of concerts featuring the very best of choral music from the Renaissance to the twenty-first century. Hear them in venues across London, the UK and beyond, on BBC Radio 3 and online.

BBC SINGERS

BBC SINGERS AT 90

O Duo

Photos: James MacMillan - Philip Gatward; BBC Singers - Sophie Laslett; O Duo - Gillan McBain; David Hill – John Wood.

BBC Singers

MILTON COURT

The BBC Singers return to Milton Court Concert Hall for a second season of concerts including delectable French songs with Chief Conductor David Hill, James MacMillan conducting his own music, and Thomas Tallis's magnificent Spem in alium. Guests include virtuoso percussionists O Duo and cellist Nicolas Altstaedt.

SINGERS AT SIX

Four concerts in the atmospheric surroundings of St Giles' Cripplegate, each complementing the BBC Symphony Orchestra's Barbican concert the same evening. A 90th anniversary concert of pieces written for the BBC Singers, music from Poland and Leipzig, and Renaissance works from Spain and England.

ST PAUL'S KNIGHTSBRIDGE

A series of free concerts in the Victorian splendour of St Paul's Knightsbridge, featuring a wide range of glorious choral music.

All concerts are broadcast on BBC Radio 3 and streamed online.

bbc.co.uk/singers for full details of all events, including our exciting learning events, to sign up for our free e-newsletter and to book tickets.

@BBCsingers
facebook.com/BBCSingers

'Clean-edged tone and impeccable musicianship.'
The Guardian

BBC RADIO 3:

EDINBURGH INTERNATIONAL FESTIVAL

8–31 August 2014

'jewel in the nation's artistic crown'

THE SUNDAY TIMES

Don't miss the unmissable... book your trip and join us

Berlioz Les Troyens with the Mariinsky Opera and Valery Gergiev / Czech Philharmonic and Jiří Bělohlávek / **Royal Concertgebouw Orchestra and Mariss Jansons** / András Schiff / **Rossini William Tell** / Rotterdam Philharmonic Orchestra and Yannick Nézet-Séguin / **Nicola Benedetti** / Paul Lewis / **Teatro Regio Torino and Gianandrea Noseda** / Britten Owen Wingrave / **Daniil Trifonov** / Ute Lemper / **Kronos Quartet** / Jordi Savall / **Harry Partch Delusion of the Fury** / The Sixteen / **Leonidas Kavakos** / Britten War Requiem / **Heiner Goebbels** / Ladysmith Black Mambazo / **Melbourne Symphony Orchestra** / Bernarda Fink / **Collegium Vocale Gent and Philippe Herreweghe** / Erin Wall…

View the full programme and book online at eif.co.uk #EdintFest

Call 0131 473 2000 for a free copy of the Festival brochure.

Supported by the City of Edinburgh Council and Creative Scotland. Charity No SC004694

EXTRAORDINARILY TALENTED PEOPLE

f www.facebook.com/royalcollegeofmusic

t www.twitter.com/rcmlatest

You Tube www.youtube.com/RCMLondon

ROYAL COLLEGE OF MUSIC, LONDON

020 7591 4300

www.rcm.ac.uk

INSIDE THE HEAD OF
RICHARD STRAUSS

A champion of progressive tone-poems and bloody operas who turned later in life to serene Romantic lyricism, a composer first courted then dismissed by the Nazi Party, Richard Strauss remains an enigma 150 years after his birth. As the Proms features three of his complete operas, among other works, **TIM ASHLEY** attempts to probe the composer's psyche

Time, that 'strange thing' of which the Marschallin speaks so eloquently in *Der Rosenkavalier*, was not always kind to Richard Strauss. In December 1948, nine months before his death, he told his friend and biographer Willi Schuh that he felt he had outlived himself. The *Four Last Songs*, his last major score, which records his love for his wife Pauline in the face of encroaching mortality, had been completed the previous September. Strauss was aware that his glory days at the forefront of Western music were long gone, and that subsequent generations had come to consider his work anachronistic. And, despite his official de-Nazification the previous June, his decision to remain, work and, for 18 months, hold public office in Hitler's Germany had resulted in charges of collaboration that were not going to go away.

Since then, of course, much has changed, though he remains controversial. The best of his music, rarely out of favour despite his fluctuating reputation, seems as fresh, startling and challenging as it always did.

The frequently voiced criticism that his output from *Der Rosenkavalier* (1909–10) onwards constitutes a rejection of modernist ideals in favour of a return to post-Romanticism has been challenged by a re-examination of the degree to which subject dictates both style and harmonic complexity in his music. And our awareness of the intimidation to which the Nazis subjected Strauss and his family from 1938 onwards has immeasurably deepened our understanding of the tragic complexity of his relationship with the Third Reich.

Relating the music to the man, however, has never been easy. The emotional immediacy of his work sits awkwardly with conventional ideas of Strauss as a bourgeois type, happily married if henpecked, with a watchful eye on his bank balance and a marked fondness for status and kudos. He was among the first composers to function under the glare of modern journalism, and seemingly enjoyed the scrutiny and speculation that initially raged about his life, work and finances. He was also one of the last great composers to spend his

formative years under the German system of aristocratic patronage, reaching the highest position (the conductorship of the Berlin Court Opera) in the recently formed Empire, despite Wilhelm II's open dislike of his work. His decision, in 1933, to accept the presidency of Goebbels's *Reichsmusikkammer* – the body promoting 'good German music' – was, in part, the result of his catastrophic equating of totalitarian policy with the monarchical system under which he had been trained to function. The Nazis dismissed him in 1935 after the Gestapo intercepted a letter to his then librettist, the Austrian-Jewish writer Stefan Zweig, which was critical of the regime.

As a man Strauss was emotionally secretive. His voluminous correspondence always tells us what he thinks, but rarely how he feels. Throughout his life he largely kept quiet about his childhood, presenting it, on occasion, as essentially happy, though it was sometimes far from being so. His father, Franz, was the principal horn player at the Munich Court Opera; his mother, Josephine,

STRAUSS'S HEROINES
Portraits of passion and despair

Throughout his life Strauss was fascinated by the female voice and the female psyche. His wife, Pauline, for whom many of his early songs were written, was a well-known dramatic soprano, and noted as a prima donna off-stage as well as on. After her retirement a series of now-legendary sopranos – Maria Jeritza, Lotte Lehmann, Rose Pauly, Elisabeth Schumann – also fired Strauss's musical imagination. He had a notable dislike of tenors, whom he once termed 'a disease', and many of his sympathetic male protagonists are played either by baritones, such as Barak in *Die Frau ohne Schatten*, or, following the example of Cherubino in Mozart's *The Marriage of Figaro*, by sopranos or mezzos in drag, such as Octavian in *Der Rosenkavalier* and the Composer in *Ariadne auf Naxos*. His female protagonists, meanwhile, are among the most complex in opera.

Salome and *Elektra* are both sometimes described in terms of Freudian psychopathology. We have no evidence, however, that Strauss was familiar with Freud's work, and both operas should be seen as contemporaneous developments along similar lines. *Salome* is based on Oscar Wilde's eponymous 1891 play. Salome is a corrupted innocent in a decadent world, whose sudden desire for the chaste, fanatically severe Jokanaan (John the Baptist) results in a catastrophic sexual awakening. She defines her experience as 'love' throughout the opera, allowing the emotion its name in a setting in which it is otherwise never mentioned. Strauss takes her at her word, forging a curious empathy with his heroine as her vocal line blossoms into an exultant lyricism. But the rending dissonances that underpin her utterances are a constant reminder of both the violence of her feelings and their nightmarish consequences in the real world in which she moves.

Elektra reworks Greek tragedy in terms of psychodrama and portrays three women locked in a repressive co-dependency. Electra's obsession with avenging her father's death erodes the sanity of her murderous mother Clytemnestra and prevents her sister Chrysothemis from finding the fulfilment she craves with a husband and children. The score is eruptive and Dionysian, its harmonic range daringly wide, whether depicting Electra's obsession or Clytemnestra's mental collapse. Chrysothemis's single-mindedness, in contrast, is designated by rapturous lyricism.

Lyricism predominates in *Der Rosenkavalier*, which inhabits a radically different world, though one which is also viewed through female eyes. The Marschallin – beautiful but no longer young, and married to a largely absentee husband – realises that her affair

Poster for a 'Richard Strauss Week' in Munich, 1910, which featured performances of both *Elektra* and *Salome*

with the teenage Octavian must end 'today, tomorrow or the day after', after he falls in love with a girl his own age. The librettist Hofmannsthal described her as the figure with whom the audience 'feel and move'. In a comedy of manners and class pretensions, she alone is conscious of the passing of time, and her awareness of its effect on human relationships dictates the opera's bittersweet tone and often unbearable poignancy.

Strauss took a provocative delight in portraying bodily reactions to desire with an explicitness that can still startle.

The amorous hero Don Juan allows himself to be killed in a duel: a colourful life captured with rapier-sharp vividness in Strauss's tone-poem of 1888–9

was a member of an affluent family of brewers. Franz fostered his son's talent by any means he could, but his views were reactionary: a Classicist at heart, he adored Mozart and Beethoven, but was violently opposed to the experimentalism of Liszt and Wagner, despite the latter's admiration for his playing. Strauss's musical education, undertaken by his father's colleagues, was informal and practical, but what often passed for encouragement on Franz's part was carping criticism and relentless fault-finding.

The wars of attrition that developed between father and son worsened when, as a young adult, Strauss became increasingly drawn to the progressive composers his father despised. Josephine, meanwhile, whose own family background was abusive, gradually developed symptoms of mental illness that on several occasions necessitated admission to a sanatorium. It is not coincidental that *Don Juan* (1888–9), the score that made Strauss famous as an orchestral composer, is based on a play in which the sensualist hero defines himself in opposition to his unseen but repressive father, nor that *Salome* (1903–5) and *Elektra* (1906–8), his first major operatic successes, depict the female psyche in extreme crisis.

Don Juan ushers in the great series of tone-poems that have remained core-repertoire works since their first performances more than a century ago. The term 'tone-poem' (*Tondichtung* in German) was Strauss's coinage, first used of his own *Macbeth* (1888, revised 1890–91). The style is usually described as 'post-Wagnerian', which is in many ways accurate, but also limiting. The influence of Liszt's flamboyant symphonic poems is equally apparent, though Strauss's deployment of vast orchestral forces to create dynamic and textural gradations of immense subtlety is very much his own.

Liszt's stress on pictoralism, however, gives way in Strauss to an emphasis on psychological portraiture, and it is only in *Tod und Verklärung* (1888–9) and *Also sprach Zarathustra* (1896) that he adopts free-flowing Listzian form. Whatever the tensions in Strauss's relationship with his father, his appreciation of the latter's Classicism was genuine. Throughout his life, he admired Mozart above all other composers. And the extravagance of many of the tone-poems – *Don Juan* and *Ein Heldenleben* (1897–8) among them – is held in check by their being rooted in Classical structure.

Don Juan was a seminal work in a number of ways. It re-introduced an eroticism into music that the 19th-century Romantics had avoided despite their emphasis on passion. Sex in Wagner is fundamentally a striving of souls towards mystical union. Strauss, who never cared for metaphysics, took a provocative delight in portraying bodily

Actor and dancer Maud Allan, transfixed by her reward, in her own dance version of Oscar Wilde's controversially lurid *Salome* (1907), on which Strauss's opera is based

reactions to desire with an explicitness that can still startle. The Lothario Don Juan himself, meanwhile, is the prototype of a figure whom we repeatedly meet in Strauss's output – the rebellious, amoral individualist, whose identity is slowly defined in opposition to normative social structures that eventually prove destructive.

Strauss's protagonists, in the tone-poems above all, have much in common with the *Übermensch* ('Superman') types of Nietzsche's philosophy, which Strauss later claimed was the most important intellectual influence in his life, though we should remember that Strauss did not discover Nietzsche until well after *Don Juan*'s completion. The Straussian parabola of assertion and collapse, meanwhile, can be found in the prankster Till Eulenspiegel's eventual punishment at the hands of the bourgeoisie whom he mocks, and in the anonymous (if autobiographical) hero of *Ein Heldenleben*, who withdraws from the world after his battles with his enemies end in stalemate. It is also true of Salome, whose sexual extremism in an already decadent society has fatal consequences.

Like the major tone-poems, *Salome*, *Elektra* and *Der Rosenkavalier* have never been out of the repertoire. *Salome* and *Elektra* are often bracketed together as works constructed round a central female protagonist, whose psychological disorder is presented in terms of the kind of aggressively modernist sound-world that Strauss is supposed to have eventually rejected. The equation of violent dissonance with extreme psychology became integral to

Librettist Hugo von Hofmannsthal (1874–1929), who collaborated with Strauss on *Elektra* and *Der Rosenkavalier*, among other operas

Sarah Connolly as the Marschallin's toy boy, Octavian, in English National Opera's 2012 revival of *Der Rosenkavalier*, directed and designed by Sir David McVicar

the apparatus of 20th-century opera. Strauss, however, unlike Schoenberg, was no theorist, and though pragmatism seems a curious quality to associate with such searing music, the harmonic and orchestral structure of both works derive from a practical need to find a musical language appropriate to the subject.

Elektra and *Der Rosenkavalier*, meanwhile, also form the first products of Strauss's long collaboration with the Austrian writer Hugo von Hofmannsthal. Hofmannsthal was able to cater for the Classicist in Strauss as well as the post-Romantic, often bringing both elements into alignment. At once contemporary and Sophoclean, *Elektra* deploys both a taut symphonic structure and the Aristotelian unities of time, place and action to constrain a convulsive yet probing exploration of obsessive violence and sexual repression. *Der Rosenkavalier*, in marked contrast, places

post-Wagnerian developments at the service of a bittersweet Mozartian comedy conceived, in part, as a sequel to *The Marriage of Figaro*, that examines, with astonishing poignancy, the relationship between sex and love, and the inevitable effect of time and change on human affairs. In his lifetime, Strauss was never to replicate its success, and it is only recently that his later stage works have begun to be fully appreciated and understood.

'I may not be a first-rate composer,' Strauss remarked in 1947, with the characteristic self-deprecation that marked some of his later utterances, 'but I am a first-class second-rate composer.' Time has, however, placed him in the front rank. This year's anniversary allows us to hear him again, to re-examine the complexities of his life and art, and, above all, to admire his greatness. ●

Tim Ashley has written on music and opera for *The Guardian* for 18 years and is the author of a biography of Richard Strauss.

RICHARD STRAUSS AT THE PROMS

Burleske; Tod und Verklärung
PROM 34 • 11 AUGUST

Deutsche Motette; Festival Prelude;
Four Last Songs
PROM 19 • 31 JULY

Die Frau ohne Schatten –
symphonic fantasia
PROM 4 • 20 JULY

Don Juan
PROM 44 • 19 AUGUST

Eight Poems from 'Letzte Blätter';
Four Songs, Op. 27 – Nos. 1, 3 & 4
PROMS CHAMBER MUSIC 5
18 AUGUST

Elektra
PROM 59 • 31 AUGUST

Ein Heldenleben
PROM 39 • 15 AUGUST

Metamorphosen (arr. R. Leopold)
PROMS CHAMBER MUSIC 6
25 AUGUST

Der Rosenkavalier
PROM 6 • 22 JULY

Salome
PROM 58 • 30 AUGUST

Suite in B flat major for
13 wind instruments
PROMS CHAMBER MUSIC 3
4 AUGUST

Taillefer
PROM 76 • 13 SEPTEMBER

Till Eulenspiegels lustige Streiche
PROM 5 • 21 JULY

RICHARD STRAUSS

21

SO BBC Symphony Orchestra

Concerts 2014–15
bbc.co.uk/symphonyorchestra

Join the BBC Symphony Orchestra at the Barbican for a thrillingly wide-ranging season of concerts featuring a unique mix of classics, opera and the very best of new music.

SAKARI ORAMO CONDUCTS NIELSEN

In his second season as Chief Conductor, Sakari Oramo conducts all six symphonies by Carl Nielsen. Expect unmissable concerts filled with elemental forces and pure energy.

OPERA

The dark splendour of Bartók's *Duke Bluebeard's Castle*, Smetana's tragedy *Dalibor* conducted by Jiří Bělohlávek, and the UK premiere of Unsuk Chin's magical *Alice in Wonderland*.

THE SOUND OF CHAPLIN

Live accompaniment of Chaplin films including *Shoulder Arms* and *Easy Street*, with scores by Neil Brand, Timothy Brock and Chaplin himself.

ARTIST IN ASSOCIATION: BRETT DEAN

Music by the BBC SO's new Artist in Association including trumpet concerto *Dramatis personae* performed by Håkan Hardenberger and *The Last Days of Socrates* with Sir John Tomlinson.

BBC SINGERS AT 90

The BBC Singers celebrate their 90th anniversary with a world premiere by Kevin Volans, music by Bach and Bruckner and concerts in St Giles' Cripplegate.

TOTAL IMMERSION & SUPERB NEW MUSIC

Total Immersion days remembering visionary composer John Tavener, marking the 90th birthday of Pierre Boulez and digging into the wonderful world of percussion. Premieres from composers including Thomas Larcher, Albert Schnelzer and Ryan Wigglesworth.

Follow us to the Barbican in September.
bbc.co.uk/symphonyorchestra for full details and to sign up to our free e-newsletter.

barbican
Associate Orchestra

Box Office: 020 7638 8891
barbican.org.uk

Follow us: twitter.com/bbcso
facebook.com/bbcso

BBC RADIO 3

BBC Symphony Chorus

Join us

One of the country's finest and most distinctive amateur choirs, the BBC Symphony Chorus enjoys the highest broadcast profile of any non-professional choir in the UK. In its appearances with the BBC Symphony Orchestra at the Barbican and BBC Proms, where it is the resident choir, the Chorus performs a wide range of exciting and challenging large-scale works.

Appearances at this year's BBC Proms include performances of Rachmaninov's choral symphony *The Bells* with Edward Gardner and Stravinsky's *Oedipus Rex* under Chief Conductor Sakari Oramo, as well as the iconic Last Night of the Proms. Following on from performances of Elgar's *The Apostles* and *The Dream of Gerontius* at the Barbican in April, the BBC SO and Chorus will reunite with Sir Andrew Davis at the First Night of the Proms to perform Elgar's *The Kingdom*.

Would you like to join us?

If you are an experienced choral singer who would like to work on new and challenging music, as well as key choral works, then the BBC Symphony Chorus would like to hear from you. Membership is free!

To find out more about the Chorus, including details of upcoming auditions, visit **bbc.co.uk/symphonychorus** or contact the Chorus Administrator by email at bbcsc@bbc.co.uk or telephone on 020 7765 4715.

Photo: Mark Allan

LEST WE
FORGET

A century after the outbreak of the First World War, the Proms features a range of works reflecting the responses of composers affected, directly or otherwise, by the conflict. **STEPHEN JOHNSON** discovers that, like the fallen soldiers, age has not wearied them

I find it too difficult to give verisimilitude to a world for which this huge bloody trap was all the while set and which childishly didn't know it!

For the novelist Henry James, writing at the end of 1914, it was clear that the changes wrought by the dawning catastrophe of the First World War would be epochal. James's immediate response was creative silence. It says a great deal about the impact of that unprecedented catastrophe that we are only now beginning to understand how the composers of James's time, and afterwards, registered it. In the case of Ralph Vaughan Williams's *Pastoral Symphony* (No. 3, 1916–21), the re-evaluation has been radical. Half a century has passed since the composer's biographer Michael Kennedy suggested that the *Pastoral* was really a 'war requiem', but only now does the message seem to be sinking in. At first we are met – perhaps surprisingly – with a relatively untroubled musical landscape. The *Pastoral Symphony* rarely raises its voice,

its contours roll like the South Downs, the scoring is at times luxuriously easy on the ear. But this landscape is full of ghosts: veiled dissonances convey troubled undercurrents, and at the heart of the nocturnal slow movement a solo trumpet tries, but fails, to sound the 'Last Post' – a memory of a young soldier Vaughan Williams heard practising the bugle on the eve of his being posted to France. Did that boy survive? Countless others didn't. For a moment the music registers the visceral shock of that thought.

The *Pastoral Symphony* was never billed as being 'anti-war'. The English composer Frank Bridge's cello concerto *Oration* (1930), however, is exactly that. A pacifist, Bridge poured all his anger and despair about the conflict and its consequences into this

one-movement masterpiece. Strikingly, *Oration* was largely ignored when it first appeared and it has only recently started to gain the attention it deserves. Bridge's pacifism, and his *Oration* in particular, did make a strong impression on the composer's brilliant pupil Benjamin Britten – of whom more later.

Holst conceived his one major hit, *The Planets*, between 1914 and 1917. Incredibly, 'Mars, the Bringer of War' was composed in 1914, before the outbreak of war.

Did the young Britten also make a connection with another important work by a composer he much admired, Gustav Holst? Holst conceived his one major hit, *The Planets*, between 1914 and 1917. Incredibly, 'Mars, the Bringer of War' was composed in 1914, before the outbreak of war. This music has accompanied scenes of mechanised mass carnage in countless documentaries and TV dramas; yet when Holst composed it, 'warfare' for most people would have meant old-

Robert Hunt Library/Mary Evans Picture Library

FIRST WORLD WAR CENTENARY | 25

WIGMORE HALL

2014–2015

SEPTEMBER 2014 – JULY 2015 WIGMORE SERIES

JOYCE DIDONATO & SIR ANTONIO PAPPANO | ALINA IBRAGIMOVA & CÉDRIC TIBERGHIEN | SIR THOMAS ALLEN
ENSEMBLE INTERCONTEMPORAIN | JOSHUA BELL | DMITRI HVOROSTOVSKY | THE SIXTEEN | ANDRÁS SCHIFF
NASH ENSEMBLE | SANDRINE PIAU | ALBAN GERHARDT | IAN BOSTRIDGE | MARTIN FRÖST | FRANCO FAGIOLI
AUGUSTIN HADELICH | ANTHONY MARWOOD | IMOGEN COOPER | PAUL LEWIS | CHRISTOPH PRÉGARDIEN
VOX LUMINIS | FLORIAN BOESCH | SIMON KEENLYSIDE & EMANUEL AX | HAGEN QUARTET | CAROLYN SAMPSON
TAKÁCS QUARTET | ENSEMBLE MODERN | KRISTIAN BEZUIDENHOUT | ANDREAS SCHOLL | JORDI SAVALL
JEAN-GUIHEN QUEYRAS & ALEXANDER MELNIKOV | MARIA JOÃO PIRES | FREIBURG BAROQUE ORCHESTRA
HILLIARD ENSEMBLE | IGOR LEVIT | SONIA PRINA | MAX EMANUEL CENČIĆ | CHRISTIAN GERHAHER | JACK QUARTET
ARDITTI QUARTET | DOROTHEA RÖSCHMANN & MITSUKO UCHIDA | MATTHIAS GOERNE | PAVEL HAAS QUARTET
MONTEVERDI CHOIR AND ORCHESTRA | GERALD FINLEY | ALICE COOTE | LE CONCERT SPIRITUEL & HERVÉ NIQUET

EUROPE'S LEADING VENUE FOR CHAMBER MUSIC, EARLY MUSIC AND SONG

ONLINE BOOKING: WWW.WIGMORE-HALL.ORG.UK · BOX OFFICE: 020 7935 2141
SIGN UP TO OUR E-LIST: WWW.WIGMORE-HALL.ORG.UK/E-LIST

DIRECTOR: JOHN GILHOOLY · 36 WIGMORE STREET, LONDON W1U 2BP · REGISTERED CHARITY NO: 1024838

Supported using public funding by
ARTS COUNCIL ENGLAND

> Butterworth could hardly have guessed that he would soon be one of Housman's 'lads in their hundreds' who would 'die in their glory and never grow old'.

fashioned infantry and cavalry charges: tanks weren't used in combat until 1915. The nightmare futuristic visions of socialist friends such as the novelist H. G. Wells would have coloured his vision, but none of that explains the brutal, inhuman intensity of 'Mars' – against which the escape into inner worlds in the final 'Neptune, the Mystic' now sounds very like an agonised reaction.

Like Frank Bridge, the Italian Alfredo Casella was a non-combatant. But that didn't prevent him from confronting the issues directly in his *Elegia eroica* ('Heroic Elegy') in 1916. Dedicated 'to the unknown soldier', it is essentially an anguished funeral march for large orchestra, haunted by memories of a mother singing a lullaby to her dead son. The message and meaning are clear enough here. But what about Rudi Stephan's *Music for Orchestra* (1912)? Knowing that this very promising young German composer was killed on the Galician front in 1915 adds poignancy to this moving, elegiac work. But is there an element of prophecy here, however oblique? Or is this music firmly rooted in a world still innocently unaware that Henry James's 'huge bloody trap' was waiting round the corner? When George Butterworth made his settings of poems from A. E. Housman's treasured collection *A Shropshire Lad*, Housman's lyrical, musically suggestive nostalgia for a lost

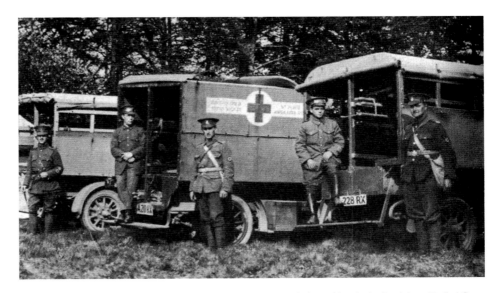

Vaughan Williams (*far right*) in Ecoivres, France (1916), serving as an ambulance driver in the Royal Army Medical Corps

and largely imaginary English Eden would almost certainly have been the main attraction. Butterworth could hardly have guessed that he would soon be one of the poet's 'lads in their hundreds' who would 'die in their glory and never grow old'. Young English men had died in conflict in every generation before the First World War, and Housman wouldn't have needed to be a prophet to sense that it would happen again. But it's hard to hear Butterworth's setting without a kind of premonitory shudder on his behalf: he was killed at the Battle of the Somme in 1916.

A few months later, Australian-born Frederick Septimus Kelly also died on the Somme, not long after the completion of his *Elegy* 'in memoriam Rupert Brooke' (1915–16) for strings and harp. Kelly is said to have begun composing his *Elegy* on a French hospital ship in the Mediterranean as his friend, the poet Brooke, lay dying nearby.

Kelly was present at Brooke's burial among olive trees on the island of Skyros. 'For the whole day I was oppressed with the sense of loss,' he wrote, 'but when the officers and men had gone … then the sense of tragedy gave place to a sense of passionless beauty, engendered both by the poet and the place.' Both qualities – 'tragedy' yielding ultimately to 'passionless beauty' – radiate from the heart of this beautiful, dignified piece.

Unlike Butterworth and Kelly, the composer and poet Ivor Gurney (1890–1937) survived combat, despite the horrific experience of being gassed at Passchendaele. Gurney had shown signs of mental instability some time before the war. Those who were close to him said that the experience of serving in the army initially gave him a sense of structure and purpose that he'd previously lacked. But after the war his balance of mind deteriorated and he was declared insane in 1922.

BALM FOR THE SOUL

Michael Trimble explores why we turn to music in times of crisis

In *The Republic*, Plato argued that music written in most modes (or scales) should be banned. He was afraid that it might arouse the passions, disturb the power of reasoning, and lead to an undermining of social order. This sentiment has been echoed down the ages — especially by some religious authorities, fearing that music may induce disorder and lasciviousness. These concerns prove one thing: that music arouses emotion, it moves us. (The word 'emotion' derives from the Latin *movere* – 'move'.) Being moved by music is, like shedding tears in response to our emotions, an exclusively human attribute, and the two go together. Both are involved in how we as human beings respond to certain life events.

All human societies use music for special occasions, and its role at times of crisis — such as during war or bereavement — has been written about since the beginning of human cultures. There is something very special about group activities: singing or playing instruments together, or moving together (as in dancing), unifies our feelings and are immediate social coalescents. Powerful, warlike strains are one aspect of music's ability to move us, to incite energy and enmity against others. But we so often also turn to music to try to make sense of things when all around us is falling apart. The feelings aroused by the beauty of music leave us literally choked: they are beyond words. As humans, our highly developed sense of compassion — and the

associated feelings of yearning brought on by loss — are fed and quelled by music. Music and tears go together: 90% of people in one study reported 'shivers down the spine' and 80% confessed to crying after listening to music. Most people experience the release of tears in such settings as cathartic. Music activates certain brain structures that are linked with positive feelings, and it also aligns physiological activities such as breathing, the heart rate and other aspects of our autonomic (or involuntary) nervous system — not only in individuals but also among people listening to music together.

The feelings stirred by music are those that are typically deeply embedded within us — ranging from when in childhood we 'mourn' the separation from our mother, to the sense of bereavement followed by the tragedy of loss. The same feelings arise from the consequences of war, and it is little surpirse that, like music, they are ineffable and epiphanic. As Alexander Pope expressed in his St Cecilia's Day ode: 'Music the fiercest grief can charm, / And Fate's severest rage disarm: / Music can soften pain to ease, / And make despair and madness please.'

Michael Trimble is Emeritus Professor in Behavioural Neurology at the Institute of Neurology. An expert in the perception of artistic experiences, he is a trustee of The Musical Brain and author of Why Humans Like to Cry.

The English idyll in a First World War recruitment poster

Not long before that, Gurney managed to complete – just about – his orchestral *War Elegy* (1920). But the manuscript proved hard to decipher and it's only thanks to the persistent efforts of conductor Mark Finch that we now have a fully performable score. The *War Elegy* is another funeral march, occasionally recalling Elgar, if in a strange, fragmentary fashion – at times it can be like listening to someone trying to recall important events and feelings, but in a confused, not-quite coherent way. The philosopher Friedrich Nietzsche spoke of works which 'bear the imprint of their time like an open wound'. It is hard to think of a more unsettling example than Gurney's *War Elegy* – most unsettling of all, perhaps, in its bleakly perfunctory ending.

In recent times, perhaps not surprisingly, we find composers more prepared to look back and take stock. Sally Beamish's Violin Concerto (1994) was composed after Beamish had been captivated by Erich Maria Remarque's First World War novel *All Quiet on the Western Front*. In one particularly memorable passage, Remarque describes a Russian prisoner playing folk songs on a violin: 'The violin continues alone. In the night it is so thin it sounds frozen.' Against a – for Beamish – unusually harsh orchestral background, the violin, as she tells us, represents 'the lone fragile voice of the soldier'. It is not a comfortable work, but it makes its point trenchantly. By contrast, Roxanna Panufnik's orchestral prelude *Three Paths to Peace* (2008), shows that composers need not always strive, in Hamlet's words, 'to hold a mirror up to nature' – there are other ways to respond artistically to strife. *Three Paths to Peace* celebrates Abraham as the father of the Jewish, Christian and Islamic faiths, and wordlessly cries for reconciliation.

How this will compare with the choral *Requiem Fragments* (2013), by the late John Tavener – to be performed on 4 August, the day on which, 100 years earlier, Britain declared war on Germany – remains to be seen, but the path to peace was always the one Tavener attempted to tread. By the time the composer Gabriel Prokofiev (grandson of the Russian composer Sergey) was born in 1975, the end of the First World War was already practically a lifetime in the past. But, as he proves in his new Violin Concerto, which carries resonances of the 1914–18 conflict, he is another of today's composers who can commemorate even if they can't remember.

Reflecting reality, registering protest, mourning loss, praying for peace – there is

Ivor Gurney in his Gloucester Regiment uniform

one great work that does all that. The conflict and reconciliation between Wilfred Owen's desolate war poetry and the Latin words of the Requiem Mass in Benjamin's Britten *War Requiem* (1961–2) is a remarkable enough fusion in itself. But the music raises it higher still. At the end Britten achieves something unique: as the two male soloists intertwine to the last words of Owen's unfinished poem *Strange Meeting* ('Let us sleep now …') soprano soloist, chorus, boys' choir and orchestra build to a rapturous climax on the words of the committal prayer, 'In paradisum' ('May Angels receive thee into Paradise'). But the vision doesn't last: dissonant questioning bells and hollow choral harmonies also register profound doubt. Hope and unbelief coexist – as both must: even, or perhaps especially, in response to the terrible negation of war. ●

Formerly a critic for both *The Independent* and *The Guardian*, Stephen Johnson writes regularly for *BBC Music Magazine* and is the author of books on Bruckner, Mahler and Wagner. For 14 years he was a presenter of BBC Radio 3's *Discovering Music*.

The BBC presents a four-year season of programmes commemorating the centenary of the First World War, featuring original dramas, documentaries and perspectives across TV, radio and online. For more details, see bbc.co.uk/ww1.

FIRST WORLD WAR-RELATED WORKS AT THE PROMS

Sally Beamish Violin Concerto
London premiere; **Gurney** War Elegy
PROM 20 • 1 AUGUST

Bridge Oration
PROM 38 • 14 AUGUST

Britten War Requiem
PROM 47 • 21 AUGUST

G. Butterworth Six Songs from 'A Shropshire Lad'; **Kelly** Elegy for strings, in memoriam Rupert Brooke; **Stephan** Music for Orchestra (1912); **Vaughan Williams** Pastoral Symphony (No. 3)
PROM 42 • 17 AUGUST

Casella Elegia eroico
PROM 29 • 8 AUGUST

Holst The Planets
PROM 56 • 28 AUGUST

Roxanna Panufnik Three Paths to Peace
European premiere
PROM 4 • 20 JULY

Gabriel Prokofiev Violin Concerto
BBC commission: world premiere
PROM 16 • 29 JULY

Tavener Requiem Fragments
BBC commission: world premiere
PROM 25 • 4 AUGUST

War Horse Prom
Programme to include: Elgar: Two Partsongs, Op. 26 – The Snow; Holst: Ave Maria; plus music by Adrian Sutton from the National Theatre's *War Horse*
PROM 22 • 3 AUGUST

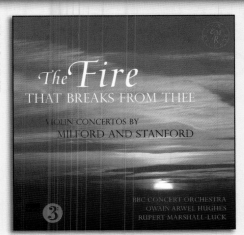

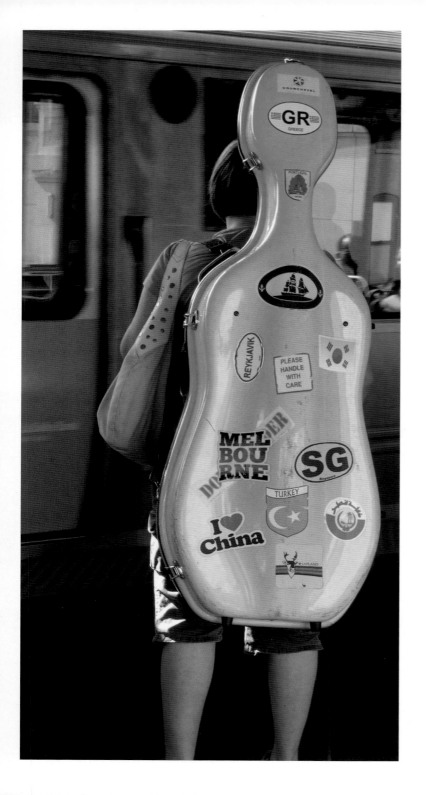

GLOBAL
VISITORS

Nearly 50 years after the first appearance of a non-British orchestra at the Proms, this summer's festival showcases a profusion of ensembles from around the world – many of which, as **FIONA MADDOCKS** explains, have only recently gained visibility in the West

Visiting orchestras are among the brightest of the jewels which adorn the BBC Proms: each year, when the programme is unveiled, many of us rush to scrutinise the list of ensembles from the Old World or the New, from East or West, to see who will enrich our listening this summer. Will they come from Vienna or Berlin, New York or San Francisco, Paris or Rome?

These are still the places predominantly associated with the Western classical tradition. Yet few music-lovers can have missed the explosion of musical life outside the mainstream Euro-American hub. From Venezuela to the Congo, the Middle East to Shanghai, a new era of musical encounters which criss-cross the globe is under way. Orchestras from afar have been appearing at the Proms for almost half a century, but this summer their presence is a central focus.

The **China Philharmonic Orchestra** is the first of the distant visitors, performing under the baton of Long Yu, who co-founded the orchestra in 2000. No strangers to the West, they embarked together on a 22-city tour of Europe and North America in 2005, and Yu himself is one of a number of Chinese musicians who grew up during the Cultural Revolution and who have now returned home, having absorbed the Western canon through studying and working in Europe. In their Prom (19 July) they appear with pianist Haochen Zhang, joint winner of the 2009 Van Cliburn competition, and with Alison Balsom, who gives the UK premiere of a new trumpet concerto by Chinese-born, French-resident Qigang Chen.

Better known to Proms audiences is the **World Orchestra for Peace**, an ensemble which performs only on special, hand-picked occasions and does so here the following night (20 July). Founded in 1995 by Georg Solti to celebrate, as he put it, 'the unique strength of music as an ambassador for peace', it brings together musicians at the peak of their careers from all over the world. The WOP first appeared at the Proms in 2000. Then, as now, it was conducted by Valery Gergiev, who perhaps spoke for all musicians when he said of the orchestra: 'There can be differences … but we are all daughters and sons of world culture.'

Another early visitor is the **Borusan Istanbul Philharmonic Orchestra** (29 July), conducted by Sascha Goetzel, its Viennese Artistic Director and Principal Conductor. Founded in 1999, it complements the longer-established Istanbul State Symphony Orchestra, and is supported by the Borusan industrial conglomerate. After first performing on the European side of the Bosphorus, it now has an enthusiastic following on the Anatolian side too, and since 2003 has been the resident orchestra of the Istanbul International Music Festival. Its Prom includes Balakirev's 'oriental fantasy' *Islamey*, inspired by folk songs from across the Turkish border in the Caucasus, as well as Mozart's take on a Turkish harem, in the overture to *Die Entführung aus dem Serail*.

The next trio of 'global' orchestras arrives in mid-August. The veteran **Melbourne Symphony Orchestra**, Australia's longest-serving professional orchestra, which gave its

Han-Na Chang, cellist, and now Music Director of the Qatar Philharmonic Orchestra, which features both Arab and European musicians

first performance in 1906, may not find it difficult to earn a special place in the hearts of Prommers: its new Chief Conductor is Sir Andrew Davis, a key figure at the Proms while he presided for 11 years (1989–2000) over the BBC Symphony Orchestra. The MSO performs frequently at Arts Centre Melbourne, a distinctive presence on the city's skyline, with its 162-metre spire, but – like most of this year's global visitors – the orchestra will be making its debut in the London landmark that is the Royal Albert Hall.

Having given 10 performances at the Proms since its debut here in 2003, the **West–Eastern Divan Orchestra**, along with its co-founder and conductor Daniel Barenboim, has become a regular fixture. Its story is well known but worth retelling: based in Seville, Spain, the orchestra was founded by Barenboim with his Palestinian friend, the writer Edward Said, to bring together Arab and Israeli musicians as an emblem of peace between nations in conflict. It consists

The Harpa concert hall and conference centre in Reykjavik's eastern harbour: its 1,800-seat concert hall is home to the Iceland Symphony Orchestra

of young musicians from all over the Middle East – Egyptian, Iranian, Israeli, Jordanian, Lebanese, Palestinian and Syrian – as well as Spanish, usually playing Western classical repertoire. On 20 August, it combines Spanish-inspired works by Ravel with two UK premieres, by the Syrian composer Kareem Roustom and by the Jerusalem-born Ayal Adler.

Iceland may have a tiny population – around 320,000, which roughly matches that of Nottingham – but it has a fine orchestra and vibrant musical tradition. The **Iceland Symphony Orchestra**, based in the capital Reykjavik, with its home in the eye-catching new steel-and-glass Harpa concert hall in the city's historic harbour area, is in its 65th season. Ilan Volkov, well known to Proms audiences as Principal Guest Conductor of the BBC Scottish Symphony Orchestra, has been

Sheila Rock/EMI Classics (above left); Arctic Images/Corbis (above right)

An erupting geyser in Iceland's Haukadalur valley, a feature of the landscape that inspired Jón Leifs's *Geysir*, which the Iceland Symphony Orchestra performs at its Proms debut

Chief Conductor since the 2011/12 season. Their Prom (22 August) makes a feature of two Icelandic pieces inspired by the country's spectacular natural landscape: *Geysir* by Jón Leifs (1899–1968) and *Magma* by Haukur Tómasson (born 1960).

Continuing to span all corners of the world, the Proms next reaches out to the Far East, welcoming the orchestras of Seoul (27 August) and Singapore (2 September). Founded in 1948, the **Seoul Philharmonic Orchestra** is South Korea's best-known orchestra, whose Artistic Director is the Seoul-born pianist and conductor Myung-Whun Chung. In recent years he has worked hard to build links with musicians in North Korea in the hope of establishing cultural ties between the two countries. Their Prom includes *Šu*, the Concerto for sheng (traditional Chinese mouth organ) by their compatriot Unsuk Chin.

Established more recently (1979) and with a mission to bridge the musical traditions of Asia and the West, the **Singapore Symphony Orchestra** prides itself on its versatility and ability to embrace eclectic musical styles. On 2 September, conducted by its Music Director since 1997, Lan Shui, it performs Russian works alongside the UK premiere of the Piano Concerto by the Chinese-American composer Zhou Long.

This celebration of global music extends to the Proms Saturday Matinee series at Cadogan Hall. **Armonia Atenea** was set up in 1991 to celebrate the inauguration of Megaron, the new Athens concert hall, where it is resident; on 2 August it performs a programme on the theme of Greek heroes in Baroque opera. The Finnish city of Rovaniemi is a world away from Athens, but it is home to the **Lapland Chamber Orchestra**. The EU's northernmost orchestra performs not only in its own Finnish province, but also acrosss the Arctic region. Its Proms performance is conducted by John Storgårds (also Principal Guest Conductor of the BBC Philharmonic).

This year's final visitor, the **Qatar Philharmonic Orchestra**, has many European players as well as musicians from the Arab region. Its new Music Director is South Korean cellist and conductor Han-Na Chang. The orchestra's stated desire is to perform Western and Arabic classical music 'to inspire the children and adults of Qatar and the Arab world to create and enjoy music'. This year (7 September) it can add Proms listeners to its audience and extend that joyful ambition to the entire world. ●

Chief Music Critic of *The Observer*, Fiona Maddocks was founder-editor of *BBC Music Magazine*. Her book *Harrison Birtwistle: Wild Tracks* is published by Faber in May.

GLOBAL ORCHESTRAS AT THE PROMS

Armonia Atenea/George Petrou
**PROMS SATURDAY MATINEE 1
2 AUGUST**

Borusan Istanbul Philharmonic Orchestra/
Sascha Goetzel
PROM 16 • 29 JULY

China Philharmonic Orchestra/Long Yu
PROM 2 • 19 JULY

Iceland Symphony Orchestra/Ilan Volkov
PROM 48 • 22 AUGUST

Lapland Chamber Orchestra
**PROMS SATURDAY MATINEE 2
9 AUGUST**

Melbourne Symphony Orchestra
PROM 44 • 19 AUGUST

Qatar Philharmonic Orchestra/
Han-Na Chang
PROM 67 • 7 SEPTEMBER

Seoul Philharmonic Orchestra/
Myung-Whun Chung
PROM 55 • 27 AUGUST

Singapore Symphony Orchestra/Lan Shui
PROM 61 • 2 SEPTEMBER

West–Eastern Divan Orchestra/
Daniel Barenboim
PROM 46 • 20 AUGUST

World Orchestra for Peace/Valery Gergiev
PROM 4 • 20 JULY

GLOBAL VISITORS

35

PERFECT MATCH

In a summer that embraces the FIFA World Cup and the Commonwealth Games as well as Wimbledon, the Proms celebrates the relationship between music and sport. **TOM SERVICE** ponders on how these outwardly divergent pursuits are in fact close partners

You might think the outright competitiveness, sheer display of physical prowess and brazen elitism of sport to exist a million miles from the realm of aesthetic contemplation that surrounds classical music. But, when you look at them as socio-cultural phenomena, they are actually rather closely related. Both are about the communion of thousands of people supporting a team of often world-class performers and a community of fans viscerally involved in what they're witnessing, so much so that they sometimes spontaneously voice their appreciation (though, thankfully, less so at the Royal Albert Hall than at Old Trafford).

Both audiences are emotionally committed, both want to see the best from the teams out on the pitch or on the stage, and both are there to will their teams to victory (and the musicians, as much as sportspeople, really do have to conquer superhuman technical demands in, say, a Strauss tone-poem or a Mahler symphony; here, equally, failure is not an option). Then there's the more abstract desire, from both audiences, for a greater goal to be achieved, something that advances the quality of the art form or of the sport in question. Even if on occasion all you want from your team is a quick win, an easy victory, most football fans also dream that, by the final whistle, their side will have also displayed the artistry that bears out the term 'the beautiful game'.

There are, of course, obvious differences, too, between the worlds of sport and musical culture. The harsh brutality of celebrating only those who jump highest, run fastest or throw furthest is surely absent in the classical music world. Or is it? What do musical competitions, still so influential in kick-starting the careers of young musicians, involve other than an assessment of technical virtuosity and musicianship, according to the criteria of an apparently objective judging panel? Compare a diving, gymnastic or figure-skating tournament to a classical music competition and the analogy is much closer than with events in the athletics stadium: in the pool, the gym and the ice rink, you also have sets of judges making assessments based not just on technical excellence but also, more subjectively, on stylistic perfection.

All that's before we get to the many ways in which composers themselves have brought their love of sport into the concert hall: Shostakovich, Honegger, Michael Nyman, Benedict Mason, Mark-Anthony Turnage have all written sport-inspired pieces, based on everything from rugby to Arsenal Football Club; Elgar was a huge Wolverhampton Wanderers fan, and wrote what may be the

PEAK PERFORMANCE

Conductor Semyon Bychkov, who for eight years played non-professionally for the St Petersburg Dynamos volleyball team, explores the connections between sporting and musical achievement

There's an enormous similarity between musicians and sportsmen – more than one at first realises. Playing volleyball was a tremendous life-school for me; engaging in sport forms character and one's ability to serve in a team. It's the same in an orchestra, choir or opera house: it requires a collective effort to go beyond our limitations in a common search for excellence.

Of course, musicians don't win matches, but in music you compete with yourself. And there's very much the element of stamina: how do you survive a marathon run, or a marathon performance, such as a Wagner opera? By knowing how to pace yourself, which comes from experience and the ability to live in a long stretch of time. You always try to reach the peak of form just at the moment when you have a match to play or a performance to give.

After a match, when players are interviewed, they will always say it was the team that won it; without the help of their teammates, they simply couldn't have done it. In a way, successful sports teams live for each other and with each other. So does a symphony orchestra – there is a human chemistry that creates this atmosphere: as with the The Three Musketeers, it's all for one and one for all.

The audience plays an important role in both endeavours. You can sense just how much it means for people to be there and the anticipation of the performance wills you to give your very best.

Semyon Bychkov conducts Strauss's *Elektra* in Prom 59 (31 August)

Sheila Rock (above left); Chris Christodoulou/BBC (above right)

Who couldn't be stirred into action by the power of 'O Fortuna' from *Carmina burana* or Parry's *Jerusalem*?

first ever football chant for the club ('He banged the leather for goal'), and we know that Mozart loved billiards and would surely have appreciated the virtuosity of Ronnie O'Sullivan if he'd been around to witness it. To pick a couple of conductors who are sports fans: Sir John Eliot Gardiner (Prom 54) can often be seen at Lord's cricket ground in north London, and Daniel Harding (Prom 57) is the most committed Manchester United supporter you're ever likely to encounter.

There's a clear alignment of the musical and sports spheres too, in the borrowing of classical favourites as football anthems. Who couldn't be stirred into action by the power of 'O Fortuna' from *Carmina burana*, Dance of the Knights from Prokofiev's *Romeo and Juliet* or that Last Night of the Proms favourite, Parry's *Jerusalem*?

Yet the deepest connections between the worlds of sport and music are suggested by the fact we use the same word, 'play', to describe what we're doing, whether we're taking part in a Saturday-morning five-a-side match or a performance with a local orchestra. To play, whether it's sport or music, might imply that we're engaged in an activity of supreme purposelessness, but we're also in a metaphorical arena that allows us to experience extremes of physicality and emotion, to push our bodies, intellects and spirits into places we wouldn't otherwise take them – even to create a heightened state of transcendent otherness.

Tenor Joseph Calleja (*centre*), joined by British Olympic and Paralympic rowing medallists to sing *Rule, Britannia!* at 2012's Last Night of the Proms

The truly great sportspeople talk of a rare but essential experience of being 'in the zone', a state of uncanny and apparently unwilled 'flow' between brain and body. The difference is that when Andy Murray is in that strange and special place, we can share only the delight or despair of his victory or defeat; but when it's conductor Sakari Oramo or violinist Janine Jansen in the Royal Albert Hall, we in the audience are taken into that transfiguring 'zone' as well. That's why, for me, the Proms will always beat the Premier League or the Commonwealth Games. Not that it's a competition, of course … ●

Tom Service writes about music for *The Guardian* and since 2003 has been the presenter of Radio 3's flagship magazine programme, *Music Matters*. His two recent books are *Music as Alchemy* and *Thomas Adès: Full of Noises*.

BBC SPORT PROM

Sporting anthems and TV themes, plus classical favourites selected by sports personalities, presented by Gabby Logan
PROM 3 • 20 JULY

UNIVERSITY OF
WEST LONDON
London College of Music

Connected.

London College of Music is an internationally recognised music institution with a long tradition of providing innovative and creative courses. Many courses are specifically designed to fit around personal and professional commitments and are offered on a full or part time basis.

Our well established links with creative industries in London, the UK and abroad ensure that your studies are real and relevant to your musical interests.

UNDERGRADUATE PORTFOLIO:
- Composition
- Music Management
- Music Technology
- Musical Theatre
- Performance

POSTGRADUATE PORTFOLIO:
- Composition
- Music Management
- Music Technology
- Musical Theatre
- Performance

 London College of Music Examinations offer a wide range of external graded exams and diplomas.
uwl.ac.uk/lcmexams

uwl.ac.uk/lcm

BEHIND THE
FAÇADE

Ahead of this year's Proms focus on William Walton, **MALCOLM HAYES** highlights the often overlooked individuality of the composer's music, in a career that took him from *enfant terrible* to Establishment figure

Musical fashion is a strange phenomenon, as William Walton spent his long creative life finding out. When early performances of his witty 'entertainment' *Façade* astonished concert-goers in the 1920s, its brilliantly talented young composer was seen in cultural circles as representing the essence of contemporary modishness.

Four decades later, a new, modernist agenda was being set by a younger generation of English composers (notably Harrison Birtwistle and Peter Maxwell Davies), with strong support from the musical press to match. When Walton conducted the first performance of his *Variations on a Theme of Hindemith* at the Royal Festival Hall in 1963, the critical consensus was now more or less that music of this kind was old hat. Over time, composers often find themselves undergoing this sort of perceived transformation, from radical new young voice into outmoded Establishment figure. But the long-term fluctuation in Walton's share price has been extreme enough to indicate a situation more complex than that. Above all, fashion loves to categorise, and the individuality at work in Walton's music makes it particularly resistant to the process.

Born in 1902, the son of a music teacher in the Lancashire town of Oldham, Walton went to the choir school of Oxford's Christ Church college on a scholarship and then, aged 16, entered the college itself. A fellow undergraduate was Sacheverell Sitwell, who introduced his siblings, Osbert and Edith, to the remarkable young musician. Failed (non-musical) examinations in 1920 meant that Walton's scholarship was not renewed, so the culture-hunting Sitwells took him to live in the family's London home in Carlyle Square. There, Walton and Edith Sitwell together devised the words-and-music sequence that would become *Façade*.

When the work received its private premiere in the Sitwells' drawing room in 1922, an authentic *succès de scandale* was achieved. *Façade*'s fantastical range of moods and colours, however, related to something deeper than a gift for magpie-like parody. Two years earlier, the Sitwell family had for the first time taken young Willie on one of their regular trips to Italy. The experience was life-changing, from the moment that the train emerged from the Alps into the Italian sunlight. ('I've never forgotten it,' said Walton many years later: 'a new world.') Thereafter, the sounds and atmosphere of the Italian south around the Amalfi coast would cross-fertilise Walton's music in a way that went much deeper than local colour. His mature style was rooted in the English tradition, reaching back through Elgar to 19th-century Romanticism – roots that coexisted with the anti-parochial, cosmopolitan streak awakened by the first of his lifelong sequence of Italian encounters.

This unique mix of elements presented both an opportunity and a problem to a young composer trying to make his way in a conservative English musical scene. *Façade*, Walton sensed, was an unrepeatable idea. Looking for a way forward, he came up with the roistering, rhythmically energised overture *Portsmouth Point* (1924–5), which brought

The English poet Edith Sitwell, whose abstract poems Walton set to music in *Façade*. Portrait from 1915, by Roger Fry (1866–1934)

him growing visibility. When the impresario Sergey Diaghilev turned down a projected score for his Ballets Russes company, Walton in 1926–7 recast the music as the *Sinfonia concertante* for piano and orchestra. The result was curiously experimental – as if the styles of Rachmaninov and Prokofiev are filtered through those of Stravinsky and Falla – yet with a surging, inventive strength very much Walton's own.

Maturity then arrived with the Viola Concerto. Coruscating rhythmic drive, poignant romanticism and moody jazz-inflected harmony are here drawn together into a lyrical statement whose mastery Walton never surpassed. Now came the sequence of masterworks on which his reputation today largely rests. The oratorio *Belshazzar's Feast* (1930–1) brought off a spectacularly successful fusion of jazz-age rhythmic swagger with the choral and orchestral grandeur of Berlioz. The First Symphony (1931–5) charted, through four turbulent movements, the course of Walton's troubled relationship with Baroness Imma Doernberg and its eventual succession by his more serene love for Alice, Viscountess Wimborne. During a winter at Ravello on the Amalfi coast, Alice persuaded Walton to turn down some lucrative film-score offers, including one from Hollywood, and to concentrate instead on the Violin Concerto (1936–9) requested by Jascha Heifetz. Posterity accordingly owes her a major debt; and it seems appropriate that the concerto's exquisite lyricism and loveliness should be Alice's musical memorial.

The Second World War found Walton coming into his own as a film composer. A major success was the soundtrack he wrote for *The First of the Few* (1942), about designer R. J. Mitchell's battle against terminal illness to create the Spitfire fighter plane; Walton later arranged the stirring title theme and busy aircraft-factory sequence as *Spitfire Prelude and Fugue*. In 1944 came Laurence Olivier's film of *Henry V*, featuring Walton's finest score for the medium. A number of shorter concert-

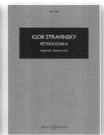

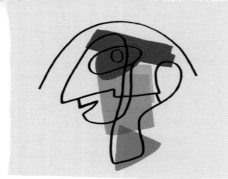

> The individuality at work in Walton's music makes it particularly resistant to categorisation.

Walton, with his wife Susana, backstage at the Royal Festival Hall in 1977

hall suites of the music have materialised, not arranged by the composer himself. These have been superseded in recent years by *Henry V: A Shakespeare Scenario*, in which Christopher Palmer assembled a comprehensive musical selection into a convincing large-scale design.

By now Walton's world was changing around him more rapidly than he could have realised. In 1945 Benjamin Britten's opera *Peter Grimes* effectively rewrote the rulebook as to where English music was now considered to be. Alice Wimborne died of cancer in 1948. Later that year, on a visit to Argentina, Walton met and married the much younger Susana Gil Passo, and together they settled on the island of Ischia in the Bay of Naples. Professionally and personally, it was a happy decision. Walton knew he would not enjoy living surrounded by a caucus of Anglo-Saxon opinion constantly telling him what a wonderful composer Britten was, however much he agreed with that assessment (through the gritted teeth of professional rivalry). And as Susana Walton once put it to me: 'No-one in England could accept that William had gone and married this Indian from South America.'

Walton continued to compose fluently until cancer treatment in 1966 (itself successful, but damaging to the rest of his health) undermined his productivity and, more disturbingly, his creative confidence. While the style of his music did not change, the tone did, into something subtler and more

finely wrought. Received opinion liked to make out (and still largely does) that Walton's music 'went off' after his move to Ischia. The ridiculousness of the assertion is made clear by his 1963 tribute to the composer-performer who, a third of a century earlier, had played the solo part in the Viola Concerto's premiere. *Variations on a Theme of Hindemith* is a statement as complete as any Walton wrote – a warmly humane utterance by a composer who felt acutely the contrary winds of fashion, and who, nonetheless, was able to keep composing as if those winds did not exist. Which, in the long term, of course, they don't. Perhaps, at this summer's Proms, the time for music of such individuality and quality has at last arrived. ●

Malcolm Hayes is a composer, writer, broadcaster and music journalist. He contributes regularly to *BBC Music Magazine* and edited *The Selected Letters of William Walton*.

WALTON AT THE PROMS

Façade
PROMS CHAMBER MUSIC 8
8 SEPTEMBER

Façade – Popular Song
PROM 76 • 13 SEPTEMBER

Henry V: A Shakespeare Scenario
(arr. C. Palmer)
PROM 32 • 10 AUGUST

Sinfonia concertante
PROM 60 • 1 SEPTEMBER

Symphony No. 1 in B flat minor
PROM 20 • 1 AUGUST

Variations on a Theme of Hindemith
PROM 10 • 25 JULY

Viola Concerto
PROM 72 • 10 SEPTEMBER

Violin Concerto
PROM 35 • 12 AUGUST

LOVE
MUSIC
**HELP
MUSICIANS**UK

**I'm a violinist and Help Musicians UK
helped me financially and emotionally
when I had cancer.**

**Your support means we can help more
people like Mandhira.
Help us help musicians.**

**helpmusicians.org.uk
020 7239 9100**

Help Musicians UK is the new name for the
Musicians Benevolent Fund. We help musicians of all genres
throughout their professional lives. Registered charity 228089.

The world's favourite miniature scores

· For students, professionals and enthusiasts

· Over 1,200 individual works

· Baroque, Classical, Romantic & Contemporary

· Orchestral, Chamber, Choral and Opera

NORTHERN KNIGHTS

As the Proms celebrates the 80th birthdays of Sir Peter Maxwell Davies and Sir Harrison Birtwistle, **JONATHAN CROSS** profiles the two composers, who rose from Lancashire roots to become pillars of the Establishment

It would surely have been unthinkable to audiences in the 1960s that the music of two Northern upstarts would, in the 2010s, be so widely acknowledged and celebrated. When Peter Maxwell Davies conducted the premiere of his large-scale orchestral work *Worldes Blis* at the Proms in 1969, it created quite a tumult. 'Most of the audience walked out,' recalls the composer, 'and most of those who stayed booed.' Harrison Birtwistle's *Nomos*, premiered by Colin Davis at the Proms a year earlier, had had a slightly smoother ride, yet, even as recently as 1995, Birtwistle still managed to ruffle Proms audience feathers with the aptly titled *Panic*, subsequently described by a *Radio Times* correspondent as 'a complete cacophony of unrhythmic, unmelodious and unmusical sounds', and by *The Spectator* as 'an atrocity of epic proportions'. While history

has proved the initial dismissal of these works to have been premature, the early reputations of these two Lancashire lads as *enfants terribles* has proved harder to shift.

Born in 1934, Birtwistle and Davies represented a new generation of English composer. As grammar-school boys from Accrington and Salford respectively, who both went on to study at the Royal Manchester (now Royal Northern) College of Music, their backgrounds were markedly different to the privileged upbringing of earlier generations of London-educated figures. They breathed a different air; they were, perhaps, less constrained by convention. Manchester in the 1950s certainly encouraged more radical thinking than the neo-Classical tradition at the Royal Academy of Music of the time. Fellow student Alexander Goehr (son of the Schoenberg pupil

Walter Goehr) wrote of 'a certain Central European feeling' about Manchester, which was more receptive to the music of the Second Viennese School as well as to the latest ideas emerging from Paris and Darmstadt. Together, Birtwistle, Davies, Goehr and others formed the New Music Manchester group in order to have their own music performed and heard; in the 1960s they were instrumental in founding the Wardour Castle Summer School and the Pierrot Players (re-formed in 1970 as the Fires of London), both of which played key roles in reshaping the landscape of British new music.

The 1960s saw, for both Birtwistle and Davies, the production of arguably their most radical works, which explicitly rejected the lyrical, pastoral traditions of English music from earlier in the century and challenged listeners (and players) with an uncompromising

Birtwistle still managed to ruffle Proms audience feathers with the aptly titled *Panic*, subsequently described by a *Radio Times* correspondent as 'a complete cacophony of unrhythmic, unmelodious and unmusical sounds'.

approach to material, form and subject matter. Medieval and Renaissance music was one shared model, Schoenbergian Expressionism another, resulting in such key works as Davies's *Revelation and Fall*, *Eight Songs for a Mad King* and *Taverner*, and Birtwistle's *Tragoedia* and *Punch and Judy*. Both composers recognised the importance of engaging with theatre as a means of speaking directly – whether that was, for instance, through the provocative use of a naked dancer to represent Christ in Davies's *Vesalii icones*, or by the movement of musicians about the concert platform to 'act out' the bold, musical juxtapositions of Birtwistle's *Verses for Ensembles*.

Since the 1970s the two composers have forged their own separate, distinctive paths. Davies's compositional activities have moved in two main directions simultaneously. The strongly expressed opposition to injustice and hypocrisy articulated in his early works continues in different ways right up to the present. While superficially it might appear

the ultimate act of betrayal for a once arch-republican to accept the role of Master of the Queen's Music, Davies has in fact used his position of influence to speak out strongly on such matters as government cuts to the arts in general, and to the provision for music education in British schools in particular. He also continues to produce what one might call *Gebrauchmusik*, that is, 'utility music' written for use by people in particular communities, whether that be stage works for young performers, choral music for liturgical use, or all kinds of pieces that pay tribute to the people and places of Orkney, where he has lived since 1971, including the joyful *An Orkney Wedding, with Sunrise*, complete with Highland bagpiper.

At the same time Davies has, like a latter-day Haydn, engaged with and rethought the principal instrumental genres of the 18th and 19th centuries. The 10 'Naxos' String Quartets for the Maggini Quartet and the 10 'Strathclyde' Concertos for the Scottish Chamber Orchestra stand as extraordinary

testimony to the close relationships he has developed with these professional ensembles. But it is surely in his cycle of (to date) 10 symphonies, starting with the First in 1973 and reaching the premiere of the 10th just this February, that one sees Davies at his most impressive. They speak, of course, to the Beethovenian legacy, and they show great courage in sustaining an intensity of musical thought across vast architectures in an age when composers are increasingly required to offer instant emotional gratification – as, for instance, in his Sibelius-inspired Symphony No. 5, premiered at the Proms in 1994 and returning this year.

Birtwistle's reputation since 1970 has been forged principally in the opera house. His radical experiments of the 1960s combined with a period spent working at the National Theatre coalesced into one monumental theatrical project that dominated the 1970s and 1980s, namely his 'lyric tragedy' *The Mask of Orpheus*, premiered in London

Harrison Birtwistle (*top left*) and Peter Maxwell Davies (*middle right*) with fellow Manchester students in the 1950s: Elgar Howarth (*top right*), John Ogdon (*centre*), Alexander Goehr (*bottom left*), Audrey Goehr (*bottom centre*) and John Dow (*bottom right*)

Loelia Goehr

Hit and myth: Punch and the Minotaur, two typically powerful characters from two of Sir Harrison Birtwistle's operas, composed 40 years apart

in 1986. Though it is designed for a standard opera house, its complex plot and musical organisation, multiple representations of character, and use of electronics, all pushed at the boundaries of what was possible in the theatre. It remains a landmark work, despite the lamentable absence of subsequent fully staged productions. And while his later operas are more conventional in form and expression – most notably his two works for the Royal Opera, *Gawain* (1990–91, revised 1994) and *The Minotaur* (2005–7) – their distinctive landscapes of shadows, dreams, mirrors and memories continue to speak profoundly of the losses of the late-modern age. Birtwistle, like Orpheus, is a melancholic, and this particular world-view has coloured a range of his most expressive works of recent decades, notably his powerful, millennial statement *Exody*, and a complementary pair of orchestral studies inspired by the Elizabethan melancholics, *The Shadow of Night* and *Night's Black Bird*.

It is really quite impossible to fathom how Max and Harry (as they are known to their friends) can be turning 80 this year. If anything, both are more productive than ever, and while their work inevitably reflects on some of the darker themes that later years bring, in many respects their music has as much youthful energy as it had in the 1950s and 1960s. Their contributions to musical modernism have been profound and their music is now heard and discussed with the respect deserved by two knights of the realm. Yet this Establishment status has not prevented them from continuing to provoke their audiences afresh, whether in Davies's outspoken opposition to the invasion of Iraq in his Third 'Naxos' Quartet (2003), or in Birtwistle's melancholic reflection on the shameful Highland Clearances of the 19th century in his string quartet *The Tree of Strings* (2007). Long may their polemics continue to flourish. ●

Jonathan Cross is Professor of Musicology at the University of Oxford, and author of, among other texts on recent music, *Harrison Birtwistle: Man, Mind, Music* (2000) and *Harrison Birtwistle: The Mask of Orpheus* (2009).

Mark Ellidge/ArenaPAL (left); Clive Barda/ArenaPAL (right)

SIR HARRISON BIRTWISTLE AT THE PROMS

Dinah and Nick's Love Song; Meridian; Verses for Ensembles
PROMS SATURDAY MATINEE 4
6 SEPTEMBER

Endless Parade
PROMS SATURDAY MATINEE 2
9 AUGUST

Exody
PROM 72 • 10 SEPTEMBER

Night's Black Bird
PROM 18 • 30 JULY

Sonance Severance 2000
PROM 33 • 10 AUGUST
(see also Proms Plus Composer Portrait)

•••

SIR PETER MAXWELL DAVIES AT THE PROMS

Caroline Mathilde – suite from Act 2
PROM 35 • 12 AUGUST

Concert Overture 'Ebb of Winter';
An Orkney Wedding, with Sunrise;
Strathclyde Concerto No. 4
PROM 70 • 8 SEPTEMBER

Linguae ignis; A Mirror of Whitening Light; Revelation and Fall
PROMS SATURDAY MATINEE 3
30 AUGUST

Sinfonia
PROMS SATURDAY MATINEE 2
9 AUGUST

Symphony No. 5
PROM 38 • 14 AUGUST
(see also Proms Plus Composer Portrait)

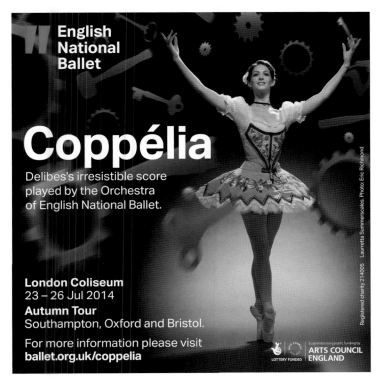
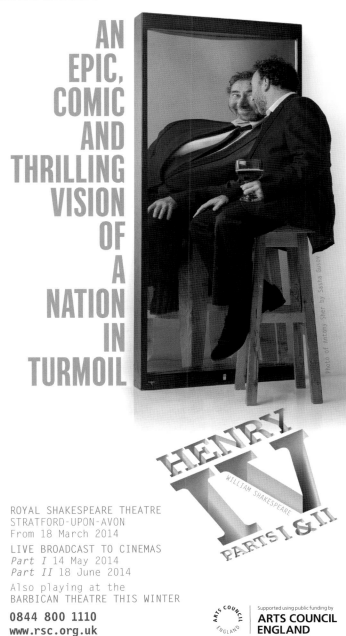

ILLUSION FOR
THE EARS

Though he views himself as a traditional composer, Benedict Mason is something of an accidental iconoclast, drawn to the element of theatre and radically redefining the concert experience. **IVAN HEWETT** looks forward to his new work, *Meld*

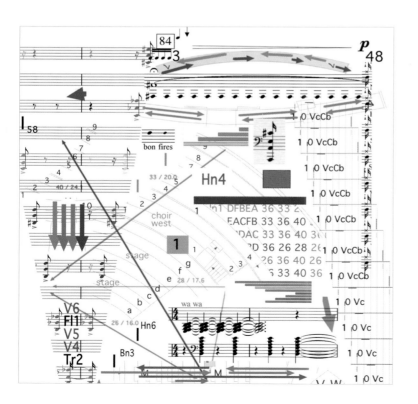

A new piece at the Proms is rarely a complete unknown. Often we have some prior notion of what the composer is about and, if we don't, at the concert the programme note will give us an idea of what the music will actually sound like.

In the case of Benedict Mason's new BBC commission, *Meld*, receiving its world premiere at the Proms, even that small reassurance isn't on offer. The nature of this piece is being kept carefully under wraps, because surprise is essential to its effect. This isn't because Mason likes to shock: it goes deeper than that. He wants each new piece to feel like a step into the unknown.

That conviction showed itself from the beginning. His early works, which appeared during the mid-1980s and early 1990s, were marked by a delightful and unsettling brilliance. Among them was *Lighthouses of England and Wales*, which took the form of a whistle-stop tour round the coast, liberally spiced with memories of nautical music. Another was the first Double Concerto for horn and trombone, which took its cue from the dizzying rhythmic complications and surreal humour of György Ligeti's late concertos, and actually outdid them. And there was the *Self-Referential Songs and Realistic Virelais*, in which the words of the songs are amusingly mirrored in the workings of the music, in 'self-referential' fashion.

All this suggested a sly post-modern sensibility, which was exactly right for the times. Mason seemed to be the coming man, yet since the mid-1990s he has been a rare presence on the musical scene in the UK. Not that he's been idle, or experienced that falling-off in creativity which sometimes dogs composers who make an especially brilliant start. On the contrary, he's been constantly productive, usually for musical organisations elsewhere in Europe. But because these recent works are ambitious in different ways, often calling for unusual resources beyond the reach of 'normal' institutions, such as orchestras, they've slipped from view.

Sometimes these pieces go beyond the typical demands that new music can place on performers and listeners. Several works have been designed around the physical characteristics of specific spaces, such as the Alte Oper in Frankfurt and the Jean Nouvel-designed concert hall in Lucerne. The players may be distributed in odd parts of the building, or they may be asked to play unusual instruments – as in his enormous, fascinating opus from 2004 curiously entitled *felt | ebb | thus | brink | here |*

array | telling, where the movements are divided up according to the sound-source. For example the first three movements are entitled 'For harmonics and helmholtz resonators', 'For glass, plastic and metal with air fire and water' and 'For hard wood and high-pitched echoes'.

This is a far cry from the ingenious cultural references of the *Self-Referential Songs* and the Schubertian glimpses of the String Quartet No. 1. And it points towards the essential difficulty and fascination of Mason's music, which go way beyond the practical problems of placing 70 or so players around an auditorium or the challenge of playing the 600 instruments required for *felt | ebb* ... It's the fact that his pieces elude every neat aesthetic pigeonhole, especially the ones they most obviously suggest.

Take the simple matter of titles. It's tempting to label a composer who names a piece *The Four Slopes of Twice Among Gliders of her Gravity* as whimsical and Satie-esque, especially as the characteristic tone of his earlier pieces is indeed light, with fleeting gestures sometimes caught in little whirling repetitive cycles, as if time has temporarily got stuck. In fact that title refers to Marcel Duchamp, another unsettler of traditional artistic categories. And quite a few pieces have unimpeachably sober titles, such as the String Quartets 1 and 2.

Then there's the matter of the sounds of his music. These can be almost punishingly simple, as in his first acknowledged piece, *The Hinterstoisser Traverse,* which consists entirely of the note G, layered and rhythmicised in myriad ways. But often Mason's works luxuriate in the glow of simple major chords and high, glistening harmonics, as in the first Double Concerto. And in some works notes disappear entirely, giving way to subtly layered rattlings, whisperings and murmurings.

A performance of Benedict Masons's *Da hleeo durum daree durum dittm da herum* – for actors, musicians and lighting – which the composer staged at the Bregenz Festival in 2009

This variety might suggest a conviction that every piece requires its own unique aural resources, as Stockhausen always insisted. But Mason is quite capable of writing for a familiar medium like the string quartet. And, though he designs certain pieces around certain spaces, he hates to be thought of as a 'site-specific' artist and says that all his pieces could be recreated elsewhere. Most of all he dislikes the suggestion that he's a kind of mad inventor of music, who ignores practicality. 'I have to be very practical,' he says, 'so I can realise all my apparently impractical ideas.'

So if he's not a teasing 'post-modernist', or a severe modernist systematiser, what is he? In the end what seems to interest Mason most – as much as music, or the element of performance – is the act of listening. It's as if listening, when liberated from the business

of guiding us round the world, can be a source of illumination and wonder in itself. It connects us in countless ways to our other senses, and also to our minds, but most of the time is in a state of slumber. It needs to be awoken, which requires that combination of surprise and wonder best described as a sense of the miraculous. Mason disclaims any intention to achieve a miracle – 'I wouldn't be so presumptuous,' he says – but in his best pieces he achieves something like it. ●

Ivan Hewett is a critic and broadcaster who for nine years presented BBC Radio 3's *Music Matters.* He writes for *The Telegraph* and teaches at the Royal College of Music.

BENEDICT MASON'S MELD AT THE PROMS

PROM 41 • 16 AUGUST

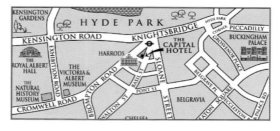

POWER OF SIX

As Sakari Oramo, the BBC Symphony Orchestra's new Chief Conductor, prepares for his first Last Night of the Proms, **HELEN WALLACE** talks to him and profiles his five counterparts in BBC groups around the country – a dream team that presides over 13 of the 76 Proms at the Royal Albert Hall

Marin Alsop may last year have become the first woman to conduct the Last Night of the Proms but, at the end of this summer, the BBC Symphony Orchestra's Chief Conductor Sakari Oramo will surely become the first Last Night conductor also to have performed earlier in the season as violinist. (He joins Last Night violinist Janine Jansen in one of the Proms Chamber Music concerts.) It's not a challenge many could take on – or bring off – but it turns out that the violin is fundamental to Oramo's music-making: 'I've played since I was 7 years old; the instrument has grown to be a part of me. When my conducting career took off, I spent a couple of years not playing at all, but it caught up with me. Losing the physical contact to sound was painful and even affected my conducting adversely. When I took up playing again, I realised that not having to do it "for a living" actually made it easier – not so much technically, but musically. I felt free to play in the way I wanted, not as I was expected to.'

No wonder Oramo has a formidable reputation as an orchestral trainer: he's one of those rare top-flight maestros who can still identify wholly with the musicians before him. Duetting with Janine Jansen is something else, though: 'It's wonderful and scary to play with Janine. She makes me want to push up my own standard as far as I can.'

Conducting was always an ambition for Oramo, who was born into a family of musicians. He made his baton-wielding debut aged just 12, for a Finnish educational TV programme, 'wearing rubber boots – it was a rainy day'. He pursued his studies through the Sibelius Academy and is still amused by the review of his graduation concert: 'Beautiful to watch, terrible to listen to.' As one of the founder-members of Helsinki's pioneering Avanti! ensemble, he shook things up with contemporary music and period-performance practice, before the need to earn a living led him into the concert-master's chair of the Finnish Radio Symphony Orchestra. Then fate intervened: in 1993 a conductor went sick, and he was pushed onto the podium for Brahms's First Symphony, which resulted in his becoming Co-Principal Conductor and later Chief Conductor of the orchestra (1994–2012). By this point, Oramo had already begun studying with the legendary Jorma Panula, teacher of his compatriots Osmo Vänskä, Jukka-Pekka Saraste and Esa-Pekka Salonen.

Back in 1999, on a train journey between Birmingham and London, I chatted with Oramo about that time: 'I fully expected a long career ahead of me as a concert-master. When I went to Panula, I was in something of a crisis musically. I had a huge number of influences coming at me from different sides and I didn't know how to boil it all down into my own musicianship. He made me see what was already inside me, but liberated my imagination through technique and a practical sense of musicianship.' Oramo concluded it was a mysterious process, that – true to Finnish form – didn't involve a lot of talking.

When I met Panula he, in turn, paid tribute to Oramo, as the very model of a modern maestro: 'a team worker, not an autocrat – he helps, but doesn't get in the way. The foundation is great ability, of course, but Sakari has the advantage of genuine good behaviour.' This may sound like a rather old-fashioned asset, but has never been a more valuable one in today's often fraught and pressurised music world.

Despite his mild demeanour, Oramo has proved to have an electrifying effect on orchestras. After only two performances with the City of Birmingham Symphony Orchestra he succeeded Sir Simon Rattle in 1998, and after only one performance with the BBC SO in 2011, he was appointed Chief Conductor

No wonder Oramo has a formidable reputation as an orchestral trainer: he's one of those rare top-flight maestros who can still identify wholly with the musicians before him.

DAVID HILL
Chief Conductor,
BBC Singers
(since 2007)

One of the UK's leading choral directors, David Hill combines the creation of challenging premiere performances with the BBC Singers with his work as Music Director of The Bach Choir, and now of the Yale Schola Cantorum. The sheer range of the Singers' repertoire demands versatility, which he finds they have in spades: 'This choir is unique – it's the only full-time chamber choir in the UK. They are fearless and will take on anything, knowing they will master it in whatever language. It's a privilege to work with them.'

The regular Singers at Six events at the Barbican provide a fascinating counterpoint to the BBC Symphony Orchestra concerts that follow, while the choir can also be heard in free concerts at St Paul's Knightsbridge, at Maida Vale and at Milton Court. This year's premieres include C.P. E. Bach's *St John Passion* in Bournemouth and *A Man from the Future*, composed by Neil Tennant and Chris Lowe of the Pet Shop Boys: no-one could deliver that range with more panache.

KEITH LOCKHART
Principal Conductor,
BBC Concert Orchestra
(since 2010)

American Keith Lockhart is equally at home with Glenn Miller's swing as he is whipping up a crystalline performance of Stravinsky. He's been the enormously successful conductor of the Boston Pops Orchestra since 1995, and brings his showmanship and open-minded perspective to his role at the BBC Concert Orchestra. He loves 'the amazing virtuosity and spirit' of the BBC CO musicians. 'If it's playable by an orchestra (and maybe even if it's not), they can perform it, with style and skill.' Recent highlights include the 2012 Diamond Jubilee concert at Buckingham Palace.

His Proms programme this year epitomises the BBC CO's range: 'I'm looking forward to bringing some of my favourite music from my native land. *Appalachian Spring* is one of the masterpieces of 20th-century music. I'm also excited that the trio Time for Three is making its UK debut with us. The piece Chris Brubeck has written for these three players fits them like a glove.'

JUANJO MENA
Chief Conductor,
BBC Philharmonic
(since 2011)

'I have a great affection for the BBC Philharmonic's home at MediaCity in Salford; the buzz of creativity there is infectious,' says Juanjo Mena, who came to the BBC Philharmonic via the Bergen Philharmonic Orchestra and, before that, the Bilbao Symphony Orchestra. His expertise in Spanish repertoire has resulted in a stream of acclaimed recordings of music by composers such as Falla, Montsalvatge and Turina, but he's also an enthusiast of English repertoire: his Proms concerts this summer include works by Sir Harrison Birtwistle, Elgar, Moeran and Walton.

Mena praises the BBC Philharmonic for 'the quality of its first reading of every score' and says if his orchestra were a car 'it would be a Bentley Brooklands coupé: classy, elegant ... it's responsive, has immense power, the ability to take risks; it's a grand tourer (all over the world) and has a beautiful sound, thanks to its Rolls-Royce twin-turbocharged V8 engine!'

Sakari Oramo at the First Night of the Proms 2013, his first concert as the
BBC Symphony Orchestra's new Chief Conductor

(astonishingly, that one concert was his debut with a London-based orchestra). Oramo was not looking for a new post at the time, but it proved an irresistible invitation: 'I actually already had more than enough work planned for the next couple of years. But how can one resist such an offer, coming out of the blue after just one concert? The quality of the orchestra and choirs, the possibility of participating in the Proms, the endless opportunities to programme challenging music!'

He made an imposing debut as Chief Conductor at the First Night of the Proms last year, sealing his British music credentials with a rousing performance of Vaughan Williams's *A Sea Symphony*. His current, highly imaginative BBC Symphony Orchestra season at the Barbican, including many UK premieres, has drawn glowing reviews. How does he want to develop the orchestra?

'It's exciting and stimulating to work and create strategies in the most competitive, dense, intense location of orchestral life – London! The BBC SO is an incredibly fun and capable group of musicians, an orchestra of virtuosity and immense capacity to give music warmth and expression. So, therefore, these are precisely the areas I want to develop. I want to give the players a self-evident confidence across all important musical styles. My dream is that one will immediately recognise the orchestra's playing: "Oh yes, this is the BBC SO!"'

It's significant that the qualities he admires in his British players mirror those for which his own interpretations are often praised: 'They don't show off but are immensely resilient in playing long lines, and developments. So much of orchestral performance nowadays is "going for the big moments". Having those moments worked into, struggled for, is equally important. The key for impact is not in the culminations themselves, but in the processes leading to them.'

A notably complete musician, Oramo is also a skilled orchestrator, as will be heard in Szymanowski's *Songs of a Fairy Princess*, to be sung by his wife, soprano Anu Komsi (Prom 49). 'Szymanowski only orchestrated three of his six songs, originally written for voice and piano, so it's natural to feel right about completing the set. I tried to study his style, to find the root of his orchestral thinking, and my aim was for the orchestrations to sound even more like Szymanowski than his own.' Drawn as he is to the many-layered subtleties of late-Romanticism, it's perhaps not surprising that Oramo has a particular affinity with British music, as shown in his luminous readings of Tippett, Britten, Bliss, Bax and Vaughan Williams. This year he presents Vaughan Williams's ballet *Job*, and he's an outspoken advocate for the work: 'Vaughan Williams was a true poet and a romantic soul. Like many of his best works, *Job* is not merely fascinating: it's truly gripping if performed well. The key to his music, as with so many composers, is *language*. I can hear English in

it, and it's vital that the phrases are shaped in English, with the correct emphases.' Spoken with the confidence of a multi-linguist, and someone who now feels as at home in London as he does in Helsinki.

Oramo is excited, not daunted, by the prospect of playing host at the Last Night, but he won't be drawn on the contents of his speech. We need not fear about the music, though: 'I'm working on my *Rule, Britannia!* and *Jerusalem* already!'. ●

Helen Wallace is Consultant Editor of *BBC Music Magazine*, and a critic, broadcaster and Kodály teacher. She is the author of *Boosey & Hawkes: The Publishing Story*, and her latest publication is *The Top 50 Works of Chamber Music* (Kings Place Music Foundation).

DONALD RUNNICLES

Chief Conductor, BBC Scottish Symphony Orchestra (since 2009)

Edinburgh-born Donald Runnicles is a true man of the theatre, combining his role at the BBC Scottish Symphony Orchestra with the music directorship of the august Deutsche Oper Berlin. He made his name with blazing performances of Wagner and Strauss during his 17 years at San Francisco Opera, and finds his two roles provide an enriching and stimulating counterpoint, from epic storytelling in Berlin to 'exploring the inevitable theatre and drama inherent in great orchestral repertoire' in Glasgow.

A memorable performance of Wagner's *Tannhäuser* at last year's Proms brought both institutions together, and is his highlight to date. But it's 'the sheer range of repertoire' he explores with the BBC Scottish that excites him, from Mozart to John Adams, Thea Musgrave to Shostakovich. His ambition for the orchestra? 'That we continue to attract the finest players in the world to join our prestigious ranks.'

THOMAS SØNDERGÅRD

Principal Conductor, BBC National Orchestra of Wales (since 2012)

Young Danish conductor Thomas Søndergård knows all about broadcasting, having arrived in Cardiff fresh from the Norwegian Radio Orchestra. He combines his BBC post with being Principal Guest Conductor of the Royal Scottish National Orchestra, and is a regular figure at the Royal Danish and Royal Swedish operas.

For him, the best thing about working with the BBC NOW is 'the dedication and musicality of the players. It's a joy to work with them each and every time', and he's had a warm reception during tours through Wales: 'When we did our North Wales tour last season, the welcome we received at each venue was very touching. People were queuing out of the door in Bangor!'

His programming is a bold mix of core classical and 20th-century masterworks. 'I'm looking forward to performing the fifth symphonies of both Sibelius and Nielsen at the Proms,' he says. 'It'll be a thrill for us, and I hope to bring some Scandinavian energy to London!'

BBC CONDUCTORS AT THE PROMS

David Hill
BBC Singers
PROM 37 • 13 AUGUST

Keith Lockhart
BBC Concert Orchestra
PROM 71 • 9 SEPTEMBER

Juanjo Mena
BBC Philharmonic
PROM 10 • 25 JULY
BBC Philharmonic
PROM 18 • 30 JULY

Sakari Oramo
BBC Symphony Orchestra
PROM 28 • 7 AUGUST
with Janine Jansen *violin*
PROMS CHAMBER MUSIC 4 • 11 AUGUST
BBC Symphony Orchestra
PROM 36 • 13 AUGUST
BBC Symphony Orchestra
PROM 49 • 23 AUGUST
BBC Symphony Orchestra
PROM 76 • 13 SEPTEMBER

Donald Runnicles
BBC Scottish Symphony Orchestra
PROM 23 • 3 AUGUST
BBC Scottish Symphony Orchestra
PROM 24 • 4 AUGUST
Deutsche Oper Berlin
PROM 58 • 30 AUGUST

Thomas Søndergård
BBC National Orchestra of Wales
PROM 34 • 11 AUGUST
BBC National Orchestra of Wales
PROM 35 • 12 AUGUST

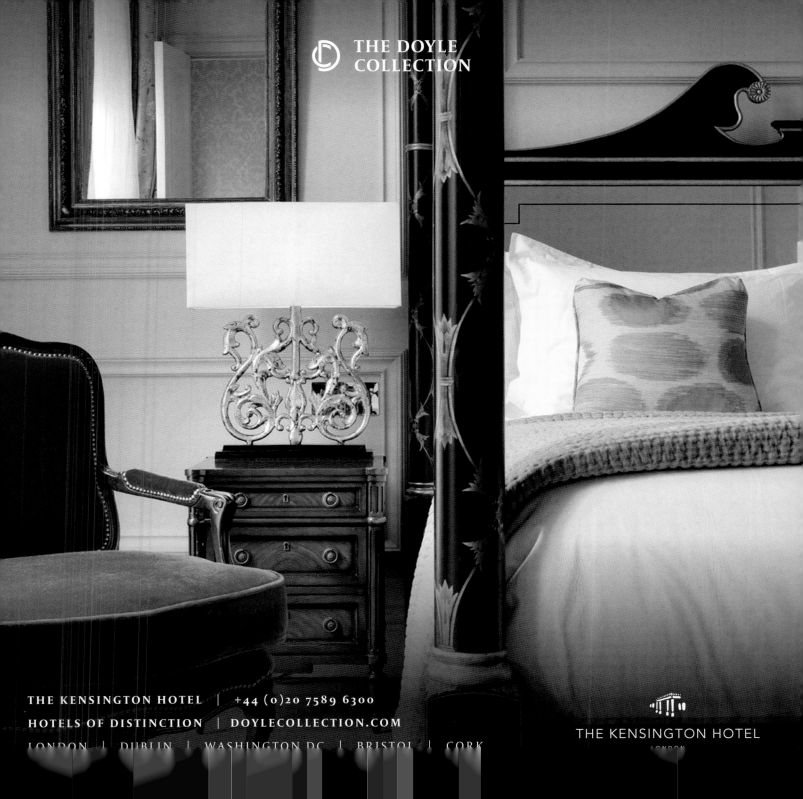

THE DOYLE COLLECTION

THE KENSINGTON HOTEL | +44 (0)20 7589 6300
HOTELS OF DISTINCTION | DOYLECOLLECTION.COM
LONDON | DUBLIN | WASHINGTON DC | BRISTOL | CORK

THE KENSINGTON HOTEL
LONDON

NEW MUSIC

This year's world, European, UK and London premieres capture the spirit of the Proms' international audience, with new works by both emerging and established British talent and by composers from traditions and cultures across the globe. **VERITY SHARP** finds out more

Verity Sharp produces and presents programmes for television and radio. She has broadcast on BBC Radio 3's *Late Junction* and *Hear and Now*, and the BBC Proms.

JOHN ADAMS

(BORN 1947)

Saxophone Concerto (2013)
UK premiere

PROM 63 · 4 SEPTEMBER

Largely ignored by many classical composers, the saxophone has always found favour with America's John Adams. Whole quartets of them turn up in his works *Nixon in China* and *Fearful Symmetries*. The saxophone sound is in his veins as, while he was growing up, barely a day went by when he didn't hear it. His father played alto and the family record collection was well stocked with jazz greats. 'I never,' Adams has said, 'considered the saxophone an alien instrument.' Yet, with the sax so tightly bound to the history of jazz, finding its orchestral voice was a challenge.

With few worthy classical models to study, Adams turned instead to the inspirational string arrangements of Stan Getz, Charlie Parker and Gil Evans. 'While the concerto is not meant to sound jazzy *per se*, its jazz influences lie only slightly below the surface. I make constant use of the instrument's vaunted agility, as well as its capacity for a lyrical utterance that is only a short step away from that of the human voice.' Adams wrote the concerto for the 'fearless' Tim McAllister, having heard about his previous incarnation as a champion stunt bicycle rider. According to McAllister, though, there are no 'stereotypical pyrotechnics' in the work. Instead, it demands huge versatility and stamina as well as the ability to produce a whole new sound for the saxophone.

AYAL ADLER

(BORN 1968)

Resonating Sounds (2014)
UK premiere

PROM 46 · 20 AUGUST

Big, dramatic contrasts are what matter to Israel's Ayal Adler. 'Contrasts,' he writes, 'between the atmosphere and mood in the course of this piece help to create in the listener a sense of intensity and dramatic moments.' He's been perfecting these ideas over the past 20 years in works for piano (he himself is a pianist), chamber ensemble and orchestra. A senior lecturer at the Jerusalem Academy of Music and Dance and a senior board member of the Israeli Composers' League, Adler is busy and in demand. At the time of writing, the finer detail of *Resonating Sounds* hasn't been worked through, but the scaffolding is clear. The piece will be a single movement, built from great differences in sound and texture.

'There are a few characteristics that reappear through my recent works,' he writes, 'such as: "dynamic" and "static" time – frequent changes versus immobility and repetition; dense masses of sound, especially within orchestral works, versus airy, transparent textures.' With such an evocative title, Adler's intentions are clear. He often plays with the nature of sound itself, experimenting with colourful effects such as overblowing, microtonal slides and playing close to the bridge. Complex interweaving lines are offset by sections 'predominated by vast harmonic chords/clusters with inner voices leading in between'.

SALLY BEAMISH

(BORN 1956)

Violin Concerto (1994)
London premiere

PROM 20 • 1 AUGUST

Although Sally Beamish's Violin Concerto was written for Anthony Marwood in 1994, its performance at this year's Proms is timely as it was inspired by her reading of Erich Maria Remarque's First World War novel *All Quiet on the Western Front*. 'Anthony sent me a copy,' she writes. 'I was immediately captivated by the book with its extraordinary juxtaposition of vivid, explosive narrative and wistful silence, coloured with bitter irony and language of heart-rending beauty. It brought to the surface my own deep-rooted sense of the futility and tragedy of war and the Violin Concerto is an expression of this.'

The concerto form has inspired Beamish for much of her career. 'I love the drama created by a central protagonist,' she says, 'the relationship between soloist and orchestra, and soloist and audience.' It's a perfect vehicle for this combative subject matter, which she here divides into three movements, each inspired by a short, hauntingly evocative passage from the novel. 'I saw Anthony as the lone, fragile voice of the soldier and his expressive, intimate and personal approach to the violin was a huge factor in the solo part. The orchestra often represents the nightmare of battle, the terrifying sounds and images. But it also creates the world of innocence from the soldier's life before war – half-remembered fragments of dance and folk music.'

BARRIE BIGNOLD

(BORN 1955)

Around Sound (2014)
BBC commission: world premiere

PROMS 11 & 13 • 26 & 27 JULY

Writing music for television is a fiercely competitive business. But Barrie Bignold has it down to a fine art. Over the past 20 years he's scored programmes as diverse as *Nigella Bites* and *The Road to Baghdad*, as well as being wholeheartedly embraced by the world of children's television. 'To be absolutely honest, I didn't initially like the idea of writing kids' music at all,' he says, 'until the penny dropped that kids live in the same world as everybody else and that "writing down" to them is completely unnecessary.' As he went on to compose music for *Tweenies*, *Wibbly Pig*, *Gigglebiz* and *Melody*, to name but a few, the realisation proved a winner. 'I don't have children myself and I think that's why my sense of humour is still around age 6. I've never had to grow up properly.'

Drawing on his solid background in theatre, Bignold has also written music for stage productions from *Twelfth Night* to *CBeebies Live!*. He says of his new piece for the CBeebies Prom, 'We'll take everyday London noises and turn them into music with the help of the orchestra and the very lively CBeebies audience and presenters! I'm always blown away by the experience of hearing a great orchestra in the Royal Albert Hall – I hope even a little of that rubs off onto the kids.'

CHRIS BRUBECK

(BORN 1952)

Travels in Time for Three (2010)
UK premiere

PROM 71 • 9 SEPTEMBER

Chris Brubeck was never going to take to an ivory tower to generate ideas for this extensive concerto suite. Jazz by its very nature is a collaborative affair, so his first move was to record a three-day jam session with the players for whom he was writing. Describing themselves as 'the world's first classically trained garage band', the young virtuosi of Time for Three can turn their hand to any kind of music.

Having mastered the 'train' theme that Brubeck penned to bind the four movements together, violinists Zach DePue and Nick Kendall with double bassist Ranaan Meyer and Brubeck himself began stylistically transforming the material, taking it back into the Baroque era and propelling it forwards through gospel, funk, classical, Cajun and Irish folk. 'Zach started playing an Irish fiddle tune in 4/4 while Ranaan, Nick and I were jamming in odd signatures like 7 and 9. It was actually an accident that we all really found intriguing.' Listening back to the session, analysing the complex material and harnessing it into an orchestral score was, even for a rhythm king such as Brubeck, 'like trying to capture lightning in a bottle. The styles shift on a dime, the common thread being the main theme and, as the music quickly leaps from the sensibilities of the 1700s to the 21st century, it almost seems as though the trio are musical "time travellers".'

DAVE BRUBECK
arr. CHRIS BRUBECK

(1920–2012)

Blue Rondo à la Turk
(1959, arr. 2014) *UK premiere*

PROM 71 • 9 SEPTEMBER

Blue Rondo à la Turk may have been released as the mere B-side to the Dave Brubeck Quartet's famous earworm *Take Five*, but the tune still managed to become legend by itself. Coming across this wonky riff while on tour in Turkey in 1958, Brubeck was told, 'This rhythm is to us what the blues is to you.'

Now, more than 50 years on, his son Chris has made a new orchestral arrangement that forgoes the need for a jazz quartet altogether. He writes, 'Dave first heard musicians jamming to this wild beat on the streets of Istanbul. It turned out, when he analysed the rhythm, that it was in 9/8 time. (My father studied with Darius Milhaud, who taught him that it was important to listen to the music of different cultures for inspiration.) So my new arrangement begins with the percussion section of the orchestra getting the 9/8 "street groove" going before the famous melody starts. When the theme begins, it is in alternating fragments with the propulsive 9/8 rhythm. That's never been done before and it should help tell the story of how Dave wrote the piece.' He continues, 'Blue Rondo is such an amazing composition that it will stand up even without the improvised elements. But I'll keep some flexibility in the chart; who knows, there might be a trumpet player who can blow his face off on the blues if given an opportunity.'

NEW MUSIC | 65

QIGANG CHEN

(BORN 1951)

Joie éternelle (2013)
BBC co-commission with the China Philharmonic Orchestra, MDR Orchestra, Leipzig, and the NTR Saturday Matinee series (the Netherlands): UK premiere

PROM 2 • 19 JULY

Qigang Chen's birthplace is ingrained in his music and, as with so many artists, 'ideological re-education' during the Cultural Revolution only made his grip on China's ancient history tighter. A childhood memory of seeing the 400-year-old epic Chinese opera *The Peony Pavilion* provided him with inspiration for *Joie éternelle*. 'The opera's original tune is delicate and graceful, yet also has an unyielding, instantly identifiable character,' he writes. 'Subsequent encounters with the tune as an adult have thus always evoked childhood memories. I have decided to use the original title of the *Qu Pai*, ['"Eternal Joy"'] because it seems to me to have a quasi-religious connotation.'

Chen learnt his craft at the Beijing Conservatory and then in Paris as the last pupil of Messiaen. His music often skilfully melds the allure and angularity of Chinese traditional music with an orchestral sensuousness that seems so very French. He frequently favours writing for voice and strings, but this is the first time Qigang has put a brass instrument centre-stage. 'I thought it was the perfect opportunity to reincarnate this tune with the sound of the trumpet, a very Western instrument. I hope to fully explore the trumpet's expressive range, from the exquisite to the muscular. I imagine the soloist conveying the wild inner character of the music while playing an elegant, beautiful melody.'

SIR PETER MAXWELL DAVIES

(BORN 1934)

Concert Overture 'Ebb of Winter' (2013)
London premiere

PROM 70 • 8 SEPTEMBER

Ebb of Winter may be Davies's 40th-birthday present to the orchestra he knows so well, but it's not sugar-coated. Complex orchestral passages and soloistic moments are designed to challenge and celebrate the undoubted brilliance of the Scottish Chamber Orchestra. As Davies has said, this is not the music 'of a tired old man'. Opening with a blazing horn fanfare, the piece is a dramatic account of a turbulent Orkney winter reluctant to yield to spring. It charts the kind of squally weather Davies knows intimately, having lived on the islands for over 40 years and walked its beaches daily. The brutal meteorological mood swings are captured with some dissonant harmonies and restless rhythms, but behind the piece is a backdrop of haunting beauty.

The past couple of years haven't been easy for Max, who was at one point given six weeks to live, following a diagnosis of acute leukaemia. He has said of *Ebb of Winter*, '[There is] some very dark music in there … I wasn't really quite aware of it. It's as if the music knew something that I didn't.' Thankfully now in the clear and back to his ebullient self, Davies at 80 recognises within him a greater spiritual awareness. 'The end of *Ebb* is optimistic and it does finish triumphantly, but I do have to keep pinching myself, thinking, "hey, you're alive!"'

JONATHAN DOVE

(BORN 1959)

Gaia (2013–14)
BBC commission: world premiere

PROM 15 • 28 JULY

Jonathan Dove's blithe, translucent music has won him many fans. His fanfares hailed the millennium and his *A Song of Joy* opened the Last Night of the Proms in 2010. His innate understanding of drama has led to a profusion of operas aimed at amateurs and professionals alike, but two of these, *The Walk from the Garden* and *The Day After*, have dealt with the darker subject of climate change. 'In 2008 I was invited to join the Cape Farewell voyage, in which musicians visited the Arctic in the company of scientists. Since then, I have been interested in finding ways of writing about climate change, looking for subjects for operas and concert pieces without trying to turn them into sermons or lectures.'

Named after the ancient Greek earth goddess, James Lovelock's Gaia Theory deals with the complex relationship of ecosystems binding Earth with its atmosphere. He once described evolution as 'a tightly coupled dance, with life and the material environment as partners'. Dove writes, 'His description of all the inter-related processes maintaining the earth in the optimum conditions for life as a kind of dance, is musically suggestive. I found myself wondering about the dance and imagining what it might sound like. How would the heat of the sun change the character of the dance? What would happen if some elements of the dance started to spin out of control?'

LUCA FRANCESCONI

(BORN 1956)

Duende – The Dark Notes (2014)
BBC co-commission with the Swedish Radio Symphony Orchestra and RAI National Symphony Orchestra: UK premiere

PROM 28 • 7 AUGUST

Anyone who has cried when least expecting it while listening to music or experiencing art, has met *duende*. It is a darkness, buried deep in the soul and often associated with the music of Andalusia, where it is evoked by performers of flamenco. According to Spanish poet Federico García Lorca, 'duende is a power, not a work. It is a struggle, not a thought', and you only have to listen to the great flamenco singers to believe it. But asking the violin to convey such a powerful spirit is, as Luca Francesconi writes, 'extremely difficult. To recover a primitive force in the instrument that perhaps most embodies the musical history of the West, it is necessary to make a perilous descent into the underworld of dark notes, or a flight beyond the orbit of the earth.'

A pupil of Berio and Stockhausen, Italy's Luca Francesconi is an arch-modernist who writes music of rich complexity and blistering virtuosity. He has the ability to let sound run free while maintaining a masterful control. 'The piece is about celebrating and at the same time about releasing the "dark notes" into oblivion,' says violinist Leila Josefowicz, for whom the piece was written. 'The general shape of the piece follows this idea, starting very high in the stratosphere and then becoming darker and darker in quality. It was thrilling to work on such extreme sounds with Luca.'

HELEN GRIME

(BORN 1981)

Near Midnight (2012)
London premiere

PROM 31 • 9 AUGUST

Having a piece heard at the Proms for the first time places a great deal of pressure on a composer, especially if, like Helen Grime's *Virga* in 2009, it is hailed soon after as one of the best classical works of the 21st century. Although Grime welcomed the attention, she was never going to be blown off course by mere flattery. Now in her early thirties, Grime has been writing music since she was 10 and, although she considered careers in archaeology and professional performance (she's a formidable oboe player), composing won out. 'I'm always striving to get closer to my ideal of what I want my music to be,' she says. 'I think this really drives me to compose. I want to write music that is emotionally direct.'

She wrote *Near Midnight* in her role as Associate Composer to the Hallé Orchestra, setting out to exploit the orchestra's 'very special, lyrical quality'. 'The initial inspiration came from a poem by D. H. Lawrence called *Weeknight Service*,' she says. 'I wanted to conjure the feelings of unrest, melancholy and reflection of the night. The poem has images of tolling bells, which became important structural points – fanfare-like brass passages come in different guises at different points of the piece.' She continues, 'A lot of the piece was written at night: I very much like the quiet and solitude that this time brings.'

GAVIN HIGGINS

(BORN 1983)

Velocity (2014)
BBC commission: world premiere

PROM 76 • 13 SEPTEMBER

Gavin Higgins knows how to pack a punch. Who isn't going to take notice of titles such as *Coogee Funk*, *Freaks* and *Dancing at the Edge of Hell*? But then brass players aren't renowned for their shy and retiring nature. Higgins played tenor horn in his local brass band in the Forest of Dean, where he grew up, before switching to the French horn. Studying performance alongside composition, he gained a Masters from the Royal College of Music in 2009. His Proms debut came three years later with *Der Aufstand*, his dark and turbulent musical response to the previous year's summer of riots. Writing music of great rhythmic force brought him to the attention of the Rambert Dance Company, which appointed him as its inaugural Musician-in-Residence.

While there is a softer side to Higgins, his preference is for high-impact, dynamic pieces. The perfect choice, then, for kick-starting the Last Night of the Proms. He says of *Velocity*, 'The piece won't be a fanfare in the traditional sense, but rather a short, fast, rhythmically fuelled tour de force for full orchestra. Blazing brass and soaring strings will characterise much of the piece. It will be a challenge to pack everything I want to say into a three-minute work, but it's going to be so exciting to hear it performed in the Royal Albert Hall.'

SIMON HOLT

(BORN 1958)

Morpheus Wakes (2011)
BBC commission: world premiere

PROM 14 • 27 JULY

The showiness of Simon Holt's music stems from student days at art school and a formative diet of everything from experimental kraut-rockers Faust to the dynamic music of Messiaen. Yet, where Holt can be flash, he can also be calm, creating pieces that demand attention while also clearing space for reflection. *Morpheus Wakes* is his fourth major Proms commission, a flute concerto written for Emmanuel Pahud. 'The title,' explains Holt, 'refers to Morpheus, a god of dreams, mentioned in Ovid's *Metamorphoses*. Capable of taking human form, he can materialise in other people's dreams. When not in human form he takes the guise of a winged demon. For this piece, I imagined him being trapped in a kind of permafrost, from which he takes flight. The question of what the god of dreams may dream about was always at the back of my mind when writing. His shape-shifting could be said to be represented by his changing from one flute to another and the interaction between the orchestral flutes.'

Holt has been Composer-in-Association with the BBC National Orchestra of Wales since 2008. 'I now know the orchestra's playing very well,' he says, 'especially that of Eva Stewart, who will be playing the piccolo. I've written a few wild piccolo lines for her over the past few years and it should be fascinating to watch her interact with Emmanuel.'

DAVID HORNE

(BORN 1970)

Daedalus in Flight (2013)
London premiere

PROM 10 • 25 JULY

This isn't the first time that the story of Daedalus and his wings famously fashioned from wax and feathers has inspired David Horne, and he doesn't think it'll be the last. The escape from the labyrinth has already spawned a string quartet and now comes *Daedalus in Flight*, a short and ebullient movement for orchestra. 'The notions surrounding the exhilaration of flight and escape are the most attractive to me,' says Horne. 'In myth, Daedalus's story is not an entirely happy one, of course, he is devastated by the loss of Icarus. My focus, by contrast, was on the success of his escape and the subsequent elation that might entail.'

He continues, 'I definitely decided on the title before I'd written a single note and I was also quite clear about the music I wanted to write: highly energetic, colourful, effervescent and driven throughout.' And those descriptive words apply just as well to Horne's overall approach to writing music. His was a precocious talent. He first appeared at the Proms at the age of 19 as soloist in Prokofiev's Third Piano Concerto. Nine years later he obtained a PhD in composition from Harvard and returned to the UK as a lecturer at the Royal Northern College of Music. Now he is busy turning his musical imagination to everything from opera to electronica – and doing it with relish.

BENEDICT MASON

(BORN 1954)

Meld (2012–13)
BBC commission: world premiere

PROM 41 · 16 AUGUST

Benedict Mason knows how to be playful – a gift so often lost in an adult world. He has the ability to think so far outside the box that any 'normal' questions about how he writes or thinks about his music are returned with a polite raised eyebrow. He uses his music to skilfully experiment with questions of style and the puzzles of rhythm, sound and perception. Between 1994 and 1997, he wrote his *Music for European Concert Halls* series, in which he explored the acoustics and 'spatial' potential of certain venues (the Royal Albert Hall included, with the Clarinet Concerto that marked his Proms debut in 1995). He has also invented instruments as a way of expanding his sound-world.

Meld was intended for the Proms in 2012, but its scale and ambition meant it has had to wait until now to be fully realised. It uses non-fictional and documentary texts. 'I wrote it for the first Saturday night of the 2012 Olympics, so I chose its text appropriately, but hopefully it is abstract enough to be non-occasional', says Mason. He added the title later. 'I find the word is rather interesting and rare in its etymology – but I don't think it has anything to do with the piece.' In an increasingly bland commercial world, it's good to know Mason is as beguilingly elusive as ever.

WILLIAM MATHIAS

(1934–92)

Violin Concerto (1991)
London premiere

PROM 27 · 6 AUGUST

It's as hard to dislike William Mathias's music as, by all accounts, it was to dislike the man himself. The gregarious Welshman immortalised his zest for life in a body of work that exudes warmth and captures the Celtic spirit. Largely self-taught and having grown up in a tradition of amateur music-making, Mathias adopted the mantra of clear communication. Through his use of unambiguous harmonies and catchy dance rhythms he ensured his music had direct appeal. Yet, despite many of his pieces being played and enjoyed the world over, the Violin Concerto is something of an enigma. Written for and premiered by György Pauk in 1992, it has rarely been performed, and never recorded. Fans of Mathias's music hunt for information on blogs and the programme note simply reads, 'a heady celebration of song and dance, in four movements that are strongly contrasted, yet highly integrated'.

Violinist Matthew Trusler sheds some light on this late work that puts the soloist firmly in the driving seat. 'It's extremely difficult,' he reports. 'The concerto has the same, fairly epic structure as Shostakovich's First Violin Concerto: slow first movement, fast scherzo second, long, unfolding climactic third and manic fourth to finish. Plus, there are several cadenzas thrown in, just to exhaust the soloist. It's terrific fun to play, full of atmosphere and extremely expressive.'

JOHN MCLEOD

(BORN 1934)

The Sun Dances (2001)
London premiere

PROM 23 · 3 AUGUST

Expressions of faith, religious or otherwise, have preoccupied a multitude of composers. Not least Scotland's John McLeod, who recognises this as a 'common thread' in many of the dramatic, sonorous and rhythmically vibrant pieces he's written over the past 40 years. But, given the abstract nature of the subject matter, his discovery of the Gaelic folk tale of Old Barbara Macphie must have been a boon. Such was the strength of this woman's faith that, one Easter Sunday morning, from the top of Ben More, the highest mountain on the Isle of Mull, she claims to have seen the sun dance for joy of Christ's resurrection: 'The glorious gold-bright sun was rising on the crest of the great hills and it was changing colour – green, purple, red, blood-red, white, intense-white and gold-white, like the glory of the God of the elements to the children of men. It was dancing up and down in exultation at the joyous resurrection of the beloved Saviour of victory.'

What a gift for McLeod and his orchestral painterly brilliance. In 2000 he set the sun dancing with dense harmonies and luscious textures, but, 'as the work progressed I began hearing in my head (for no apparent reason) the old Scottish psalm tune known as "Martyrs". This became so powerful that it found its way into the piece – at first as fragments and then in full glory at the climax of the piece.'

ROXANNA PANUFNIK

(BORN 1968)

Three Paths to Peace (2008)
European premiere

PROM 4 · 20 JULY

'Hello, PANUFNIK CENTENARY YEAR!! (Dad's, cheeky! x)' tweeted Roxanna Panufnik at the beginning of 2014, launching a year of celebrations with much father–daughter programming. Juggling a packed family life with the demands of a fruitful career means Roxanna Panufnik only banks on getting about five minutes of music written a month. So, when the World Orchestra for Peace requested a new work in 2008 at short notice, it was going to be disappointed. That is, until the idea came up to carve an orchestral prelude from her existing and much-acclaimed violin concerto, *Abraham*. The result, *Three Paths to Peace*, is a dignified 12 minutes of tightly honed music that binds together Sephardic chant, Christian plainsong and the Islamic call to prayer.

'*Abraham* is considered the father of all these three faiths,' Panufnik has explained. 'The whole concept behind it is that, despite all the conflict in the world between the three monotheistic faiths – Christianity, Judaism and Islam – we do all believe in the same one God.' Skilfully weaving fine orchestral textures from church bell patterns, Sufi drum rhythms and the sound of the Jewish shofar (ram's horn), *Three Paths* is an achingly restrained, deeply soulful vision of hope. It moves through five rich scenarios towards what she has described as, 'a homogenous, harmonious and joyful conclusion'.

GABRIEL PROKOFIEV

(BORN 1975)

Violin Concerto (2014)
BBC commission: world premiere

PROM 16 • 29 JULY

Gabriel Prokofiev's love/hate relationship with classical music has led to his treading some innovative pathways. As a DJ, dance music producer and classical composer, he has often focused on finding common ground where these seemingly diverse musical disciplines can meet. With his record label and club night Nonclassical, he's created new platforms on which both musicians and listeners can experiment. In 2011 he used his Proms debut to introduce DJ Switch to the National Youth Orchestra of Great Britain, for his rhythmically savvy Concerto for turntables and orchestra.

Three years on, Prokofiev is in a more contemplative, even traditional, mood. His Violin Concerto marks the centenary of the First World War (the war that would eventually lead to his grandfather Sergey Prokofiev leaving Russia for America). 'The work uses full symphonic orchestra,' writes Gabriel Prokofiev, 'with a particular focus on pairing the solo violin with different sections of the orchestra to create distinctly different images. In one section the violin is accompanied by four snare drums positioned in different parts of the stage. I'm using the soloist to paint the intimate picture of the human experiences during the First World War. There are musical references both to the old Europe, and in particular to the peoples and places that were particularly significant in 1914.'

BERNARD RANDS

(BORN 1934)

Concerto for Piano and Orchestra (2013)
UK premiere

PROM 39 • 15 AUGUST

Bernard Rands is one of contemporary music's towering figures, with over 100 pieces to his name and his 80th birthday earlier this year. English born but resident in America since the mid-1970s, he's a rigorous technician whose music and teaching have inspired many. And yet, 'For me,' he says, 'the creative process is never easy.' You wouldn't think it listening to his music, which takes impressive command of the orchestra and delivers lucid pieces time and again.

Ever mindful of the listener, Rands believes the opening of a work is particularly crucial. 'The concerto begins with a majestic, almost strident theme on the strings – that permeates the entire first movement and is "commented upon" by the piano, which is only gradually seduced into the discourse.' Three movements ensue, 'but there the similarities with the convention end! Each movement is a unique form appropriate to and deriving from the musical ideas themselves.' And take note, this is not a piano concerto. 'It seems appropriate to call it what it is,' says Rands, 'a concerto for piano and orchestra, implying a less conventional role for both forces – the orchestra has as much of a concerto character as the soloist, it's not simply an accompaniment to the piano. I'd say that the general character of this work is one of gracious understatement rather than requiring Romantic grand climaxes.'

BEHZAD RANJBARAN

(BORN 1955)

Seemorgh – The Sunrise (1991)
European premiere

PROM 67 • 7 SEPTEMBER

Behzad Ranjbaran is a master of musical storytelling. His Persian Trilogy has an effect similar to that of reading a child's book of fantasy stories complete with brilliantly drawn pictures of fearless heroes, irksome villains and fiery mythical beings. The music is bursting with character, skilfully orchestrated and cinematic in scope. Ranjbaran was 10 years old when he first became 'transfixed' by the stories of the *Shahnameh* ('The Book of Kings'). This is Persia's epic national poem that, in some 60,000 verses, recounts the country's legends and myths, from the beginning of time to the Arab conquest of the 7th century. Tales that Ranjbaran recalls, 'captured my imagination forever'.

One of the stories retold in the Persian Trilogy is that of the Seemorgh, a magical bird that rescues an abandoned baby and nurtures him in her nest on the highest point of Mount Alborz. 'As a child in Tehran,' writes Ranjbaran, 'I was very impressed with Mount Alborz, the mountain on which Seemorgh supposedly lived. I used to gaze at the mountain, thinking that she actually lived there. Watching the mountain during sunrise and sunset with its white peak full of snow was truly fascinating. In writing the third movement ("The Sunrise") of *Seemorgh*, I felt as if I were still under the spell of those images.'

KAREEM ROUSTOM

(BORN 1971)

Ramal (2014)
UK premiere

PROM 46 • 20 AUGUST

Kareem Roustom is as comfortable making string arrangements for pop stars as he is writing music for cinema screen and concert hall. Born in Damascus to an American mother and Syrian father, he has a love of jazz, plays the Arabic oud and is well versed in both Eastern and Western musical languages. He hasn't returned to beleaguered Syria since 2008, but his homeland is never far from his thoughts.

Ramal takes its name from a classical Arabic poetic metre. Roustom explains, 'an epic mystical poem, titled *The Conference of the Birds*, by the 13th-century Iranian Sufi poet Farid ud-Din Attar, was composed on this metre. Although [my piece] is not programmatic *per se*, it does reflect themes from *The Conference of the Birds* – especially the ways in which the personal and spiritual journeys of different individuals can co-exist or collide. *Ramal* is also a meditation on the inevitability of change, and the very human impulse to resist change. As I watch the tragic changes in Syria today, it feels ever more important to hold on to some traditions that speak to me of its rich and vibrant culture and history. When one leaves a country, by force or by choice, one cannot bring the stones of the family home. However, one can keep alive the poetry, music and culture.'

Alicia Clarke (Prokofiev); Elias Roustom (Roustom)

JOHN TAVENER

(1944–2013)

Gnosis (2013)
BBC commission: world premiere

PROM 7 • 23 JULY

Greek for 'knowledge', gnosis defines a belief that cites metaphysics rather than faith as a route to spiritual enlightenment. Metaphysics also guided Tavener's compositional approach. He once wrote, 'All music already exists. When God created the world, he created everything. It's up to us as artists to find that music.' This led to his composing with great speed and fluency (what he called 'divine dictation'), but also to an abhorrence of music in which he heard only the composer's ego rather than the divine.

He softened this view in later years: 'I've come to realise that it is part of God's plan that one suffers,' he said. 'It's up to one to somehow transcend it and to produce a kind of ecstasy through the suffering.' He also began to acknowledge that quest in other composers' works. *Gnosis* 'was largely inspired by a performance of Mahler's 'Der Abschied' from *Das Lied von der Erde*,' says mezzo-soprano Sarah Connolly, to whom the piece is dedicated. 'There's a *pianissimo* low C on double bass throughout, with recurring varied vocal melismatic patterns above. The strings are largely chordal with occasional short manic outbursts. John's directions in the score, in no particular order, are; ''apocalyptic'', ''suddenly violent'', ''full of grace'', *dolcissimo possibile*, ''suddenly still'', ''with rapture and bliss'', ''rapt and intense''.'

JOHN TAVENER

(1944–2013)

Requiem Fragments (2013)
BBC commission: world premiere

PROM 25 • 4 AUGUST

Requiem Fragments is not, as the title might suggest, an incomplete work, nor is it a reduced version of Tavener's *Requiem* of 2007. It is a new, complete piece in which Tavener actively decided to omit some of the traditional movements and reflect his interest in a multitude of faiths. Dedicated to the Tallis Scholars, it bookends a fruitful working relationship that began in the early 1980s with *Ikon of Light*.

Peter Phillips's thoughts about *Requiem Fragments* offer acute insight. 'When I last visited Tavener, just before he died, he asked me to bring the score of Josquin's 24-voice canon *Qui habitat*. In the *Fragments* the Latin (and Greek) texts of ''Requiem aeternam'', ''Kyrie eleison'' and ''Sanctus'' are overlaid with references to Hindu philosophy. The massive last movement, which consists largely of a triple-choir canon, until the very end only uses two words: ''Manikarnika'' (the ghat on the Ganges where funeral pyres burn); and ''Mahapralaya'' (meaning Great Dissolution). It is interesting that the handwriting in the score changes noticeably before ''Manikarnika'' starts, as does the style of the music. Suddenly we're back in the sound-world of *Ikon of Light* and even of Josquin's *Qui habitat*. Perhaps I arrived at John's house with my Josquin score at a crucial moment and, if he'd been asked, he would have said my visit had been divinely ordained – he liked to think in those terms.'

NEIL TENNANT/ CHRIS LOWE

(BORN 1954 / BORN 1959)

A Man From the Future (2012–14)
world premiere

PROM 8 • 23 JULY

There's something very apt about the Pet Shop Boys, famous for using state-of-the-art computer technology, paying homage to the pioneer who started it all. *A Man from the Future* is Neil Tennant and Chris Lowe's tribute to the mathematician and computer genius Alan Turing, who 'in his attitudes to both science and sexuality,' Tennant asserts, 'was decades ahead of his time'. Turing helped break the Enigma code during the Second World War, but also formulated the concept of the digital computer, going on to pioneer work in artificial intelligence. Refusing to hide his homosexuality, he was prosecuted in 1952, forced to take chemical 'treatment' and committed suicide.

Using voice, orchestra, spoken word, electronic instruments and chorus, *A Man from the Future* lays out Turing's life in eight chapters. 'The challenge of writing the piece was to blend music, singing and narrative,' says Tennant. 'It consists mainly of words taken from Andrew Hodges's biography of Turing, chosen to spotlight key moments in his life and for the poetic quality of the writing.' In a single-movement preview in 2012, the choir applied ethereal shading to Tennant's distinctive voice and the Pet Shop Boys' hallmark electronic washes and beats were mixed over dense beds of orchestral sound. Tennant described the result as 'very different from anything else we've ever done'.

JUKKA TIENSUU

(BORN 1948)

Voice verser (2012)
UK premiere

PROM 49 • 23 AUGUST

Finland's Jukka Tiensuu is a musical chameleon. Composer, conductor, pianist and harpsichordist, he turns his hand to any style, from Baroque to free jazz. Each piece he writes is different, tackling a particular facet of sound that's awakened his curiosity, be it acoustic or electronic, spatial or complex. This makes describing his overall music problematic but has resulted in a catalogue of breathtaking scope. As he declares, 'When seeking the fundamental essence of music, one cannot confine oneself to a narrow approach.'

Tiensuu rarely likes to discuss pieces and when he does, keeps descriptions to a bare minimum. This is not some arch pretension, but in line with the belief he has stated that 'an open mind is the shortest way to understanding'. To describe a piece in words could prejudice the listener, whereas his preference is to communicate purely through sound. To that end he creates pieces with a clarity and cohesion that speak to those willing to listen. So, what does he have to say about *Voice verser*? Simply, '*Voice verser* for soprano and orchestra consists of three songs: ''Desparia'', ''Come'' and ''Riitti''. The orchestra part includes two groups of musicians placed at or near the back corners of the audience.' And now all we can do is listen with an open mind.

HAUKUR TÓMASSON

(BORN 1960)

Magma (1998, rev. 1999)
UK premiere

PROM 48 • 22 AUGUST

There are few people in sparsely populated Iceland who aren't up to something creative, be it painting, writing, sculpting or experimenting with music. And it's little wonder. Geographically isolated, Iceland's provocative, volcanic landscape of mountains, lava fields and glaciers positively demand a reaction, and provide an endless source of inspiration. None more so for musical purposes than magma, the blisteringly hot molten rock that squirms beneath Earth's surface, occasionally making itself known as volcanic lava outflow.

Haukur Tómasson's piece is not a direct description of magma, but feeds off it. 'I mostly get some kind of energy from experiencing something sublimely beautiful in nature,' he says, using the words 'animated, *cantabile* and rigorous' to characterise the various chapters of the piece. Over its 15 minutes, two forceful ideas are pitted against each other, 'one thick, floating, magma-like and one rhythmically congealing, which slowly takes over'. Here are the Tómasson hallmarks. Restless rhythms, vibrant orchestrations and powerful unifying climaxes are the elements he forges deftly into works of sound logic and strength. It is the kind of impressive, coherent language that won him the Nordic Council Music Prize in 2004 and that marks him out as one of Iceland's most powerful voices.

JUDITH WEIR

(BORN 1954)

Day Break Shadows Flee (2014)
BBC commission: world premiere

PCM 7 • 1 SEPTEMBER

No fewer than 19 pieces by Judith Weir have been heard at the Proms over the years. An impressive tally for a living composer and indicative of her warm, stylish command of melody that has won listeners over time and time again. She is rightfully respected as one of Britain's leading and best-loved contemporary composers, compact simplicity is key to her success – taking an idea and distilling it until only the fundamental ingredients are left for close examination. True to form, her aim with this solo piano piece was 'to avoid fistfuls of notes which have so often been the default setting of contemporary piano music in the past' and instead to create 'something linear, made up of melody lines of many kinds, fast and slow, jagged and smooth'.

The words 'Day Break Shadows Flee' came to her as she began sketching the piece's two contrasting ideas: 'firstly fast, nervous, scurrying, mysterious music which I thought of as nocturnes – and secondly, a more confident, warmer, arching phrase, appearing in many musical guises. I realised the warm-phrase music was a kind of *ritornello* appearing between the nocturnes. Or perhaps there were two different pieces playing on different channels simultaneously, with the warm music bursting in from time to time to drive away the nervous mystery music.'

BILL WHELAN

(BORN 1950)

Riverdance: A Symphonic Suite (2012)
UK premiere

PROM 51 • 25 AUGUST

To mark 20 years of *Riverdance*, Bill Whelan has fulfilled a long-held ambition: to carve a full-length concert piece from the music of his world-famous show. But letting orchestras in on the *craic*, has meant forgoing not only the breathtaking dancing, but also the distinctive traditional instruments, such as uilleann pipes, Balkan gadulkas and Spanish guitars. 'All of these had to be substituted,' he writes, 'and replaced when bringing this music to the symphonic stage. The reeds of the oboe and cor anglais seemed such natural and expressive replacements for the pipes. Flutes and piccolos were ideal surrogates for the whistles, the harp and piano for the guitars.

'The Symphonic Suite,' he continues, 'weaves through different moods and colours – from sombre slow airs and songs to energetic and climactic dances. The story of *Riverdance* is about the journey of the Irish into the wider world, and the music has been about finding points of connection between our traditional music and the music of other cultures – from flamenco and Eastern European music to choral and jazz. All of these influences are discernible in 21st-century Ireland. I think the pure tradition is still robust and very visible, and I believe that Irish artists will always seek to reach into that tradition to find ways for individual and contemporary expression.'

JÖRG WIDMANN

(BORN 1973)

Flûte en suite (2011)
UK premiere

PROM 68 • 7 SEPTEMBER

'Tradition is tending the flame, not worshipping the ashes.' The words are Mahler's but the sentiment is well illustrated by Jörg Widmann's work. The German composer is aware of his place in a long line of German greats. But, rather than revere the masters from a distance, he takes every opportunity to seize their ideas and mould them to a 21st-century outlook. *Flûte en suite* is a series of eight dances with titles such as 'Allemande', 'Courante' and 'Badinerie'. The form is familiar but the content is far from Baroque. Instead, the movements act as gilt frames, displaying what Widmann describes as 'the exciting dark timbre' of the Cleveland Orchestra's principal flautist Joshua Smith.

'I simply wanted,' writes Widmann, 'to create a piece in which he is heard, a form where you can hear him almost every second.' Flutes in the low register cloak the opening in mystery before other sections of the scaled-down orchestra are introduced with careful consideration. Edgy harmonies build steadily, delivering some blistering chords at timely climaxes. 'Sunken worlds suddenly emerge, only to reach the surface, hover in dangerously distorted fashion and then sink back to the bottom.' Yet, at the end of the concerto there is humour, as if Widmann, scared by his own ghosts, has packed up his musical Ouija board and headed home with a grin.

JÖRG WIDMANN
(BORN 1973)

Teufel Amor (2009, rev. 2011)
UK premiere

PROM 69 • 8 SEPTEMBER

Jörg Widmann's passion, whether through composition or his work as a virtuoso clarinettist, is to take a fresh look at the ideas of the past. Not to revere or reject them, but to understand and use them as solid foundations on which to build a highly modern future. To this end, his music is often challenging, dramatic and tightly packed with ideas. He was the Cleveland Orchestra's Daniel R. Lewis Young Composer Fellow from 2009 to 2011. During that time he worked on this ambitious orchestral piece that grapples with the extreme nature of love itself, from agony to ecstasy.

Based on a poem by Frederich Schiller of which only a fragment survives, *Teufel Amor* translates as 'devil love'. Tackling the contradiction inherent in the title, Widmann also took inspiration from the surviving line: *Süsser Amor, verweile im melodischen Flug* ['Sweet Amor, remain in melodic flight'] which he describes as 'an exceedingly poetic and also musical fragment. A movement as a state of being and a state of being as movement: an apparently contradictory pair, just like the title of the poem.' He continues, 'My imagination was fired by Schiller's fragment; his conception of the flight of Amor as the heights and depths of a melodic progression inspired me to compose a symphonic hymn which praises the marvels of love – even in its devilish incarnation.'

Christopher Peter/Schott Music (Widmann)

ZHOU LONG
(BORN 1953)

Postures (2013–14)
European premiere

PROM 61 • 2 SEPTEMBER

The idea behind *Postures* stems from the Chinese martial art of kung fu. As Hollywood would have us believe, the external display of physical brilliance in this ancient discipline is important, but so too is the internal training of the mind, spirit and breath. 'I always consider the piano as a rhythmic and hammered instrument,' writes Pulitzer Prize-winning composer Zhou Long. 'With this in mind, *Postures* reflects some movements in different animal gestures in kung fu. This piece not only illustrates those energies, but the meditation of the mind.'

Zhou Long has mastered the art of combining ancient Chinese tradition with modern Western ideas. He often tempers his serene melodies with gritty chromatic harmonies to create 'otherworldly atmospheres' – music that, rather than romanticising the past, seems to embody it positively. 'For the Chinese,' he once said, 'the past does not freeze in time: its spiritual and philosophical essence flows continuously into the present as an unbroken long river, transcending historical boundaries.' The tantalising images embedded in the three movements of *Postures* include a shaman dance in which dancers 'wearing the masks of five animals (tiger, leopard, bear, deer and roe deer) … express their joy of work and life'; 'bells borne on the wind from valleys and canyons'; and the antics of the Peking Opera monkey.

International Orchestra Series 2014/15

Great orchestras from around the world at Southbank Centre

Daniel Barenboim

Martha Argerich © Adriano Heitmann

Gustavo Dudamel © Adam Latham

Gustavo Dudamel

Simón Bolívar Symphony Orchestra of Venezuela

Simon Rattle

Berliner Philharmoniker

Daniel Barenboim

Staatskapelle Berlin

Iván Fischer

Budapest Festival Orchestra

southbankcentre.co.uk/orchestra
0844 847 9934

Media partner

THE TIMES

Supported using public funding by
ARTS COUNCIL ENGLAND
LOTTERY FUNDED

SOUTHBANK CENTRE

Talented Dancer or Musician?

Yes, TALENT is ALL you need for a place at a Music and Dance School.

All our schools are dedicated to encouraging talented young people from all financial and cultural backgrounds... we can offer up to 100% Government funding for places.

Music and Dance Schools are committed to the highest teaching standards in music and dance, as well as an excellent academic education.

If you are interested in one of the Music and Dance Schools just visit our website for contact details.

www.musicanddanceschools.com

There are nine Music and Dance Schools throughout the UK

• Chetham's School of Music, Manchester
• Elmhurst School for Dance, Birmingham
• St Mary's Music School, Edinburgh
• The Hammond, Chester
• The Purcell School for Young Musicians, Herts
• The Royal Ballet School, London
• Tring Park School for the Performing Arts, Herts
• Wells Cathedral School, Somerset
• Yehudi Menuhin School, Surrey

MUSIC
& DANCE
SCHOOLS
ACCESS TO EXCELLENCE

SINGAPORE SYMPHONY ORCHESTRA

'This could be one of the great orchestras of the 21st century'

THE SPECTATOR

'Come back soon!'

THE TIMES

Come hear the SSO's Proms debut on 2 Sep 2014!

GLINKA
Overture to *Russlan and Ludmilla*

ZHOU LONG
Piano Concerto
UK PREMIERE

RACHMANINOV
Symphony No. 2 in E minor, Op. 27

Lan Shui music director
Andreas Haefliger piano

14/15 season includes:

Vladimir Ashkenazy | Krystian Zimerman
Yefim Bronfman | Paul Lewis
Stephen Hough | Midori

SINGAPORE
SYMPHONY
ORCHESTRA

www.sso.org.sg

BIRTHDAY BATONISTS

With four of Britain's most noted conductors celebrating significant birthdays this year, **HUGH CANNING** looks at over 175 years of their collective conducting experience – and the reasons behind their continued success

There's a commonly held belief that conductors, like fine wines, get better as they mature. An aura of magisterial wisdom accrues to the most celebrated podium stars the older they get. One thinks of the Indian-summer career of the excellent German Kapellmeister Günter Wand, whose Bruckner performances with the BBC and North German Radio Symphony orchestras enriched the Proms in the 1980s and 1990s, and the near-sanctity conferred on the late, great Claudio Abbado – whose reading of Mahler's Third Symphony in 2007 is spoken of by those who heard it live at the Proms in awe-struck tones. Yet such feats shouldn't surprise us. The longer great musicians ponder the mysteries of the masterpieces they interpret, the more profoundly they can reveal them to their audiences. It is with good reason that we revere our octogenarian maestros.

A nonagenarian is more of a rarity and it comes as something of a shock to realise that Sir Neville Marriner reached this venerable age on 15 April (it's hard to think of many great conductors who have been active in their nineties, other than Leopold Stokowski, who was still performing in public at 93 and making recordings two years later). Three other British conductors at this year's Proms are celebrating significant birthdays as well – Sir Roger Norrington is 80 this year, Sir Andrew Davis 70 and Donald Runnicles 60. Marriner's Prom on 10 August reunites him with the orchestra he founded in 1958, the Academy of St Martin in the Fields, in a programme featuring Beethoven's First Symphony, Bruch's First Violin Concerto and Christopher Palmer's arrangement of Walton's film score, *Henry V: A Shakespeare Scenario* – something of a Marriner party-piece, the idea for this version for speaker, chorus and orchestra having originated with him.

From the 1960s to the 1990s, the ASMF and Marriner recorded – and toured – a vast repertoire of music for chamber orchestra, from the Baroque to 20th-century classics. Their performances of Bach, Handel, Haydn, Mozart and Beethoven were regarded as exemplary at the time, ideally proportioned in comparison to the big-band sound of traditional symphony orchestras. Although Marriner never embraced the period-instrument movement, he is, in a very real sense, a pioneer of period-performance practice, preparing the way for succeeding generations of conductors

Sir Neville Marriner

Sir Roger Norrington

Taken as a mini-festival of Proms podium birthday boys, these programmes reflect the versatility – as well as the individual special interests – of four British conductors of divergent musical backgrounds.

who preferred to play Baroque and Classical music on instruments of the time.

Norrington is one of the leading lights of that movement – like Sir Neville he has been Music Director of the Stuttgart Radio Symphony Orchestra, which he brings to the Proms, now as Honorary Conductor, in a programme of Beethoven, Berlioz and Dvořák (3 September). After 15 years as founder-director of Kent Opera – during which period he conducted repertoire ranging from Monteverdi and Purcell to Britten and Tippett – Norrington rose to international prominence with the foundation of his period-instrument orchestra, the London Classical Players, whose weekend-long 'Experiences' – focusing on a major work of Haydn (*The Creation*), Beethoven ('Choral' Symphony), Berlioz (*Symphonie fantastique*) and many others – enlivened London's concert scene in the 1980s and 1990s and won Norrington a huge following for his knowledgeable explications of the music and performance practice. He encouraged audiences to applaud between movements, as that's what Haydn's, Beethoven's and

Berlioz's would have done. Now Principal Conductor of the Zurich Chamber Orchestra, he brings this ensemble and its associate Sing-Akademie to an earlier Prom (26 July) for Bach's *St John Passion*, with a distinguished team of soloists, headed by James Gilchrist as the Evangelist and Neal Davies as Christus.

Sir Andrew Davis, who celebrated his 70th birthday in February, needs no introduction to Promenaders. Even before his 11-year stewardship of the BBC Symphony Orchestra (1989–2000), he was a regular visitor to the Proms, from 1988 also as Music Director of Glyndebourne. During the last decade of the 20th century he conducted a vast repertoire of symphonic music and opera, making a speciality of the very big pieces – Mahler's Eighth Symphony, Schoenberg's *Gurrelieder* and Verdi's *Requiem* – for his opening concerts. He became a consummate master of ceremonies at the Last Night, memorably saying his farewell as the BBC SO's Chief Conductor in 2000 with an unforgettable 'speech' in the form of a

parody of the Major-General's Song ('I am the very model of a modern Major-General') from Gilbert and Sullivan's *The Pirates of Penzance* – a virtuoso piece of patter 'singing' that endeared him to millions beyond the core live audience at the Proms. Now Music Director and Principal Conductor of the Lyric Opera of Chicago, Davis opens this year's festivities in grand style with a First Night performance of Elgar's *The Kingdom* (18 July), completing the composer's triptych of oratorios, after having given performances of *The Dream of Gerontius* and *The Apostles* with the BBC SO and Chorus at the Barbican in April. His second Prom introduces his new (since 2013) partnership with the Melbourne Symphony Orchestra (19 August) in a programme comprising two Davis specialities in the first half – Strauss's *Don Juan* and Elgar's Cello Concerto, with Truls Mørk as soloist – and Berlioz's *Symphonie fantastique* in the second.

Donald Runnicles, 60 in November, is the Benjamin of the quartet, but, like Davis, heads both an opera house – the Deutsche Oper in

Sir Andrew Davis

Donald Runnicles

Berlin – and an orchestra – the BBC Scottish Symphony Orchestra – both of which appear with him in separate Proms. Last year, they joined forces, the Deutsche Oper sending its chorus, the BBC SSO supplying the orchestra, for a memorable concert performance of *Tannhäuser* for the Wagner bicentenary celebrations. This year, the Proms celebrates Richard Strauss's 150th anniversary, so the choice of Runnicles and the Deutsche Oper for *Salome* (30 August) – with last year's thrilling Brünnhilde, Nina Stemme, in the title-role – is a natural one. Opera has always been central to Runnicles's career – he spent 10 years in Germany as a Kapellmeister in Mannheim and Generalmusikdirektor in Freiburg, before landing the job of San Francisco Opera's Music Director and Principal Conductor in 1992 (eventually spending 17 years there, conducting German, Italian, French and British operatic repertoire). His conducting of Wagner's *Ring* cycle for the Deutsche Oper in 2007 led to an invitation to become the company's Music Director in 2009, the same year he took up his post

as Principal Conductor of the BBC SSO. Runnicles' two Proms with the orchestra naturally highlight his affinity for German music, with Beethoven's Fourth Symphony and Mozart's *Requiem* on 3 August and Mahler's valedictory Ninth Symphony the following evening, although both concerts open with a British work: the London premiere of Scots composer John McLeod's *The Sun Dances* and Vaughan Williams's *Fantasia on a Theme by Thomas Tallis*.

Taken as a mini-festival of Proms podium birthday boys, these programmes reflect the versatility – as well as the individual special interests – of four British conductors of divergent musical backgrounds. But, affinities can be discerned between Marriner and Norrington as pre-Classical performance-practice pioneers and between Davis and Runnicles as maestros who have found a perfect equilibrium for their work on the concert platform and in the opera house. So, many happy returns to all of them. ●

Hugh Canning writes about classical music for *The Sunday Times*.

Chris Christodoulou/BBC/BBC (Davis); Bettina Stöss/Deutsche Oper Berlin (Runnicles)

BIRTHDAY BATONISTS AT THE PROMS

Sir Andrew Davis

BBC Symphony Orchestra
PROM 1 · 18 JULY

Melbourne Symphony Orchestra
PROM 44 · 19 AUGUST

• • •

Sir Neville Marriner

Academy of St Martin in the Fields
PROM 32 · 10 AUGUST

• • •

Sir Roger Norrington

Zurich Chamber Orchestra
PROM 12 · 26 JULY

Stuttgart Radio Symphony Orchestra (SWR)
PROM 62 · 3 SEPTEMBER

• • •

Donald Runnicles

BBC Scottish Symphony Orchestra
PROMS 23 & 24 · 3 & 4 AUGUST

Deutsche Oper Berlin
PROM 58 · 30 AUGUST

BRUSH UP YOUR
SHAKESPEARE

As John Wilson and his orchestra return for a complete semi-staged performance of *Kiss Me, Kate*, **DAVID BENEDICT** marvels at how the composer-lyricist Cole Porter transformed *The Taming of the Shrew* into a Broadway hit

Photofest (Patricia Manson and Alfred Drake in the original Broadway production of 'Kiss Me, Kate,' 1948)

The switchback ride of the John Wilson Orchestra strings, woodwind and brass hurtling though the fiendishly difficult music for *Tom and Jerry* cartoons would have been enough, but the virtuoso percussionists snoring, screaming, smashing plates and firing a gun assured last year's Hollywood Rhapsody Prom a place in the history books. Given these musicians' success with some of Hollywood's finest film scores, you might expect them to return with another shimmering selection of screen gems. But no: this year Wilson is heading back to the 16th century and Shakespeare. Really? Well, Shakespeare re-imagined by Cole Porter as the 1948 hit musical *Kiss Me, Kate*.

Wilson has been plotting to bring this to the Proms for some time. 'We had such fun performing Lerner and Loewe's *My Fair Lady* at the Proms in 2012 that we decided we had to do another complete musical.' The Proms debut of *Kiss Me, Kate* – 50 years after the composer-lyricist's death – is recognition of Porter's biggest hit (1,077 performances in its original run), and the strongest musical he ever wrote. No less a figure than W. H. Auden proclaimed it better than Shakespeare's *The Taming of the Shrew*, on which it is based.

Although Wilson is a passionate expert in this genre, he is actually more cautious than many imagine him to be. 'There are musicals I've loved all my life but there's only a handful I really want to conduct: this is one of them.' He knows whereof he speaks, having conducted the hit-packed score back in 2000 in a co-production between students and alumni of the Royal College of Music and the London Academy of Music and Dramatic Art.

So what's the attraction? 'Everything! The tunes, the scoring, the snappy dialogue … it's all so deftly done and the comedy is genuinely funny.'

> There are musicals I've loved all my life but there's only a handful I really want to conduct: this is one of them.

This wasn't the first musical to be based on Shakespeare: Rodgers and Hart got there first in 1938, turning *The Comedy of Errors* into the chirpy *The Boys from Syracuse*. But great source material is no guarantee of a great musical – *Music Is*, a 1976 adaptation of *Twelfth Night*, lasted just eight performances; *Rockabye Hamlet*, first staged on Broadway in 1976, only managed seven. But the quality of the writing in every area of *Kiss Me, Kate* makes it a stand-out, especially when you consider that construction was not Porter's strong suit.

As he often said, 'I have no book sense.' By 'book' he meant 'script'. He'd become vastly successful in the 1930s, when musicals were almost universally air-headed affairs with no properly developed sense of plot or drama. He made his name adding songs to what the book-writer provided – as in, for example, his barely remembered 1935 show *Jubilee*. That included the song 'Begin the Beguine'. Daringly, it was 108 bars long – over three times the length of most songs. It wasn't popular – until clarinettist Artie Shaw recorded his swing version, which promptly sold over six and a half million copies.

But Broadway changed almost overnight in 1943 when *Oklahoma!* ushered in the era of properly dramatic musical plays. Porter's style got left behind and his scores grew increasingly lacklustre. Offered Samuel and Bella Spewack's script for this tale of the backstage/onstage bickerings of a diva-like husband-and-wife

team touring a musical production of the *Shrew*, Porter found himself aboard a vehicle with true dramatic potential and rose magnificently to the challenge.

'We're doing the complete score, from overture to exit music, in its original Broadway orchestration,' Wilson reveals, 'and it's bigger than anything else Porter wrote. It's all fresh, whether in the production numbers, the musical comedy numbers or the ballads. These songs are all cut from high-grade musical cloth. You don't ever feel that he settled for second best.'

He's not exaggerating. The score includes such perennial favourites as 'So in Love', 'Too Darn Hot', 'Always True to You in My Fashion' and, of course, Porter's famous pun-bonanza, 'Brush Up Your Shakespeare'.

It's not just the comic zing of the lyrics that makes this score so memorable. Porter's music has a highly distinctive harmonic flavour. The closest he got to describing it was in his song 'Ev'ry Time We Say Goodbye', from the 1944 flop *Seven Lively Arts*, which includes the lyric, 'There's no love song finer/ But how strange the change from major to minor.' Switching between major and minor for added pathos is a Porter hallmark.

Doing justice to all that, John Wilson's raft of soloists and chorus will be accompanied by the lush sound of 50 orchestral players from the John Wilson Orchestra. That's a size of band unheard of in today's West End, where the number of players that managements can afford is nearer 15 than 50.

'Theatre audiences have been short-changed on that front,' says Wilson. 'This is the kind of sound that scores like these deserve.' •

David Benedict is the UK critic for *Variety* and has written and broadcast extensively about musical theatre, including for BBC Radio 4's *Front Row*.

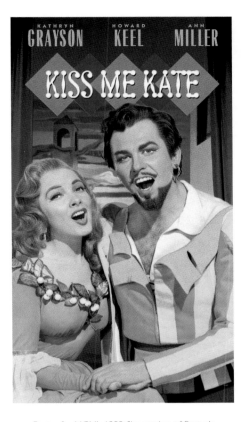

Poster for MGM's 1953 film version of Porter's *Kiss Me, Kate*, featuring Kathryn Grayson as Lilli/Kate and Howard Keel as Fred/Petruchio

KISS ME, KATE
AT THE PROMS

John Wilson conducts the
John Wilson Orchestra in the complete
original 1948 Broadway score
PROM 21 • 2 AUGUST

RESURRECTING
THE PASSION

As Peter Sellars's innovative and intimate staging of Bach's *St Matthew Passion* comes to the Proms, choral director **SIMON HALSEY**, who collaborated with Sellars and Sir Simon Rattle on the production, looks back over a remarkable rehearsal process

We knew we had a winner on our hands when, at the first whirlwind encounter with Peter Sellars in 2010, many choir members were moved to tears. The build-up had been intense. We had spent 20 days learning Bach's *St Matthew Passion* from memory. The chorales were the challenge: all those words! And what would be expected of us once we took to the stage? No lighting or costumes to speak of – the drama was to unfold through our movement and expressions; maximum intensity from minimal resources!

Peter blew into our rehearsal room like an electric storm. He challenged us to think about the meaning of every word, the weight and direction of every phrase; to place every idea in both its historical and contemporary context; to each imagine that we had ourselves taken part in the drama of the Passion.

Simon Rattle devoted an entire month to the project too and between all of us (and I mean *all* of us – every singer was a creative partner, contributing ideas) we discussed and

experimented with every nuance in the text and in the score. We played with vocal colour ('more lemon juice in the sound here', 'put on 20 kilos' weight to sing this phrase'), dynamics and tempos in the most thrillingly collaborative rehearsal period I have ever experienced.

The soloists and continuo players also arrived early on in the process. We watched entranced as they found their individual characters, and the whole international team worked daily to mine every expressive and dramatic nuance from the German text. For example, the alto and soprano soloists have very different reactions to Christ himself, the former being more emotionally involved and the latter watching from a greater distance. And wait for the last bass aria! I never saw a man carry such responsibility on his shoulders!

There are lots of small but vital solo roles for the Chorus and for Peter; accordingly Simon lavished hours on Pilate, Peter, the maids and Pilate's wife. They became surprisingly major figures in the whole.

St Thomas's Church, Leipzig, where Bach was Cantor from 1723 until his death, and where the *St Matthew Passion* was first performed, probably in 1727

DIRECTOR PETER SELLARS ON BACH'S ST MATTHEW PASSION

Imagine the first followers, broken and bereft the night after the Crucifixion. After a triumphal entry into Jerusalem, their leader was executed in public following a sham trial by a discredited government. How could everything have gone so wrong?

Bach wrote the *St Matthew Passion*, not as a concert work and not as a work of theatre, but as a transformative ritual reaching across time and space, uniting disparate and dispirited communities. His achievement is one of the most powerful acts of remembrance in human history. In the *St Matthew Passion*, there are no spectators, only participants. We are all present as witnesses, all called upon to testify. Our own internal conflicts are exposed as the larger contradictions of the world, and our gradually expanding levels of personal and collective recognition lead to a heightened sense of personal and collective responsibility. The sheer scale of the

work tests our endurance and becomes an overwhelming exercise in compassion.

My ritual 'staging' is primarily focused on Bach's spatial imagination and the moral energies that his dialogues and juxtapositions release. Bach's musical images are often vividly pictorial; but they also move beyond the visual, passing through the tactile, to find their redemptive and healing power in the act of making music itself, which is its own kind of spiritual path of concentration, shared attention and transcendent achievement.

By now there was an extraordinary openness to the whole process – suggestion and counter-suggestion from all the performers – the choir thrilled to be so intimately involved.

The highlight? The first day with the orchestra, the Berlin Philharmonic. Everyone was nervous but Simon Rattle (calm as always) just began at the beginning and presided over the kind of process that only occurs under the very greatest conductors: guiding and listening, encouraging these great singers and musicians to give, share and take; cajoling, encouraging and developing. Arias were often unconducted, choruses guided with the lightest touch.

During rehearsals, Simon often invited the choir to sing unaccompanied and the orchestra to then find its supporting role, before highlighting those thrilling flute and oboe solo lines that so often go unheard.

The boys in Berlin came from the Staats- und Domchor (the choristers of Berlin's Cathedral). They have a tradition that stretches back centuries and they sing with a splendid vigour and colour. As they rushed in and out of the Philharmonie to deliver their fervent chorales I felt very close to Bach, as well as to Mendelssohn, who once conducted this choir and who famously revived the *St Matthew Passion*, giving a performance in 1829 that was the first for a century.

At the premiere of our staging in Berlin we had no idea what to expect, or how the

public would react. The silence, in a riveted Philharmonie, said it all. Peter, Simon, everyone had got to the heart of this great work and we were all simply stunned that Bach in Leipzig all those years ago could speak to us so clearly in 21st-century Berlin. ●

Simon Halsey is the Chief Conductor of the Berlin Radio Choir, which collaborated with Sir Simon Rattle, Peter Sellars and the Berlin Philharmonic on a staging in 2010 of Bach's *St Matthew Passion*.

BACH'S ST MATTHEW PASSION AT THE PROMS

Staging by Peter Sellars
PROM 66 • 6 SEPTEMBER

L'EAU DE RAMEAU

Composer, theoretician, organist, violinist …
Jean-Philippe Rameau, who died 250 years
ago, boasted a heady cocktail of talents.
IGOR TORONYI-LALIC sniffs out Rameau's
essential qualities, to profile a composer
who got up the noses of some critics,
but ended up smelling of roses

As Parisians took their seats for the 1733 premiere of Jean-Philippe Rameau's first opera, expectations can't have been high. Though 50 years of age and author of a widely acclaimed treatise on harmony (that would remain a central text to Western musical theory into the 20th century), the wiry theoretician was a toddler when it came to composition. Few would have thought that he could pose a challenge to Jean-Baptiste Lully, whose *tragédies en musique* still dominated the stage half a century after his death. But challenge the status quo Rameau's *Hippolyte et Aricie* did. 'My Lord!', exclaimed composer André Campra following the premiere. 'There is enough music in this opera to make 10 of them; this man will eclipse us all.' The 30 operas that followed bore this out. For the educated 18th-century Frenchman, then, it would have come as little surprise that Rameau was still being celebrated 250 years after his death.

The Proms marks the anniversary with three concerts. Two of these focus on chamber and operatic works written at the height of Rameau's powers. The third, a Late Night Prom, explores his religious motets written before fame had hit.

With the success of *Hippolyte*, the floodgates opened. A composer who had gone 50 years without writing a single note for the opera stage found himself unable to stop. Six operas followed in as many years. Rameau's facility for melodic, orchestral and harmonic invention never flagged. Among his most vivid works of this period was his opera-ballet *Les Indes galantes* (1735), which investigates love in the furthest reaches of the planet. It quickly established his popular credentials. Within six months, 'every tune, from the overture to the last gavotte, had been parodied and was known by all', noted one writer.

With originality and success, however, came trouble. Having seemingly triumphed where so many others had failed in rejuvenating French opera, Rameau provoked the start of what would become the Querelle des Bouffons, a 20-year war of words that saw stylistic disputes between the perceived Italianate or French, modern or conservative, aesthetic concerns of Rameau and others used as a proxy for larger political and intellectual battles. Occasionally it got physical. In 1742, police were called to a café where Rameau and rival Joseph-Nicolas-Pancrace Royer were brawling.

It failed to halt Rameau's progress. Fallouts merely precipitated clever changes of tack. In 1741, during a hiatus in his relationship with the Paris Opéra management, he decided to capitalise on the chamber music craze that had swept the city. The result was an elegant series of *Pièces de clavecin en concerts* for harpsichord, violin (or flute) and viol (or second

> With the success of *Hippolyte*, the floodgates opened. A composer who had gone 50 years without writing a single note for the opera stage found himself unable to stop.

violin). These, and the celebrated solo harpsichord pieces, were the only works by him that continued to be performed into the 18th century.

By 1750, Rameau was one of Europe's most celebrated musical figures. Pre-eminent in France (to the extent that the Opéra had to limit him to two productions a year), he could boast of a royal pension and academic renown. In the eyes of the *philosophes*, his theoretical works, which codified tonality, saw him join Descartes, Newton and Voltaire in the Enlightenment pantheon. It was a celebrity that no amount of stylistic squabbling could quell. Uniquely for composers of this era, it even (for a period) survived his death in 1764 at the age of 80.

But, while Rameau's flame burnt brighter and longer than all of his contemporaries (he and Lully were the first composers to enter into a repertoire), it didn't survive the violent changes in fashion and politics at the turn of the 19th century.

Not until the 1880s Rococo revival, allied to a resurgence in French nationalism in the face of the Prussian threat, did the resuscitation of Rameau begin. Debussy recruited him for his crusade against Wagner. The state enlisted *Castor et Pollux* as part of the war effort, reviving it amid a bombardment of Paris in March 1918. New economic and political priorities allowed French Baroque opera to flourish. Much of this still required lobbying from lonely fanatics. And in this climate it became the exclusive privilege of the period specialists, who increasingly had the best means to recreate the environment in which these works made most sense.

The past decade has seen this monopoly challenged, with large orchestras such as the BBC Scottish Symphony Orchestra (which performs a suite from *Les Indes galantes* on 15 August) acquiring knowledge of period performance practice in order to include the characterful orchestral music from Rameau's operas in their concert programmes.

We understand Rameau's genius far better today. The image of him as an operatic parvenu coming to the stage for the first time as an old man might not be quite right. He almost certainly took part in oratorios at his Jesuit school and toured with an opera company as a violinist.

His motets, receiving a rare outing at the Proms from the French Baroque crusaders William Christie and Les Arts Florissants, play a part in this story too. A missing link is offered in these religious works, written when Rameau was still a jobbing provincial organist. They connect the callow early work to the magisterial late operas. And though they are small in scale, no-one who listens to *In convertendo Dominus*, for example, written while Rameau was still in his thirties, can doubt that this was a composer destined for great things. ●

Igor Toronyi-Lalic is the editor of Culture House at *The Spectator*, author of Benjamin Britten (Penguin, 2013) and co-director of the London Contemporary Music Festival.

Exotic note: a costume design for the 1735 opera-ballet *Les Indes galantes*, which quickly brought Rameau to popular attention in Paris

RAMEAU AT THE PROMS

Grands motets: Deus noster refugium;
In convertendo Dominus;
Quam dilecta tabernacula
PROM 17 • 29 JULY

Les Indes galantes – suite
PROM 39 • 15 AUGUST

Pièces de clavecin en concerts
PROMS CHAMBER MUSIC 1
21 JULY

We supply quality instruments for the professional pianist.

We provide spacious rehearsal rooms for the working musician.

"After trying out dozens of instruments around the country, I found my dream piano at Peregrine's Pianos in London" - "The practice rooms are some of the quietest and best stocked in the city" - "The quality of tone and the sheer playability of their instruments make them an absolute delight for the beginning pianist and for the concert pianist" - "Schimmel's concert grands are some of the finest in the world" - "Peregrine's Pianos is a business with friendly staff who are driven by a genuine passion for pianos" - "The Schimmel presentation and tour of the workshop was absolutely fascinating and truly inspirational" - "The team at Peregrine's Pianos gave us all the help and advice we needed" - "Peregrine's Pianos is one of my favorite London treasures" - "We hire our pianos from Peregrine's Pianos because we always get a fast, friendly service and top of the range, reliable instruments" - "We would happily recommend Peregrine's Pianos to families near and far" - "Owning a grand piano was a long held dream. Peregrine's Pianos were able to make it a reality"

All quotes are taken from our website: www.peregrines-pianos.com

SCHIMMEL
PIANOS
Exclusive dealer in London

Peregrine's Pianos, 137A Grays Inn Road, London WC1X 8TU   Tel: 020 7242 9865

THE NIGHT
THING

Bach, Rameau and Reich feature in the Late
Night Proms but so do Paloma Faith, Rufus
Wainwright, Laura Mvula and the Pet Shop Boys.
TIM RUTHERFORD-JOHNSON introduces
the pop artists appearing after hours

Yes, it's a huge, reverberant and awe-inspiring building but, for some, the Royal Albert Hall really comes into its own after 10pm, once the early-evening crowd has dispersed into South Kensington. The orchestra chairs and conductor's podium are cleared away and the stage is reset for the Late Night Prom. The Hall transforms into a different space: intimate, unpredictable and even magical.

As usual, this season's Late Night Proms – 11 in all – offer a chance to sample some more alternative music alongside the classical repertoire that is the core of the evening concerts, from a 'Battle of the Bands' to an evening of Rameau with William Christie's Les Arts Florissants or a tribute to the composer John Tavener who died in November last year. Three other composers receive concerts dedicated to their music – Steve Reich, Sir Peter Maxwell Davies (80 this year) and Beethoven (a performance of the *Missa solemnis* with the Monteverdi Choir and English Baroque soloists), and there is also an unusual concert by the Aurora Orchestra under Nicholas Collon, featuring music by Mozart, the British-Bulgarian composer Dobrinka Tabakova and a new work by the English composer Benedict Mason. Expect the unexpected.

But what's really special about the Late Night Proms is that they're a chance to sample artists, sounds and genres outside the classical mainstream. The first, in 1970, set the template, when members of The Soft Machine played music by Terry Riley and others. Since then, artists featured have included Wynton Marsalis, Nitin Sawhney and

Jamie Cullum, and this year is no less diverse. If there is a focus, however, it is to get great popular singers in front of an orchestra, in a way no-one else can.

Laura Mvula already has Proms form, having appeared as part of last year's Urban Classic Prom ('So at home she kicked off her golden stilettos,' wrote *The Daily Telegraph*). This year she returns for her own show, with awards and acclaim for her debut album *Sing to the Moon* under her belt. Mvula's backing comes from the Netherlands-based Metropole Orchestra, which is already recording an instrumentally scaled-up version of *Sing to the Moon*. This will be a perfect chance to hear a collaboration that Mvula describes as 'a dream come true'.

Fellow Brit-nominated singer **Paloma Faith** is known for mixing a burlesque-inspired stage presence with deep soul music. Her third album, *A Perfect Contradiction*, released in March this year, was produced by dance-pop darling Pharrell Williams, but for the Proms she will be joined by the Urban Voices Collective and the Guy Barker Orchestra: her partnership with the latter has already earned comparisons with the glorious orchestral soul of Tom Jones and Shirley Bassey.

Night sounds: Clare Teal (Prom 30, Battle of the Bands), Steve Reich (Prom 37), Sir Peter Maxwell Davies (Prom 70)

When he was young, **Rufus Wainwright** was sent by his mother to study music, on the principle that that was what Bob Dylan had done (for a year, anyway). In many respects her plan worked: Wainwright managed just 18 months of music school but is now one of the finest singer-songwriters of his generation. Despite great success in pop, his first musical love has always been opera. (As a child he would re-enact scenes from Puccini with his cousins. 'Of course, I was [the villain] Scarpia,' he says.) And it is the sweep, complexity and melodrama of opera and music theatre, particularly in their 19th-century and Broadway manifestations, that distinguish his pop writing. 'I definitely feel there's some force for good that's been with me through life, and I think that comes from all the dead great composers,' he said in a recent *Guardian* interview.

Wainwright's own opera, *Prima Donna* (2009), was staged in Manchester, London, Toronto and New York, and he has begun writing a second, *Hadrian*, for the Canadian Opera Company. His Proms set-list will be drawn from a large pool, whether numbers from *Prima Donna*; tunes from hit musicals, as in his Judy Garland tribute concerts; or, of course, songs from any of his seven studio albums.

If anyone can compete with Wainwright for the crown of operatic pop, it is Neil Tennant and Chris Lowe of the **Pet Shop Boys**. They may be famous for their wryly observed pop/electronica, but the duo has previously taken on influences from classical music. Their lyrics namecheck Pavarotti, Stravinsky and Debussy, and they have already composed an original score for Sergey Eisenstein's silent-film masterpiece, *Battleship Potemkin* (2004), and a ballet (based on Hans Christian Andersen's *The Most Incredible Thing*, 2011) for Sadler's Wells. Their concert on 23 July features the BBC Singers and BBC Concert Orchestra in the world premiere of a 45-minute orchestral song-cycle on the life of the mathematician, code-breaker and father of computer science and artificial intelligence Alan Turing. One song from the cycle, 'He Dreamed of Machines', has already been performed with the BBC Philharmonic and the Manchester Chamber Choir, and it is a sumptuously ambiguous mix of strings, vocals and electronics, part love story, part dystopian vision, a perfect blend for the strangeness of the Royal Albert Hall after dark. ●

Tim Rutherford-Johnson is a writer, and editor of the *Oxford Dictionary of Music*. He is currently preparing a book on music since 1989 for the University of California Press.

LATE NIGHT PROMS

Pet Shop Boys
with the BBC Concert Orchestra
and BBC Singers
PROM 8 • 23 JULY

William Christie
conducts Rameau's Grands Motets
PROM 17 • 29 JULY

The Tallis Scholars
performs John Tavener
PROM 25 • 4 AUGUST

Battle of the Bands, with Clare Teal:
Count Pearson Proms Band vs
Duke Windsor Proms Band
PROM 30 • 8 AUGUST

Steve Reich:
The Desert Music; It's Gonna Rain
PROM 37 • 13 AUGUST

Mozart, Dobrinka Tabakova and
Benedict Mason
PROM 41 • 16 AUGUST

Laura Mvula
with the Metropole Orchestra
PROM 45 • 19 AUGUST

Sir John Eliot Gardiner
conducts Beethoven's 'Missa solemnis'
PROM 54 • 26 AUGUST

Paloma Faith
with the Guy Barker Orchestra
PROM 65 • 5 SEPTEMBER

Sir Peter Maxwell Davies at 80
PROM 70 • 8 SEPTEMBER

Rufus Wainwright
with the Britten Sinfonia
PROM 74 • 11 SEPTEMBER

CADOGAN HALL
COMPLEMENT

The series of Monday-lunchtime Proms has delighted audiences at Cadogan Hall for the past decade. **PETROC TRELAWNY** surveys this year's offering, which reflects anniversaries and artists featured at the Royal Albert Hall concerts

Backstage there are clocks accurate to a fraction of a second, high-tech digital links to Broadcasting House and an experienced production team. But it's not until a disembodied voice starts reading the weather forecast that I really know we are good to go. 'Drizzle in the south, dry and sunny in Scotland and Ulster ...' – I turn to the artists and wish them well – ' ... maximum temperature 22 degrees in Glasgow ... ' The doors open and I stride out onto the stage, the voice continuing in my ear – 'Now on Radio 3 we go live to Cadogan Hall for today's Proms Chamber Music concert.'

Chamber music used to be an occasional guest at the Proms. In the 1970s a Mozart string quartet might find itself scheduled alongside a performance of a Mahler symphony. The Gabrieli Quartet played Brahms in 1975, with Mendelssohn's 'Scottish' Symphony sharing the bill. But these were relatively rare occurrences in the vast space of the Royal Albert Hall. Gradually, other venues were embraced: St Augustine's Church, Kilburn; St Luke's, Chelsea; and Kensington

Town Hall, although these settings tended to be used for choral concerts or early music. It wasn't until 1996 that Proms Chamber Music concerts became weekly events and were established as an essential part of the season.

The Arditti Quartet gave the first Proms Chamber Music recital, playing works by Beethoven and Dutilleux and giving the London premiere of Elliott Carter's Fifth Quartet at the Royal College of Music's Britten Theatre. The following year the concerts moved to the grand Lecture Theatre of the Victoria and Albert Museum, where the walls are covered with allegories of Art, Poetry, Science and Philosophy and performers shared the stage with priceless treasures from the V&A's collection. With the seating limited to just 300, the tickets were snapped up within a few days of going on sale. It was the opening of Cadogan Hall in 2004 that finally gave this rich festival-within-a-festival a home that truly suits its grand ambition.

The Proms Chamber Music series is programmed by Proms Director Roger Wright

and Edward Blakeman, Editor, BBC Radio 3 and Proms, whose year-round responsibilities also include running Radio 3's nightly *Live in Concert* series and its New Generation Artists scheme. 'What's special about Cadogan Hall,' Blakeman says, 'is that it has a great acoustic and the unusual advantage of a big stage in a medium-sized venue. So, you can push at the boundaries of what defines chamber music.' The Hall was built as a Christian Science Church, its large windows filled with stained glass designed by a Danish nobleman who had worked for Tiffany in New York. 'Chamber music is often performed to an audience in a room with dimmed lights,' adds Blakeman, 'but Cadogan is so bright that you feel really connected to the world outside. It's great for a programmer to think, "Now, what do I want to hear at 1.00pm on a summer's day?" '

The Proms Chamber Music concerts allow artists also appearing at the Royal Albert Hall to show a different side to their music-making. The French Baroque ensemble **Les Arts Florissants** plays works by anniversary composer

Alice Coote (PCM 5); Benjamin Grosvenor (PCM 7); Janine Jansen (PCM 4); Louis Schwizgebel (PCM 6)

Jean-Philippe Rameau in Cadogan Hall (21 July) then gives a performance of Rameau's liturgical music in a Late Night Prom in the Royal Albert Hall a few days later (Prom 17). 'We get to hear Rameau writing for Louis XV in his private apartments and then at his most public, composing for the King at worship at Versailles,' Blakeman points out. The mezzo-soprano **Alice Coote** sings Elgar's *Sea Pictures* at the Royal Albert Hall (Prom 31), before returning to Cadogan to give a recital with **Julius Drake** (18 August), featuring songs by Richard Strauss, marking 150 years since his birth. **Benjamin Grosvenor** performs Chopin's First Piano Concerto with the BBC Philharmonic (Prom 29), while his lunchtime appearance (1 September) features a newly commissioned work by Judith Weir. There is even an exciting chance to see a conductor showing off his skill as an instrumentalist when the BBC Symphony Orchestra's Chief Conductor **Sakari Oramo** – who conducts four Proms at the Royal Albert Hall this year, including the Last Night – takes up the violin to play Prokofiev alongside his friend **Janine Jansen** (11 August).

'Having just eight PCMs is a constraint in some ways,' says Blakeman, 'but it's also a fantastic challenge. We aim to offer the broadest range of chamber music.' He is particularly pleased with a concert by some of BBC Radio 3's

New Generation Artists past and present (25 August): pianist **Louis Schwizgebel** plays a Mozart sonata before joining the **Royal String Quartet** for Mahler's Piano Quartet, and the Royals in turn combine with three other colleagues to perform Strauss's *Metamorphosen* for septet, realised from the composer's original short score. Blakeman explains, 'We always urge people to collaborate during their time on the NGA scheme – this is a perfect example.'

Strauss's anniversary is also highlighted in a concert by **Michael Collins** and the **London Winds**, who perform his Suite in B flat major (4 August), while the 300th anniversary of the birth of C. P. E. Bach is celebrated with a performance of his quirky solo and trio sonatas by **Rachel Podger**, **Kristian Bezuidenhout** and friends (28 July).

The 'last lunchtime' of this year promises to be a riotous performance of Walton's *Façade* by the **Nash Ensemble** and reciters **Ian Bostridge** and **Dame Felicity Palmer**. By then, it may feel as if autumn is nigh. Then again, we may be enjoying an Indian summer. I'll know for sure as the tinny feed of the weather forecast in my ear confirms we're on standby for another hour of great music-making. ●

Petroc Trelawny presents BBC Radio 3's *Breakfast* and *Live in Concert* and broadcasts on BBC Four. This year he presents the Proms Chamber Music concerts from the Cadogan Hall stage.

PROMS CHAMBER MUSIC
Mondays, 1.00pm

PROMS CHAMBER MUSIC 1 • 21 JULY
Les Arts Florissants/
Paolo Zanzu *harpsichord/director*

PROMS CHAMBER MUSIC 2 • 28 JULY
Rachel Podger *violin*,
Kristian Bezuidenhout *fortepiano*

PROMS CHAMBER MUSIC 3 • 4 AUGUST
London Winds/Michael Collins *clarinet/director*

PROMS CHAMBER MUSIC 4 • 11 AUGUST
Janine Jansen, Sakari Oramo *violins*,
Itamar Golan *piano*

PROMS CHAMBER MUSIC 5 • 18 AUGUST
Alice Coote *mezzo-soprano*, Julius Drake *piano*

PROMS CHAMBER MUSIC 6 • 25 AUGUST
Royal String Quartet, Louis Schwizgebel *piano*

PROMS CHAMBER MUSIC 7 • 1 SEPTEMBER
Benjamin Grosvenor *piano*

PROMS CHAMBER MUSIC 8 • 8 SEPTEMBER
Ian Bostridge, Dame Felicity Palmer *reciters*,
Nash Ensemble/John Wilson

• • •

PROMS SATURDAY MATINEES
Saturdays, 3.00pm

PROMS SATURDAY MATINEE 1 • 2 AUGUST
Myrsini Margariti *soprano*,
Irini Karaianni *mezzo-soprano*,
Armonia Atenea/George Petrou

PROMS SATURDAY MATINEE 2 • 9 AUGUST
Håkan Hardenberger *trumpet*,
Lapland Chamber Orchestra/John Storgårds

PROMS SATURDAY MATINEE 3 • 30 AUGUST
Rebecca Bottone *soprano*, Timothy Gill *cello*,
London Sinfonietta/Sian Edwards

PROMS SATURDAY MATINEE 4 • 6 SEPTEMBER
Christine Rice *mezzo-soprano*, Exaudi,
Birmingham Contemporary Music Group/
Oliver Knussen

Proms Chamber Music and Proms Saturday Matinee concerts are broadcast live on BBC Radio 3; Proms Chamber Music concerts are also repeated the following Sunday at 1.00pm.

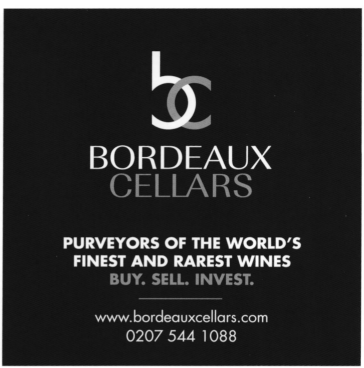

SOUND &
VISION

JAMES JOLLY explores the myriad ways in which the Proms are available to audiences across BBC Radio, TV and online, while some of those who make it happen reveal their highlights and ambitions for 2014

When the BBC Symphony Orchestra takes to the stage of the Royal Albert Hall at the First Night of the Proms on 18 July, it will mark the start – for most of us, at least – of a new Proms season. For a number of departments at the BBC, however, it will be merely another staging post in a process that has been under way for months – in some cases, years – and which will continue long after the Last Night.

Broadcasting the BBC Proms is an immensely complex undertaking, particularly in this digital age, and if you wanted a guiding principle that links the aims of everyone involved, then you couldn't do better than the words of BBC TV's Jan Younghusband, Head of Commissioning, Music and Events: 'If the audience says, "I really felt I was there", then we've done our job. "I wish I could have been there" isn't quite the same.'

The Proms revolves around the music and few things ensure that 'I felt I was there' experience better than great sound. Thankfully, that is one of the BBC's strengths. Senior Studio Manager Neil Pemberton has been working on the Proms since 1980. 'We go into the Royal Albert Hall on the Monday before the opening Friday night and get all the

> Once the music starts, the complexity of the Proms undertaking becomes clear – not just for radio and television but also for the many digital platforms.

microphone slings set up, get the Radio 3 presenter's booth miked, get the audio truck into position and gather all the extra equipment that might be needed – and we're ready by the Thursday, in time for First Night rehearsals. One year we had a Doctor Who Prom on the Saturday and it was very complex, so we had technical rehearsals before the First Night, as well as getting the hall ready. Those are the kind of challenges that are increasing each year. It's so much more challenging than when I started 30 years ago.' Each Prom requires a minimum of three studio managers – one

based in the truck outside the hall, to balance the orchestra; one in the production box in the hall to mix that balance with the live presentation, ambient sound and any pre-recorded material that will be played into the broadcast; and a third one on stage to move microphones during rehearsals and during the concert itself. If any amplification is needed, that number generally increases.

The complexity of accommodating the extraordinary mix of different ensembles and styles at the Proms presents its own challenges – one day a huge opera, the next a chamber orchestra, then an unaccompanied choir – and the initial rigging has to allow for all these different configurations. As Neil Pemberton says, the process starts in February, 'when we meet with the Proms team and look specifically at things that are going to be difficult technically'.

Once the music starts, the complexity of the Proms undertaking becomes clear – not just for radio and television but also for

Radio 3's Petroc Trelawny in the presenter's box at the Royal Albert Hall

the many digital platforms through which people can experience the concerts. Steve Bowbrick is Editor of 'Multiplatform' for the Proms and he's charged with putting in place what the BBC's Director General Tony Hall is referring to as the 'Digital Proms'. And, says Bowbrick, 'this year there will be more content available online; it will be more accessible, across more platforms. One of the things we learnt last year is just how many of our users are now enjoying our content through a range of platforms. Well over 50% of our audience accesses our content online, whether on a mobile or a tablet, so the desktop computer experience is now becoming a minority pursuit. Across the board it's about tablets and mobiles and we'll definitely be supporting those much more completely.'

And if you thought the traditional Proms audience might lag behind when it comes to new technologies, think again. 'Often, they're very touch-screen-centric. There's a real sense that their tablets are accompanying them

EMMA BLOXHAM
Lead Producer,
BBC Proms (Radio 3)

The Proms really is the highlight of our year: it's a time when teams across the BBC come together to

produce some amazing results. For an orchestra, playing for the first time at the Royal Albert Hall can be a thrilling experience, but nothing can prepare them for that very special audience, particularly the Prommers standing in the Arena and Gallery. Performers always talk about the audience's attentiveness. It generates an incredible atmosphere.

The John Wilson Orchestra's Prom is always a highlight: *Kiss Me, Kate* will be a real treat! I'm also really looking forward to Mahler's Third Symphony from the Leipzig Gewandhaus Orchestra. It'll be fascinating to hear orchestras

from China, South Korea and Turkey this year; one of the things I love about the Proms is how the atmosphere changes backstage with musicians from different countries. I'm also looking forward to the appearances by some of Radio 3's fabulous New Generation Artists.

Radio 3 will be there to catch every musical moment. We will also take listeners both backstage to talk to the performers, and across the road to the Royal College of Music for many of the Proms Plus events, which will be broadcast during the Proms intervals and after the concerts.

MARK COOPER

Head, BBC Music Television (London)

As always, this season has some really exciting concerts. There's a mix of core and unfamiliar repertoire, some fascinating visits from far-flung orchestras making their Proms debuts, some rich themes – from Strauss to composers' responses to the First World War – and some Late Night Proms, too, which really build on the Proms' desire to keep reaching out with an eclectic spirit.

These Lates have a very distinctive atmosphere, which depends enormously on the kind of artists playing. The main early-evening concerts draw a very lively, intently listening crowd but the Late Night Proms can be very different – they're often looser and that's reflected in the way we present and shoot them for TV.

We were delighted with the success of the *Proms Extra* magazine programme last year and now we want to build on that sense of drawing in the artists themselves and hearing about what they do, how they feel about particular performances and composers, but also how they feel about their working lives. We want to share their intellectual and artistic concerns: 'This is what my life is like'. It was very fresh last year and I know that, when the series returns this summer, it'll feel just as exciting and new.

Katie Derham *(far left)* talks to guests *(left to right)* Tine Thing Helseth, Mary King and Laura Mvula on the *Proms Extra* couch

around the house and they're already thinking of them as a companion to what they listen to on the radio and what they watch on the TV – which is really interesting to us.'

Making the televised offering as clear as possible – with well-defined, regular slots – proved highly successful last year and will be refined further in 2014. The Proms will feature over four days each week on TV, Thursdays to Sunday, with each evening strongly themed. Thursday nights, hosted by Tom Service, will focus on the 'Masterworks', great music introduced by the players. As Jan Younghusband explains, people love hearing musicians talk about what they do: 'It's wonderful when you watch a concert and feel that you've met some of the players and feel a connection with them. You're hearing about the music from the engine room, if you like.' Friday nights will feature popular repertoire, familiar music to kick back to at the end of a long week – and expect to see a few new faces presenting them, too.

Saturday nights will be the home of *Proms Extra* on BBC Two, with Katie Derham joined by musicians on the couch to talk about concerts that have recently taken place, and looking ahead to the coming week. 'It'll be similar to last year – it was such a success with viewers – and we decided to add an extra week of it, so it'll run from the second weekend of the season until the penultimate weekend.' Katie Derham will then introduce the Sunday-night concerts, which this year will include a focus on the dizzying array of international orchestras making their first visits to the Proms. And then, Younghusband reveals, 'We're going to throw in a themed weekend of English music – which will include works by Butterworth, Elgar, Vaughan Williams and Walton – and, for the final weekend of the Proms, we're taking three concerts live. The point of this live weekend is to adopt a slightly different approach so, rather than a sort of contextualised concert, it'll be about being down on the ground at the Proms. It'll

ANDREW DOWNS

Editorial Lead,
BBC Proms Multiplatform

My job is not only to develop a destination for Proms-lovers on the web and on mobile, but also to take the Proms – perhaps the best classical music content in the world – and make it as findable as possible both for existing fans and for potentially new ones.

Last year, views of BBC Proms video clips on YouTube more than doubled to over one million. We publish clips of the televised Proms on YouTube as well as on the BBC website because it's one of the key places people go to discover music. This year we'll present our video highlight clips on mobile for the first time.

Recommending the Proms is going to become easier. The means are growing for taking the Proms into online spaces for music discovery. The BBC now offers Playlister, a new service that we, and trusted guides, can use to create and share playlists in Spotify of the music played in the Proms.

Our aim through all of this activity is to lead listeners on journeys to broaden their experience of classical music through the Proms and Radio 3's unsurpassable archive of content.

Claudia Kappenberg

feel very different, more of a Glastonbury approach, perhaps!'

The other area that exercises the Proms team is the look of the event: everything from the dressing of the hall to the lighting. As Jan Younghusband explains: 'Usually when you go to an orchestral concert you're sitting there in stark white light because the players have to see their music. That's quite cold on TV, so we have the dilemma of how to make the Hall look atmospheric but still let the musicians see their music. Two years ago we started lighting the concerts differently and there was a really positive response from the audience. The LED screens behind the orchestra were partly put in to provide a more energy-efficient lighting source, but they also provide us with a chance to explore some complementary images. These can't be too active once the music's playing, though: the audience in the Hall can't be distracted by them. We also move our presentation position around because we like to feel that we're showing the event itself. We've

really liked the high presentation positions because the Hall looks so breathtaking.'

We all experience our Proms in different ways: you might go along to the Royal Albert Hall and soak up the unique atmosphere of a packed hall. You might watch the Proms on TV, listen on the radio (or even experience them in HD sound on the Radio 3 website – something you can do wherever you are in the world, a useful tip if you're on holiday!), or on your phone or tablet. Or you may want to listen again: Radio 3's digital team added an innovative response to this area last year, and created an archive of single works – sometimes with video as well as sound – on the Radio 3 website, allowing you either to revisit a performance or just to enjoy it at your leisure.

At the end of the day, as Steve Bowbrick puts it, 'We're just part of an operation to get the full range of amazing music to the largest possible number of music-lovers.' ●

James Jolly is Editor-in-Chief of Gramophone *and a regular voice on Radio 3 as a presenter of* Sunday Morning.

THE PROMS ON BBC RADIO 3

- Every Prom broadcast live on BBC Radio 3 (available on digital radio, via TV, mobile, laptop and tablet as well as on 90–93 FM)
- Many Proms repeated during *Afternoon on 3* (weekdays, 2.00pm) and on most Sunday afternoons at 4.00pm, plus a series of repeats over the Christmas period
- Listen on-demand for seven days after broadcast via bbc.co.uk/proms
- Proms-related programmes during the season, including *Breakfast* (weekdays, 6.30am; weekends 7.00am), *In Tune* (weekdays, 4.30pm) and *Composer of the Week* (weekdays, 12.00pm and 6.30pm)

THE PROMS ON BBC TELEVISION

- 28 Proms broadcast across BBC One, BBC Two, BBC Four and CBeebies
- Regular Thursday-, Friday- and Sunday-evening broadcasts on BBC Four, starting 25 July
- *Proms Extra* on Saturday nights, BBC Two
- The Last Night of the Proms – first half on BBC Two and second half on BBC One – plus Proms in the Park events around the country via the red button

THE PROMS ONLINE

- Visit bbc.co.uk/proms for your definitive guide to the 2014 BBC Proms season
- Listen to every Prom live in HD Sound and on-demand for seven days after broadcast, and watch every televised Prom via the BBC iPlayer.
- Get easy access to via a dedicated Proms button on the BBC iPlayer Radio app
- Keep up to date with the latest news and insights on the Proms blog, by subscribing to the email newsletter, finding us on Facebook (facebook.com/theproms) or following us on Twitter (@bbcproms; #bbcproms)
- Access the Proms on the move via the Proms mobile site
- Search the online Proms Archive, detailing every Proms concert since they began in 1895

Box office
0121 345 0602
www.thsh.co.uk

Birmingham International
Concert Season 2014/15

Igor Levit. Photo © Felix Bröde.

Barbara Hannigan. Photo © Elmer de Haas.

Marie-Elisabeth Hecker. Photo © Benjamin Ealovega.

Valery Gergiev. Photo © Marco Borggreve.

Yundi

Maria Schneider. Photo © Jimmy and Dena Katz.

Highlights include...

Australian Chamber Orchestra / Richard Tognetti
Barbara Hannigan
Borodin Quartet
Camerata Salzburg / Ben Gernon
Czech Philharmonic / Jiří Bělohlávek
Daniil Trifonov
Dresden Philharmonic / Michael Sanderling
Europa Galante / Fabio Biondi
Fisk Jubilee Singers
Hong Kong Philharmonic Orchestra / Jaap van Zweden
Igor Levit
Marc-André Hamelin
Mark Padmore / Paul Lewis
Maria Schneider Jazz Orchestra
Marie-Elisabeth Hecker / Martin Helmchen
Mariinsky Stradivarius Ensemble / Valery Gergiev
Paul Jacobs
St Petersburg Philharmonic Orchestra / Yuri Temirkanov
Takács Quartet
Yundi

For full details on all the season's events please visit:
www.thsh.co.uk/bics-2014-15

Search 'Town Hall Symphony Hall' @THSHBirmingham #BICS1415
Search 'townhallsymphonyhall'

Funded by
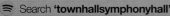
Birmingham City Council

Town Hall renovation also funded by
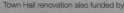 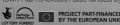
LOTTERY FUNDED
PROJECT PART-FINANCED BY THE EUROPEAN UNION

Supported using public funding by
ARTS COUNCIL ENGLAND

BIRMINGHAM
BACH Choir
Inspiring Performances

unfinished REMEMBERING

World premiere & special centenary concert to commemorate the outbreak of the First World War 1914

September 13   7.30 pm
Symphony Hall
Birmingham

Unfinished Remembering - Paul Spicer
Dona Nobis Pacem - Vaughan Williams

Soprano - Johane Ansell
Baritone - William Dazeley
Orchestra of the Swan

Birmingham Bach Choir
Conductor - Paul Spicer

Midlands Military Community Choir
A Shared Singing - Paul Spicer

Tickets from £10 - £25
THSH Box Office 0121 780 3333

www.birmingham.bachchoir.com

CHAMBER CLASSICS UNWRAPPED

TOP 50 CHAMBER WORKS AS VOTED BY YOU

FEATURING

SIR JAMES GALWAY
BRODSKY QUARTET
AURORA ORCHESTRA
SACCONI QUARTET
ACADEMY OF ST MARTIN
IN THE FIELDS
IMOGEN COOPER
JAMES EHNES
META4
ARONOWITZ ENSEMBLE
DANTE QUARTET
NAVARRA QUARTET
THE SCHUBERT ENSEMBLE
SONIA WIEDER-ATHERTON
JACK LIEBECK
LONDON SINFONIETTA
THOMAS GOULD

AND MANY MORE

Online Savers £9.50 | kingsplace.co.uk/chamber-classics-unwrapped

IN ASSOCIATION WITH

BBC music MAGAZINE

kings place
music+art+restaurants

A WORLD OF
WONDER

CHARLOTTE GARDNER delves into the array of family and pre-concert events at the Proms, from Bank Holiday classics to workshops for all the family, from literary talks to the CBeebies Prom. Let a little curiosity take you a long way

If the Proms each year were simply about two months of world-class classical music performances, at prices that everyone can afford, then nobody would be complaining. However, the fact that there are so many extra events and initiatives running alongside the main concerts is, for many, not just the icing on the cake, but the jewel in the festival's crown.

Whether you're an adult or a child, whether you're new to classical or have been an avid follower for decades, whether you want to have your head filled with new knowledge and ideas or whether you want to get alongside the musicians and have a go yourself, there's a wealth of opportunities to take your personal Proms experience to another level. For some, it will be simply be the variety of different concert styles across the summer. For others, it will be Proms Plus, a series of pre-concert talks and events based across the road from the Royal Albert Hall at the Royal College of Music. All Proms Plus events are free, and whether you choose to go on afterwards to the Prom linked to that event is up to you.

New concert experiences

People of all musical (and non-musical) backgrounds will find Proms to stretch their horizons this year.

First in the list of concerts to tempt first-timers has to be the seventh annual free Prom. This year, you pay nothing to hear a matinee performance from the Ulster Orchestra on August Bank Holiday Monday (25 August), the programme including Grieg's much-loved Piano Concerto and Bill Whelan's *Riverdance: A Symphonic Suite*. Why not make a day of it, and bring a picnic to have in nearby Hyde Park too?

Night owls should swoop on the Late Night Proms, which continue to push the boundaries of what to expect at a classical festival. The not-to-be-missed performances this summer include a new work from Neil Tennant and Chris Lowe (better known as the Pet Shop Boys), based on the life of codebreaker Alan Turing. Other late night events feature Paloma Faith, Laura Mvula and Rufus Wainwright (*see pages 90–91*).

For something entirely different, Proms Plus Lates take place in the Royal

Albert Hall's Elgar Room immediately after a number of main-evening Proms. These relaxed, intimate gatherings present a combination of jazz and poetry alongside a late-night bar. The good news for this year is that you have eight opportunities to make it to one, and all but one of them are on Saturdays. No excuses, then.

Classical newcomers might find that a themed Prom helps them get into the swing of things. If that's you, then you won't do better than the War Horse Prom on 3 August, the eve of the centenary of the First World War being declared in Britain. Guaranteed to appeal and stimulate on many different levels, this matinee Prom features music and life-size *War Horse* puppets from the National Theatre's stage production based on Michael Morpurgo's novel, and wartime songs from Gareth Malone and the Proms Military Wives Choir.

Further Exploration

For some, the beauty of the Proms is the opportunity to learn for sheer enjoyment's sake, which means making a beeline for the

PROMS PLUS EVENTS FOR ALL THE FAMILY

PROMS PLUS FAMILY*

Royal College of Music (see page 167)

Workshop-introductions to the music of the evening's Prom. Bring an instrument, or just sit back and take it all in.

Monday 21 July • 5.30pm–6.30pm
Monday 28 July • 5.30pm–6.30pm
Sunday 10 August • 5.45pm–6.45pm
Saturday 23 August • 5.30pm–6.30pm
Thursday 28 August • 5.30pm–6.30pm
Tuesday 9 September • 5.30pm–6.30pm

PROMS PLUS FAMILY ORCHESTRA AND CHORUS†

Royal College of Music (see page 167)

Play or sing alongside professional musicians, whatever your age or ability.

Sunday 3 August • 1.30pm–3.30pm
Sunday 10 August • 1.00pm–3.00pm
Saturday 23 August • 2.00pm–4.00pm
Monday 25 August • 11.30am–1.30pm

PROMS PLUS SING†

Royal College of Music (see page 167)

Explore the season's choral works by having a go yourself, whatever your singing experience.

Suitable for ages 16-plus, except 2 August and 13 September (suitable for ages 7-plus)

Saturday 19 July • 2.00pm–4.00pm
Saturday 26 July • 2.00pm–4.00pm
Saturday 2 August • 2.00pm–4.00pm
Sunday 17 August • 2.00pm–4.00pm
Saturday 6 September • 1.30pm–3.30pm
Saturday 13 September • 5.00pm–5.45pm

All events are free and suitable for family members aged 7-plus, unless otherwise indicated.

No ticket required; entry is on a first-come first-served basis (doors open 30 minutes before the event begins; capacity is limited)
†*Places must be booked in advance: sign up at bbc.co.uk/proms, or call 020 7765 0557*

Proms Plus Intro talks. In these you'll hear conductors, composers, performers or other experts in conversation with a BBC Radio 3 presenter on a wide variety of subjects. Find out about the experiences of musicians around the world in any of five events centred on this year's series of global visiting orchestras; or, if history is your thing, then the First World War theme is also well covered. For those who really want to delve into the nitty-gritty of a specific musical work, genre or composer, there is plenty to tempt you. Key among these are events honouring the life of John Tavener, who would have been 70 this year, and Richard Strauss in the 150th anniversary year of his birth. There couldn't be a better time and opportunity to explore these two composers in more detail.

In a similar vein, the series of Proms Plus Literary discussions explores the relationship between writers and composers. Poet Owen Sheers and novelist Pat Barker discuss how writers, musicians and painters have responded to war, while other events in the series feature politician Dame Shirley Williams, novelist Martin Amis, former Poet Laureate Andrew Motion and actress and director Janet Suzman. Plus, if you feel inspired to sharpen your own pencil, the Proms Poetry Competition is back, judged this year by the poet Daljit Nagra. Entrants are invited to write a poem inspired by any of the music performed at the 2014 Proms, and the winners will be announced on Friday 12 September at a special event at the Royal College of Music.

Do you know a budding young composer aged 12 to 18 who should be entering the BBC Proms Inspire Young Composers' Competition? Whatever their style of music or experience, this is a chance for them to be inspired and could lead to having their music performed at the BBC Proms and heard on BBC Radio 3. The judging panel spans a range of composers and music-industry professionals. The deadline for entries is Thursday 22 May.

The winning pieces will be performed by the Aurora Orchestra at the Inspire Young Composers' Concert on Wednesday 20 August (5.00pm–6.30pm), at the Royal College of Music.

For more information about the competition and workshops, visit www.bbc.co.uk/proms or email promslearning@bbc.co.uk.

Getting a grip at a Proms Plus Family workshop

Lots of really useful singing tips as well as deeper insight into the music. Wish I was coming to another Proms Plus Sing!

Families

The big news for the youngest concert-goers (aged 0 to 5, though older family members are sure also to be fans) is that CBeebies will be coming to the Proms for the first time. Two identical morning Proms (26 and 27 July) bring together CBeebies themes and attention-grabbing classical favourites, while Robert the Robot (Steven Kynman) takes everyone on an adventure around London, discovering the sounds around us, helped by specially filmed television clips. Mr Bloom (Ben Faulks), Swashbuckle's Gemma Hunt and Show Me Show Me's Chris Jarvis will also be on hand, as will the BBC Philharmonic, conducted by Stephen Bell, who will also perform a brand-new London-themed piece by Barrie Bignold. Proof that no-one is too young to enjoy a classical premiere!

Older children will enjoy the interactive Proms Plus Family workshops. With the emphasis very much on fun, presenters guide families through the music of the upcoming Prom, with help from professional musicians.

For all-ages enjoyment, the Proms Family Orchestra and Chorus sessions are back, in which whole families are invited to create music inspired by what they can hear at the Proms, alongside professional

For anyone wanting to flex their vocal cords, the Proms Plus Sing workshops are a brilliant way to get to know a work from the inside, with choral leaders guiding you through highlights of some of this season's key choral works, often supported by members of the BBC Singers. Workshops include Bach's dramatic St John and St Matthew Passions, Janáček's vividly coloured Glagolitic Mass and Cole Porter's musical Kiss Me, Kate, based on Shakespeare's The Taming of the Shrew.

Perhaps your mission for 2014 is to engage with the classical music being written right now. If so, then get along to the Proms Plus Portraits, where composers discuss their music with a presenter, and introduce live chamber performances of their works. This year, the all-British composers taking part are Sir Harrison Birtwistle and Sir Peter Maxwell Davies (both celebrating their 80th birthdays); and David Horne and Sally Beamish, who both have works being premiered.

Hands-on fun in the Proms Family Orchestra

musicians. All standards are welcome – there's no music to read – as is absolutely any instrument, as long as it's portable and acoustic. In fact, part of the excitement in previous years has come from the sight and sound of the wonderful and sometimes wacky combinations of instruments all performing together.

PROMS POETRY COMPETITION

Poet Daljit Nagra and Radio 3 presenter Ian McMillan introduce the winning entries in this year's Proms Poetry Competition – and welcome some of the winners on stage to read them (12 September). In association with the Poetry Society.

For full details, visit bbc.co.uk/proms.

All in it together: discovering a choral classic at Proms Plus Sing

Nurturing Talent

The Proms continues to be as much about nurturing the talent of the future as celebrating the established names of today.

Young performers this year include the National Youth Orchestra of Great Britain performing Stravinsky's *Petrushka* and Sir Harrison Birtwistle's *Sonance Severance 2000*. It's also Year 3 of the Proms Youth Choir project, which brings together youth choirs from across the country. This year the choir turns to Britten's *War Requiem*.

Inspire, the BBC Proms' annual scheme for young composers aged between 12 and 18, continues to go from strength to strength. Participants have been attending the Inspire Lab composing workshops around the country since January, and these draw to a climax with the BBC Proms Inspire Young Composers' Competition, judged by a panel including composers Anna Meredith and Stuart MacRae. It may not be too late to enter (*see box, page 106*). The winners,

announced on the Proms website on 4 July, will not only have their work performed by the Aurora Orchestra as part of the Proms Plus series and on BBC Radio 3, they will also receive a BBC commission. However, whether you win or not you'll still benefit enormously. All entrants and participants in the Inspire scheme are invited to attend a series of workshops exploring areas such as arranging, electro-acoustic composition, composing for solo instruments and contemporary composition techniques.

Don't forget that the Proms can be about your future too. Wouldn't it be wonderful if this year, as the final notes of 'Land of Hope and Glory' sound on the Last Night, you were thinking of beginnings rather than of culminations, and looking forward to pursuing new interests and talents? So, what will you try this year? ●

Charlotte Gardner is a freelance writer, journalist and critic. In addition to writing programme notes for UK orchestras and publications, she is the author of Touch Press's *The Liszt Sonata* app, performed by Stephen Hough.

RCM SPARKS

The Royal College of Music's Learning and Participation programme provides opportunities for young people and families to engage in inspiring musical activities this summer.

RCM Sparks Family Discovery (all ages)
25 July, 5, 13 August; tickets £10 (1 adult plus 1 child, £3.75 for each extra participant)
Discover musical treasures in fun hands-on sessions, including storytelling, music-making in the RCM Museum and Mini Sparks for the youngest members of the family.

Igniting Sparks – workshops for ages 6 to 9
13 and 14 August; tickets £12
Delve deeper into music featured at the Proms with the help of RCM musicians, play as an exciting ensemble and create a masterpiece in a day. Hear the music come alive in concert with a linked £5 Proms ticket offer for families.

RCM Sparks Explorers – course for ages 10 to 12 28–30 July; tickets £75 (includes a pair of tickets to the Prom on 28 July for course participant plus accompanying adult)
Unleash creativity and uncover the magical world of myths in music, take inspiration from music at the Proms and have fun writing and performing brand-new pieces as an eclectic new ensemble.

RCM Sparks Springboard Composition Course – course for ages 13 to 18
7–11 August; tickets £125 (includes a pair of tickets to the Prom on Sunday 10 August for course participant plus accompanying adult)
Learn exciting new ways of approaching composition, harness the expertise of professionals, work and perform with young RCM composers and bring creative ideas to life.

All RCM Sparks events must be booked in advance through the RCM Box Office (020 7591 4314). Free-ticket scheme available for all events, subject to eligibility. For more information about the events please see www.rcm.ac.uk/summermusic.

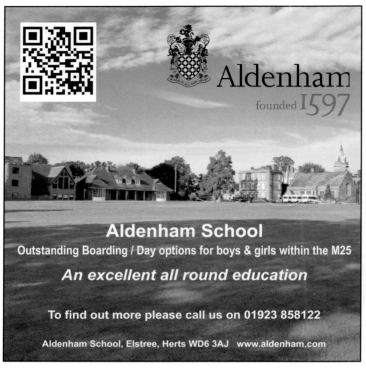

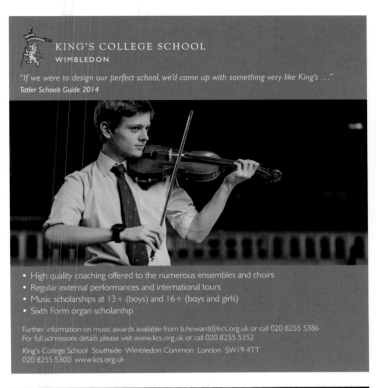
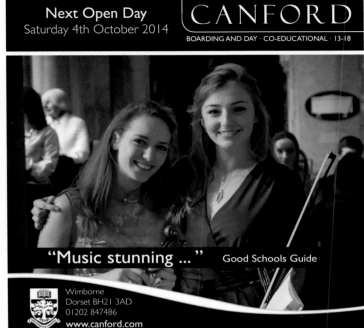

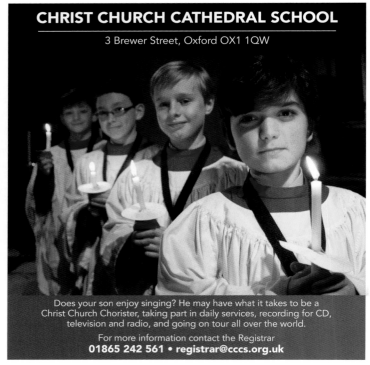
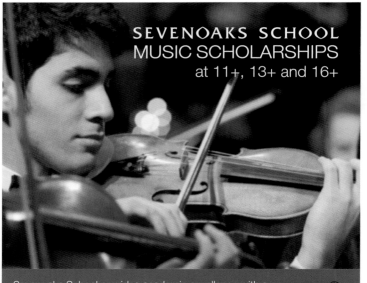

PIERINO

37 Thurloe Place, London SW7 2HP
Tel:0207 581 3770

Monday to Saturday
12 noon – 11.30pm

Sunday
12 noon – 11pm

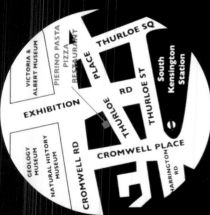

Prompt service guarenteed for you to be in time for the performance

We are within walking distance of the Royal Albert Hall, near South Kensington tube station.

You are welcome before and after the performance.

EXPERIENCE OF SERVING GENUINE ITALAN FOOD AND FOR HOME-MADE PASTA AND THE BEST PIZZA IN LONDON

CONCERT LISTINGS

BOOKING

Tickets will go on sale at 9.00am on Saturday 17 May – online, by telephone and in person. Tickets may also be requested by post.

(Promming Season Tickets and Weekend Promming Passes will go on sale at 9.00am on Friday 16 May – online, by telephone and in person.)

Plan your Proms concert-going online, before tickets go on sale, by using the Proms Planner at bbc.co.uk/proms from 2.00pm on Thursday 24 April until midnight on Friday 16 May.

ONLINE bbc.co.uk/proms
TELEPHONE 0845 401 5040*

For full booking information, see pages 158–169

*see page 163 for call-cost information

PRICE CODES Ⓐ ▸ Ⓗ

Each concert at the Royal Albert Hall falls into one of eight price bands, colour-coded for ease of reference. For a full list of prices and booking fees, see page 160. For special offers, see page 164.

Please note: concert start-times vary across the season – check before you book

The BBC: bringing the Proms to you – in concert, on radio, television and online

---

FRIDAY 18 JULY

PROM 1
7.30pm–c9.10pm • Royal Albert Hall

PRICE BAND Ⓑ *Seats £9.50 to £46 (plus booking fee*)*
WEEKEND PROMMING PASS *see page 164*

Elgar
The Kingdom   90'

Erin Wall *Blessed Virgin*
Catherine Wyn-Rogers *Mary Magdalene*
Andrew Staples *St John*
Christopher Purves *St Peter*

BBC National Chorus of Wales
BBC Symphony Chorus
BBC Symphony Orchestra
Sir Andrew Davis *conductor*

There will be no interval

The largest classical music festival in the world, the BBC Proms also boasts one of the mightiest venues. The Royal Albert Hall is a monument to the same Victorian pomp and splendour that swells through Edward Elgar's music. What better way to open this season than with the composer's biblical oratorio *The Kingdom* – the beautiful 'slow movement' of a musical triptych that started with *The Apostles*, but that would remain unfinished at Elgar's death. Celebrated Elgarian and Proms favourite Sir Andrew Davis, a Conductor Laureate of the BBC Symphony Orchestra, returns in his 70th-birthday year, joined by a distinguished cast of soloists. See 'Birthday Batonists', pages 78–79.

SIR ANDREW DAVIS

BROADCAST
RADIO *Live on BBC Radio 3*
ONLINE *Listen live and on-demand at bbc.co.uk/proms*
TV *Broadcast on BBC Two later this evening*

PROMS PLUS IN TUNE
4.30pm • Royal College of Music A live Proms edition of BBC Radio 3's drivetime programme, *In Tune*, presented by Sean Rafferty – with interviews and live performances from artists appearing this season. *Tickets available from BBC Studio Audiences, bbc.co.uk/tickets. Broadcast live on BBC Radio 3*

SPOTLIGHT ON...
Catherine Wyn-Rogers • Prom 1

Mezzo-soprano Catherine Wyn-Rogers has been part of Sir Andrew Davis's 'team' in former performances of Elgar oratorios at the Proms. But her relationship to the music goes back to her earliest student days: 'I was lucky enough at the Royal College of Music to have a singing teacher, Meriel St Clair, who had seen Elgar rehearse *The Dream of Gerontius*, and my director was Sir David Willcocks, who had been conducted by the composer as a choirboy and had seen him conduct *Gerontius* at the Three Choirs Festival, so I was helped in my first performances by two people with great insight. Andrew himself is a very exacting but hugely enthusiastic and inspiring conductor of Elgar's music. Over the years, these great oratorios have come to mean more and more to me; I think they express so much of Elgar's own soul.'

Wyn-Rogers has great empathy for the character of Mary Magdalene: 'Who could not have sympathy with someone who wishes to repent and be forgiven? There's also a sense in which she becomes a companion to the Virgin Mary and the disciples, and her perspective as a woman in that company is significant to me.' Elgar would no doubt have identified with Wyn-Rogers's love of rural Gloucestershire, where she and her husband have their home: 'It is a complete antidote to my crazy lifestyle and refreshes me for the next onslaught.'

SATURDAY 19 JULY

PROM 2
7.30pm–c10.25pm • Royal Albert Hall

PRICE BAND Ⓐ *Seats £7.50 to £38 (plus booking fee*)*
WEEKEND PROMMING PASS *see page 164*

Elgar
Pomp and Circumstance March No. 4 in G major   *6'*

Tchaikovsky
Fantasy-Overture 'Romeo and Juliet'   *20'*

Liszt
Piano Concerto No. 1 in E flat major   *19'*

INTERVAL

Qigang Chen
Joie éternelle   *25'*
BBC co-commission: UK premiere

Mussorgsky, orch. Ravel
Pictures at an Exhibition   *35'*

Haochen Zhang *piano*
Alison Balsom *trumpet*

China Philharmonic Orchestra
Long Yu *conductor*

East meets West as the China Philharmonic Orchestra launches our series of global orchestras making their debuts at the 2014 Proms. See 'Global Visitors', pages 32–35; 'New Music', pages 64–73.

BROADCAST
RADIO Live on BBC Radio 3
ONLINE Listen live and on-demand at bbc.co.uk/proms
TV Recorded for broadcast on BBC Four on 27 July

PROMS PLUS SING
2.00pm • Royal College of Music
Sing excerpts from Janáček's *Glagolitic Mass* (see Prom 9), led by Mary King, with members of the BBC Singers. Suitable for ages 16-plus. See pages 104–109 for details of how to sign up

PROMS PLUS LITERARY
5.45pm • Royal College of Music 'What is Chinese culture today?' Novelist Xiaolu Guo in discussion with Rana Mitter. *Edited version broadcast on BBC Radio 3 during tonight's interval*

PROMS PLUS LATE
Elgar Room, Royal Albert Hall Informal post-Proms music and poetry, featuring young talent. *For details see bbc.co.uk/proms*

SPOTLIGHT ON...
Haochen Zhang • Prom 2

Following studies at the Conservatory in his native Shanghai, Haochen Zhang went to Philadelphia's Curtis Institute before being catapulted into the spotlight by winning the Gold Medal at the 2009 Van Cliburn Competition. He was the first Chinese pianist to gain the title, and he was aged only 19.

This year he makes his Proms debut playing Liszt's Piano Concerto No. 1: 'For me, this work exemplifies the perfect balance between poetry and virtuosity,' he says, 'which is perhaps the fundamental balance a concert pianist must try to achieve. It's free and extremely personal in style, but also opens up room for countless different interpretations.'

As Artist-in-Residence at the Shanghai Symphony Orchestra he has had a shaping role in his region's music scene. 'Shanghai has an interesting culture, which I miss when I'm away – a combination of traditional Chinese and Western colonial influences.' Zhang takes a keen interest in contemporary Chinese composers and looks forward to hearing Qigang Chen's new trumpet concerto: 'I've met Mr Chen and know his music. Alongside other noted Chinese composers in the West, such as Tan Dun and Bright Sheng, he has successfully blended traditional Chinese tunes, stories and ethos with modern Western compositional techniques to form a unique means of expression.'

SUNDAY 20 JULY

PROM 3
10.30am–c12.45pm • Royal Albert Hall

PRICE BAND C *Seats £14 to £57 (plus booking fee*)*
WEEKEND PROMMING PASS *see page 164*

BBC SPORT PROM

Programme to include:

Mozart
A Musical Joke – Presto   5'

Orff
Carmina burana – 'O Fortuna'   5'

Prokofiev
Romeo and Juliet – Montagues and
Capulets (Dance of the Knights)   6'

Josef Strauss
Sport Polka   2'

John Williams
Summon the Heroes   6'

*plus TV themes including 'Match of the Day',
'Test Match Special' and 'Wimbledon'*

Gabby Logan *presenter*

Crouch End Festival Chorus
BBC Concert Orchestra
Rebecca Miller *conductor*

In a busy summer of sport that
includes the World Cup, the
Commonwealth Games and
Wimbledon comes the first
ever BBC Sport Prom. Gabby
Logan hosts an evening
combining classical favourites
recalling great sporting events
with memorable TV themes.
Sporting celebrities select
their favourite classical items
and we relive unforgettable sporting moments on
screens in the Hall. See 'Perfect Match', pages 38–39.

GABBY LOGAN

BROADCAST
RADIO *Live on BBC Radio 3 and Radio 5 live*
ONLINE *Listen live and on-demand at bbc.co.uk/proms*

SUNDAY 20 JULY

PROM 4
7.30pm–c10.00pm • Royal Albert Hall

PRICE BAND D *Seats £18 to £68 (plus booking fee*)*
WEEKEND PROMMING PASS *see page 164*

Roxanna Panufnik
Three Paths to Peace   12'
European premiere

R. Strauss
Die Frau ohne Schatten –
symphonic fantasia   20'

INTERVAL

Mahler
Symphony No. 6 in A minor   77'

World Orchestra for Peace
Valery Gergiev *conductor*

The World Orchestra for Peace returns with its
conductor Valery Gergiev for its fourth Proms
appearance and its only UK appearance this year,
the first of three UNESCO 2014 Concerts for
Peace in Europe. This classical supergroup
celebrates Strauss's 150th anniversary with the
colourful, fairy-tale soundscapes of his operatic
masterpiece *Die Frau ohne Schatten*. Fantasy
gives way to reality in the prescient tragedy
of Mahler's Sixth Symphony, the glorious agony of
its final movement foreshadowing the composer's
own personal heartbreaks. Roxanna Panufnik's
Three Paths to Peace, commissioned by tonight's
orchestra, meshes Christian, Jewish and Islamic
musical traditions to tell the story of Abraham and
Isaac. See 'Inside the Head of Richard Strauss', pages
16–21; 'Lest We Forget', pages 24–29; 'Global Visitors',
pages 32–35; 'New Music', pages 64–73.

(circle) **SAME-DAY SAVER** Proms 3 & 4 *(see page 164)*

BROADCAST
RADIO *Live on BBC Radio 3*
ONLINE *Listen live and on-demand at bbc.co.uk/proms*
TV *Recorded for broadcast on BBC Four on 14 August*

PROMS PLUS LITERARY
5.45pm • Royal College of Music Novelist Pat Barker, author
of the *Regeneration* trilogy based on the First World War,
and poet Owen Sheers discuss writers', musicians' and
painters' responses to war.
Edited version broadcast on BBC Radio 3 during tonight's interval

---

SPOTLIGHT ON...

World Orchestra for Peace, Fionnuala Hunt • Prom 4

The World Orchestra for Peace, which returns
to the Proms this summer, contains players
from 24 countries. But that is no obstacle to
communication, says Irish violinist Fionnuala
Hunt, one of the ensemble's 12 leaders. 'Players
don't always get much opportunity to work
with their counterparts from around the world,
so we're very curious to meet each other.'

The conductor Georg Solti founded the WOP
in 1995, to promote harmony between cultures
and, in its 20 concerts under the baton of Valery
Gergiev, it has continued to prioritise that ideal.
In 2010 it became the first major symphony
orchestra to be designated UNESCO Artist
for Peace. Although many of its members are
concert-masters and section leaders in their own
right, hand-picked from the best orchestras in
the world, 'none of us is there to profile ourselves
individually,' says Hunt.

There is no fixed seating plan; all players –
including the concert-masters – change places
for each piece. The reward, says Hunt, is
getting to play 'in the middle of a glorious wall
of sound, as Valery waves his magic wand'.
What's more, since rehearsal periods are so
short and intensive, 'it's not routine music-
making. When you sit in an orchestra for
a long time, it can become a bit "ho-hum"
at times. But this isn't like that at all.'

Matrix Studios (Logan); Amelia Stein (Hunt)

MONDAY 21 JULY

PROMS CHAMBER MUSIC 1
1.00pm–c2.00pm • Cadogan Hall

Seats £10 / £12 (plus booking fee*)

Rameau
Pièces de clavecin en concerts   53'

Les Arts Florissants
Paolo Zanzu *harpsichord/director*

Leading period-instrument ensemble Les Arts
Florissants launches the Proms Chamber Music
series with the first of its
two Proms appearances
marking 250 years since the
death of Jean-Philippe
Rameau. France's leading
Baroque composer, whom
some have called the
'French Bach', proved more
progressive than Lully, more
virtuosic than Couperin.
This lunchtime Les Arts
Florissants appears on an
intimate scale, performing Rameau's only chamber
music – the lively and virtuosic *Pièces de clavecin en
concerts*. With movements named after people,
places and moods, each is a miniature character
study, an evocative musical portrait. See 'L'Eau de
Rameau', pages 86–87; 'Cadogan Hall Complement',
pages 92–93.

PAOLO ZANZU

There will be no interval

BROADCAST
RADIO *Live on BBC Radio 3*
ONLINE *Listen live and on-demand at bbc.co.uk/proms*

MONDAY 21 JULY

PROM 5
7.30pm–c9.50pm • Royal Albert Hall

PRICE BAND C *Seats £14 to £57 (plus booking fee*)*

R. Strauss
Till Eulenspiegels lustige Streiche   18'

Dvořák
Violin Concerto in A minor   32'

INTERVAL

Beethoven
Symphony No. 6 in F major, 'Pastoral'   40'

Julia Fischer *violin*

Tonhalle Orchestra Zurich
David Zinman *conductor*

From the pastoral landscapes of Beethoven's
Symphony No. 6 to the vibrant folk scenes of
Strauss's tone-poem and Dvořák's Violin Concerto,
tonight's Prom takes a vivid journey across Central
Europe. Celebrated Straussian David Zinman
appears in his final concert as Chief Conductor of
Zurich's Tonhalle Orchestra, stepping down after
almost 20 years. Strauss appears at his playful,
joyous best in the exploits of folk-hero/prankster
Till Eulenspiegel, while Julia Fischer makes a welcome
return to the Proms in the
last of the great Romantic
violin concertos – an
inventive and idiosyncratic
work previously too often
neglected in favour of
Mendelssohn or Bruch. See
'Inside the Head of Richard
Strauss', pages 16–21.

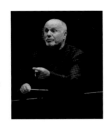

DAVID ZINMAN

BROADCAST
RADIO *Live on BBC Radio 3*
ONLINE *Listen live and on-
demand at bbc.co.uk/proms*
TV *Recorded for broadcast on BBC Four on 25 July*

PROMS PLUS FAMILY
5.30pm • Royal College of Music Join Rachel Leach and
professional musicians for a family-friendly introduction to
tonight's Prom. Bring your instrument and join in! See pages
104–109 for details

SPOTLIGHT ON...
Julia Fischer • Prom 5

Dvořák's Violin Concerto holds a special
place in Julia Fischer's heart: 'I first got to
know it when I was 6 or 7 years old. My
mother comes from the Czech Republic,
so, naturally, it was the most important
concerto in the repertoire. I remember hearing
a recording of Josef Suk playing it when I
hardly even played the violin.' It was the first
concerto the German violinist studied, and
one which she's championed in concert halls
around the world ever since. And, happily,
for a work that used to be overshadowed by
its cello counterpart, Fischer thinks that this
1879 piece has been given the recognition it
deserves in recent years.

   She recorded the work last year with the
Tonhalle Orchestra Zurich and David
Zinman, whom she joins again for this Prom.
'David and I met 10 years ago and he's been
part of my entire career. And the Tonhalle is
one of my favourite orchestras, not least
because many of my friends play in it.'
So, when Fischer steps out onto the stage,
is there a particular moment she'll be looking
forward to? 'I like the two opening cadenzas
the best. It's the greatest beginning of any
violin concerto. After the few bars in the
orchestra, there's this fantastic virtuosic
cadenza. And if that first cadenza isn't
enough, you then get to repeat it!'

TUESDAY 22 JULY

PROM 6
6.30pm–c10.40pm • Royal Albert Hall

PRICE BAND **C** *Seats £14 to £57 (plus booking fee*)*

R. Strauss
Der Rosenkavalier   185'
(semi-staged: sung in German)

Kate Royal *Marschallin*
Tara Erraught *Octavian*
Lars Woldt *Baron Ochs*
Teodora Gheorghiu *Sophie*
Michael Kraus *Herr von Faninal*
Miranda Keys *Marianne*
Christopher Gillett *Valzacchi*
Helene Schneiderman *Annina*
Gwynne Howell *Notary*
Andrej Dunaev *Italian Singer*
Robert Wörle *Innkeeper*
Scott Conner *Police Inspector*

Glyndebourne Festival Opera
London Philharmonic Orchestra
Robin Ticciati *conductor*

There will be two intervals of 20 minutes

Glyndebourne marks its own 80th anniversary and Strauss's 150th with the composer's richly melodic *Der Rosenkavalier* – the first of a trilogy of Strauss operas at this year's Proms. Vienna has rarely sounded more beguiling, more gilded with nostalgia, than in this tragicomedy that combines romance with riotous farce. Glyndebourne's new Music Director Robin Ticciati conducts an international cast, led by British soprano Kate Royal. See 'Inside the Head of Richard Strauss', pages 16–21.

ROBIN TICCIATI

BROADCAST
RADIO *Live on BBC Radio 3*
ONLINE *Listen live and on-demand at bbc.co.uk/proms*

PROMS PLUS INTRO
4.45pm • Royal College of Music Sara Mohr-Pietsch is joined by Hugo Shirley for an introduction to *Der Rosenkavalier*.
Edited version broadcast on BBC Radio 3 during tonight's first interval

SPOTLIGHT ON...
Kate Royal • Prom 6

It's over 30 years since Strauss's *Der Rosenkavalier* was last performed at Glyndebourne, a fact which hasn't passed Kate Royal by. 'It makes me feel quite terrified, really! It's one of those pieces that people have such affection for.' But the British soprano is also full of enthusiasm for this year's new production, which sees Royal both take on the role of the Marschallin for the first time and make her Strauss opera debut. 'This piece is a singing-actor's dream. Sometimes in opera you have to pad out a character, but the Marschallin is wonderfully written.'

How would Royal describe her? 'She's the wife of the head of the Austrian army, and has a fairly dull existence, really, having to do what's expected of her,' she explains. 'But she's very bright and passionate, a thinker who is searching for answers and who enjoys life. Yet she knows she will never be free from her position in society, and the opera is about her coming to terms with that.' It might be Royal's first outing with operatic Strauss, but it was hearing Elisabeth Schwarzkopf's recording of the composer's *Four Last Songs* that inspired her to become a singer: 'Something about the line and melody just struck me. I didn't in a million years think I'd perform a Strauss role at Glyndebourne, but I can't think of a more pleasurable thing to sing.'

WEDNESDAY 23 JULY

PROM 7
6.30pm–c9.00pm • Royal Albert Hall

PRICE BAND **A** *Seats £7.50 to £38 (plus booking fee*)*

Tavener
Gnosis   c12'
BBC commission: world premiere

Bartók
Violin Concerto No. 2   38'

INTERVAL

Shostakovich
Symphony No. 10 in E minor   53'

Sarah Connolly *mezzo-soprano*
Isabelle Faust *violin*

BBC Symphony Orchestra
Jiří Bělohlávek *conductor*

Isabelle Faust's association with Bartók extends back to her very first recording. Now, fresh from an acclaimed disc of both the composer's violin concertos, she joins the BBC SO and Conductor Laureate Jiří Bělohlávek for Bartók's Second Violin Concerto. Written under the threat of Fascism, it's a passionate national statement, lively with folk rhythms. By the early 1950s and Shostakovich's 10th Symphony, threat had become reality. This violent, despairing work paints a vivid portrait of the horrors of Stalin's Russia. The evening opens with the first of two posthumous premieres this season from the late John Tavener – some of the last works from England's great musical mystic. See 'New Music', pages 64–73.

SAME-DAY SAVER
Proms 7 & 8
(see page 164)

BROADCAST
RADIO *Live on BBC Radio 3*
ONLINE *Listen live and on-demand at bbc.co.uk/proms*

PROMS PLUS LITERARY
4.45pm • Royal College of Music Poet and librettist Michael Symmons Roberts and the Revd. Richard Coles on the literary works that inspired the composer John Tavener, from William Blake to John Donne, from Yeats, Shakespeare and Tolstoy to the Sufi poet Rumi.
Edited version broadcast on BBC Radio 3 during tonight's interval

Mirco Borggreve (Ticciati); Sussie Ahlburg (Royal)

WEDNESDAY 23 JULY

PROM 8
10.15pm–c11.40pm • Royal Albert Hall

PRICE BAND **F** *Seats £18/£24 (plus booking fee*)*

Neil Tennant/Chris Lowe
Overture to 'Performance' (arr. R. Niles)   8'

Pet Shop Boys songs
(orch. A. Badalamenti)   20'

A Man from the Future (orch. S. Helbig)   c45'
world premiere

Pet Shop Boys

BBC Singers
BBC Concert Orchestra
Dominic Wheeler *conductor*

There will be no interval

The legendary Pet Shop Boys make their Proms debut in this Late Night Prom, joining the BBC Singers and BBC Concert Orchestra for the world premiere of *A Man from the Future*, a new piece for electronics, orchestra, choir and narrator. The piece is inspired by the life and work of Alan Turing, who helped break the German Enigma code during the Second World War and formulated the concept of the digital computer, but was prosecuted in 1952 for his homosexuality, receiving a posthumous pardon last year. It comes as a timely homage, 60 years after Turing's death. The concert also includes new orchestral arrangements by renowned film composer Angelo Badalamenti of five Pet Shop Boys songs chosen by Tennant and Lowe, as well as the exuberant overture to their 1991 tour, *Performance*, heard live in concert for the first time. See 'New Music', pages 64–73; 'The Night Thing', pages 90–91.

SAME-DAY SAVER
Proms 7 & 8
(see page 164)

PET SHOP BOYS

BROADCAST
RADIO *Live on BBC Radio 3*
ONLINE *Listen live and on-demand at bbc.co.uk/proms*

THURSDAY 24 JULY

PROM 9
7.30pm–c9.45pm • Royal Albert Hall

PRICE BAND **B** *Seats £9.50 to £46 (plus booking fee*)*

Brahms
Piano Concerto No. 1 in D minor   49'

INTERVAL

Janáček
Glagolitic Mass (original version, reconstr. P. Wingfield)   43'

Barry Douglas *piano*
Mlada Khudoley *soprano*
Yulia Matochkina *mezzo-soprano*
Mikhail Vekua *tenor*
Yuri Vorobiev *bass*

London Symphony Chorus
London Symphony Orchestra
Valery Gergiev *conductor*

BARRY DOUGLAS

'In the tenor solo I hear a high priest,' Janáček said of his *Glagolitic Mass*, 'in the soprano solo a girlish angel and in the chorus our people.' These elements, combined with organ and orchestra, yield a huge, passionate secular oratorio celebrating life, nationhood and peace. In the first half Barry Douglas, whose relationship with the Proms goes back almost 20 years, returns with Brahms's elemental First Piano Concerto – a work that distils all the conflict of the composer's relationship with the troubled Robert Schumann and his wife Clara.

BROADCAST
RADIO *Live on BBC Radio 3*
ONLINE *Listen live and on-demand at bbc.co.uk/proms*

PROMS PLUS INTRO
5.45pm • Royal College of Music Andrew McGregor talks to Jan Smaczny, who gives an insight into Janáček's epic *Glagolitic Mass* and its influences.
Edited version broadcast on BBC Radio 3 during tonight's interval

---

FRIDAY 25 JULY

PROM 10
7.30pm–c9.50pm • Royal Albert Hall

PRICE BAND **A** *Seats £7.50 to £38 (plus booking fee*)*
WEEKEND PROMMING PASS *see page 164*

Walton
Variations on a Theme by Hindemith   23'

Moeran
Violin Concerto   33'

INTERVAL

David Horne
Daedalus in Flight   11'
London premiere

Elgar
'Enigma' Variations   29'

Tasmin Little *violin*

BBC Philharmonic
Juanjo Mena *conductor*

Moeran's lyrical Violin Concerto meshes the composer's English heritage with his love of the Irish landscape. The English theme continues with Elgar's 'Enigma' Variations – his affectionate musical portraits of friends and family – and Walton's *Hindemith Variations*, another intensely personal homage and the first work in this year's focus on the music of William Walton. British music comes right up to date with the shifting soundscapes of David Horne's *Daedalus in Flight*. See 'Behind the Façade', pages 42–45; 'Power of Six', pages 58–61; 'New Music', pages 64–73.

BROADCAST
RADIO *Live on BBC Radio 3*
ONLINE *Listen live and on-demand at bbc.co.uk/proms*

PROMS PLUS PORTRAIT
5.45pm • Royal College of Music David Horne, in conversation with Andrew McGregor, discusses his *Daedalus in Flight* and introduces performances of his chamber works.
Broadcast on BBC Radio 3 after tonight's Prom

SATURDAY 26 JULY

PROM 11

11.00am–c11.50am • Royal Albert Hall

PRICE BAND **H** *Seats £6/£12 (plus booking fee*)*

CBEEBIES PROM

Programme to include:

Barrie Bignold
Around Sound   c3'
BBC commission: world premiere

Holst
St Paul's Suite – Finale (The Dargason)   4'

Wood
Fanfare on British Sea-Songs – Hornpipe   2'

plus music from CBeebies programmes

Presenters to include:

Ben Faulks *(Mr Bloom)*
Gemma Hunt *(from 'Swashbuckle')*
Chris Jarvis *(from 'Show Me, Show Me')*
Steven Kynman *(Robert the Robot)*

BBC Philharmonic
Stephen Bell *conductor*

There will be no interval

Following on from the sell-out success of last year's Doctor Who Prom and 2011's Horrible Histories Prom, this year parents are invited to join their children for the first ever CBeebies Prom. Take a journey through London with some of your favourite CBeebies characters and explore the sounds of the orchestra, as well as the everyday sounds around us. This morning's adventure combines live music from the BBC Philharmonic and video action on screens around the hall. The next generation of classical music fans starts here. *See 'New Music', pages 64–73; 'A World of Wonder', pages 104–109.*

MR BLOOM

SATURDAY 26 JULY

PROM 12

8.00pm–c10.15pm • Royal Albert Hall

PRICE BAND **C** *Seats £14 to £57 (plus booking fee*)*
WEEKEND PROMMING PASS *see page 164*

J. S. Bach
St John Passion *(sung in German)*   120'

James Gilchrist *Evangelist*
Neal Davies *Christus*
Lucy Crowe *soprano*
Clint van der Linde *counter-tenor*
Andrew Kennedy *tenor*
Rudolf Rosen *baritone*

Zürcher Sing-Akademie
Zurich Chamber Orchestra
Sir Roger Norrington *conductor*

There will be no interval

In the first of two Proms appearances, leading Bach interpreter Sir Roger Norrington – celebrating his 80th birthday this year – directs his Zurich Chamber Orchestra in the *St John Passion* (bookended later this season by Peter Sellars's staging of the *St Matthew Passion*, conducted by Sir Simon Rattle) – a work noted for its dramatic sweep and emotional immediacy in the recounting of events leading to the crucifixion of Christ. It is realised here by a cast led by tenor James Gilchrist, a distinguished Evangelist of his generation.

SAME-DAY SAVER
Proms 11 & 12
(see page 164)

BROADCAST
RADIO *Live on BBC Radio 3*
ONLINE *Listen live and on-demand at bbc.co.uk/proms*
TV *Recorded for broadcast on BBC Four on 31 July*

PROMS PLUS SING
2.00pm • Royal College of Music Sing excerpts from Bach's *St John Passion*, led by Mary King, with the BBC Singers. Suitable for ages 16-plus. *See pages 104–109 for details of how to sign up*

PROMS PLUS INTRO
6.15pm • Royal College of Music Ian Skelly in conversation with Giles Fraser about the core aspects of the theology surrounding Bach's *St John Passion*. *Edited version broadcast on BBC Radio 3 before tonight's Prom*

PROMS PLUS LATE
Elgar Room, Royal Albert Hall Informal post-Proms music and poetry, featuring young talent. *For details see bbc.co.uk/proms*

SPOTLIGHT ON...
James Gilchrist • Prom 12

'I think the *St John Passion* is as close as Bach ever got to writing an opera,' says James Gilchrist, 'not least because the choir acts as a character in its own right. It's interesting that the solo arias are mostly at the beginning and the end, and in the middle the choir springs forwards and takes over in an alarming way. It's exciting to be the Evangelist, carrying the momentum through each scene.'

The British tenor, a veteran of the role, is always struck by the raw, contemporary feel of this work: 'Sadly, it seems to be a constantly repeating human fault that we get swept up in crowd mentality, and overlook the humanity of the individual with appalling results. Just look at the world today. Bach not only depicts the masses baying for blood, but those in authority sanctioning destruction. As artists, we can't just bewail it, we need to move our listeners, to make them conscious of its relevance.' While he often performs the Evangelist with period instruments at Baroque pitch (where A is tuned to 415Hz, rather than the standard 440Hz), he's looking forward to working with a modern orchestra under Sir Roger Norrington. 'The higher pitch increases the tension, and can make for a very powerful performance. It's a delight to work with Roger. I admire his fearlessness, the way he's willing to stick his neck out and be different.'

26–27 JULY

124

BOOK ONLINE AT BBC.CO.UK/PROMS • BY TELEPHONE 0845 401 5040† • IN PERSON AT THE ROYAL ALBERT HALL • BOOKING OPENS 9.00AM ON 17 MAY

SUNDAY 27 JULY

PROM 13
11.00am–c11.50am • Royal Albert Hall

PRICE BAND **H** *Seats £6/£12 (plus booking fee*)*

CBEEBIES PROM

Presenters to include:

Ben Faulks *(Mr Bloom)*
Gemma Hunt *(from 'Swashbuckle')*
Chris Jarvis *(from 'Show Me, Show Me')*
Steven Kynman *(Robert the Robot)*

BBC Philharmonic
Stephen Bell *conductor*

There will be no interval

For programme details, see Prom 11

BROADCAST
RADIO *Live on BBC Radio 3*
ONLINE *Listen live and on-demand at bbc.co.uk/proms*
TV *Recorded for future broadcast on CBeebies*

ROBERT THE ROBOT

SUNDAY 27 JULY

PROM 14
7.30pm–c9.45pm • Royal Albert Hall

PRICE BAND **A** *Seats £7.50 to £38 (plus booking fee*)*
WEEKEND PROMMING PASS *see page 164*

Ravel
Valses nobles et sentimentales   17'

Simon Holt
Morpheus Wakes   c15'
BBC commission: world premiere

Ravel
La valse   13'

INTERVAL

Duruflé
Requiem   42'

Emmanuel Pahud *flute*
Ruby Hughes *soprano*
Gerald Finley *baritone*

BBC National Chorus of Wales
National Youth Choir of Wales
BBC National Orchestra of Wales
Thierry Fischer *conductor*

Ravel's *La valse* turns the Viennese waltz into a darkly tinged rhapsody, while his *Valses nobles et sentimentales* reflects the iconic dance in softer tones. Duruflé's *Requiem* is the musical cousin of Fauré's more familiar *Requiem* and anchors its 20th-century harmonies in the same arching plainchant melodies of the past. Flute virtuoso Emmanuel Pahud joins the orchestra for the world premiere of Simon Holt's flute concerto *Morpheus Wakes* – written for Pahud himself, who represents the god of dreaming 'as if slowly waking from a deep, troubled sleep'. See 'New Music', pages 64–73.

SAME-DAY SAVER
Proms 13 & 14
(see page 164)

BROADCAST
RADIO *Live on BBC Radio 3*
ONLINE *Listen live and on-demand at bbc.co.uk/proms*

PROMS PLUS INTRO
5.45pm • Royal College of Music A discussion of the sacred and secular traditions in French music during the time of Ravel and Duruflé, with Martin Handley and Richard Langham Smith.
Edited version broadcast on BBC Radio 3 during tonight's interval

SPOTLIGHT ON...
Ruby Hughes • Prom 14

'Duruflé's unique and distinctive style is present throughout this magical work,' says singer Ruby Hughes, one of the soloists for this year's Proms performance of the *Requiem*. 'He conveys peace, beauty, transparency, light and profound reconciliation, as well as grief, agony and the great mystery and sadness of death and loss.'

Written in 1947, this sacred masterpiece for four-part choir, two soloists and, in this version, full orchestra, draws heavily on Gregorian plainchant and rhythms, colouring them with 20th-century French harmonies. Perhaps one of its most famous moments is the 'Pie Jesu Domine', a movement featuring a solo mezzo-soprano. So why is Hughes, a soprano, taking on this mezzo part? 'The lower registers of my voice have been developing in recent years and this in no way prevents me being a soprano,' she explains. 'It simply brings some mezzo-soprano roles within my range. If we as performers feel a profound connection to particular pieces of music, why should we not find a way of singing and sharing it?' And what is it like to sing? 'The challenge is to keep a beautiful legato and natural warmth in the sound, and to communicate the words with feeling,' says Hughes. 'Duruflé movingly evokes the fragility of the human soul with an earthly humble atmosphere. It's a gentle prayer for eternal rest.'

PROMS CHAMBER MUSIC 2
1.00pm–c2.00pm • Cadogan Hall

Seats £10/£12 (plus booking fee*)

C. P. E. Bach

Trio Sonata in A major, Wq 146   *13'*

Violin Sonata in C minor, Wq 78   *17'*

Keyboard Sonata in E minor ('Kenner
und Liebhaber' Collection No. 5), Wq 59/1   *8'*

Trio Sonata in C minor, 'Sanguineus
and Melancholicus'   *14'*

Rachel Podger *violin*
Katy Bircher *flute*
Bojan Čičić *violin*
Tomasz Pokrzywiński *cello*
Kristian Bezuidenhout *fortepiano*

There will be no interval

This year marks the 300th anniversary of the birth of C. P. E. Bach. Second son of J. S. Bach and godson of George Philipp Telemann, he was also the most musically rebellious of the younger Bachs, propelling music from the Baroque style of his father's time into the Classical era. When Mozart wrote, 'Bach is the father, we the children', he was referring not to Johann Sebastian but Carl Philipp Emmanuel. Baroque violinist Rachel Podger is joined by musical friends in a programme to explore the weird and wonderful musical world of this fascinating musician. At its core is the extraordinary and unpredented C minor Trio Sonata – an instrumental dialogue between a 'sanguine' man and a 'melancholic', in which each tries to persuade the other to change his mood. *See 'Cadogan Hall Complement', pages 92–93.*

KRISTIAN
BEZUIDENHOUT

BROADCAST
RADIO *Live on BBC Radio 3*
ONLINE *Listen live and on-demand at bbc.co.uk/proms*

SPOTLIGHT ON...
Rachel Podger • PCM 2

Baroque violinist Rachel Podger, famous for her questing approach to repertoire, needs little excuse to explore further avenues, and C. P. E. Bach's 300th anniversary presents a welcome challenge. His music has always struck her as mysteriously unpredictable: 'Sometimes he seems to be out to shock, needing to prove something – utterly understandable with a father such as his! He represented the *empfindsamer Stil*, an aesthetic which took hold during the mid-18th century, the main aims of which were to "touch the heart and move the affections". His violin-writing is at times tuneful and singing, but also angular and ungainly and requires a certain agility and quick musical reaction – contrast of expression seems to be the name of the game.'

Her chamber music concert with Kristian Bezuidenhout includes the fascinating Sonata 'Sanguineus and Melancholicus', a dramatic dialogue between the two humours and one of his most programmatic works. 'C. P. E. was not afraid of demanding from instrumentalists the range of expression he would expect from singers, and tells us in his treatise that a good performance is a matter of "portraying rage, tenderness and other passions". Performing his music, you need to be ready to soar, leap, dismiss, indulge and dodge as well as laugh heartily.'

PROM 15
7.30pm–c10.05pm • Royal Albert Hall

PRICE BAND A *Seats £7.50 to £38 (plus booking fee*)*

Jonathan Dove

Gaia   *c20'*
BBC commission: world premiere

Mozart

Piano Concerto No. 23
in A major, K488   *27'*

INTERVAL

Ravel

Daphnis and Chloe   *60'*

Ingrid Fliter *piano*

BBC Symphony Chorus
BBC Symphony Orchestra
Josep Pons *conductor*

Turbulent mythical love and poised Classical elegance come together in a concert that shifts from Jonathan Dove's large-scale orchestral work *Gaia* to the intimacy of the Viennese salon in Mozart's ever-popular Piano Concerto No. 23. Commissioned by Serge Diaghilev, Ravel's ballet *Daphnis and Chloe* is rich in all the colours and rhythms of turn-of-the-century Paris – a masterpiece that announced its composer as a force with which to be reckoned. *See 'New Music', pages 64–73.*

INGRID FLITER

BROADCAST
RADIO *Live on BBC Radio 3*
ONLINE *Listen live and on-demand at bbc.co.uk/proms*
TV *Recorded for broadcast on BBC Four on 1 August*

PROMS PLUS FAMILY
5.30pm • Royal College of Music Join professional musicians for a family-friendly introduction to tonight's Prom. Bring your instrument and join in! See pages 104–109 for details

TUESDAY 29 JULY

PROM 16

6.30pm–c8.55pm • Royal Albert Hall

PRICE BAND **A** *Seats £7.50 to £38 (plus booking fee*)*

Balakirev, orch. Lyapunov
Islamey – oriental fantasy   9'

Holst
Beni Mora   15'

Gabriel Prokofiev
Violin Concerto   c25'
BBC commission: world premiere

INTERVAL

Mozart
Die Entführung aus dem Serail
– overture   6'

Handel, arr. Beecham
Solomon – The Arrival of the
Queen of Sheba   4'

Respighi
Belkis, Queen of Sheba   25'

Daniel Hope *violin*

**Borusan Istanbul
Philharmonic Orchestra
Sascha Goetzel** *conductor*

Tonight's visitors from Istanbul make their
Proms debut, bringing the intoxicating East as
filtered through Western ears. Sneak into Mozart's
harem and witness the magnificent Queen of Sheba
(in views by Handel and Respighi). Balakirev and
Holst offer folk colourings from further afield.
*See 'Lest We Forget', pages 24–29; 'Global Visitors',
pages 32–35; 'New Music', pages 64–73.*

BROADCAST
RADIO *Live on BBC Radio 3*
ONLINE *Listen live and on-demand at bbc.co.uk/proms*
TV *Recorded for broadcast on BBC Four on 31 August*

PROMS PLUS INTRO
4.45pm • **Royal College of Music** As we continue our focus
on global orchestras, Petroc Trelawny considers Turkish
culture and Western classical music's place within it.
Edited version broadcast on BBC Radio 3 during tonight's interval

---

TUESDAY 29 JULY

PROM 17

10.00pm–c11.15pm • Royal Albert Hall

PRICE BAND **F** *Seats £18/£24 (plus booking fee*)*

Rameau
Deus noster refugium   27'
Quam dilecta tabernacula   21'
In convertendo Dominus   23'

Rachel Redmond *soprano*
Katherine Watson *soprano*
Reinoud Van Mechelen *high tenor*
Cyril Auvity *tenor*
Marc Mauillon *baritone*
Cyril Costanzo *bass*

**Les Arts Florissants
William Christie** *conductor*

There will be no interval

In its second Proms appearance this year, the
Baroque ensemble Les Arts Florissants returns at
full strength with its conductor William Christie.
While its earlier Proms Chamber Music concert
marked 250 years since Rameau's death with the
composer's small-scale chamber works, in this Late
Night Prom the Royal Albert Hall is transformed
into the gilded splendour of the Chapel Royal
in Versailles, combining
choir, orchestra and
soloists for Rameau's
grands motets. Most
celebrated for his theatrical
works, here Rameau proves
his skill at sacred drama.
Exuberant choruses give
way to the meditative
lyricism of solo movements,
chromatic embellishments
keeping the music constantly
poised between joy and sadness. *See 'L'Eau de
Rameau', pages 86–87.*

WILLIAM CHRISTIE

BROADCAST
RADIO *Live on BBC Radio 3*
ONLINE *Listen live and on-demand at bbc.co.uk/proms*

*SAME-DAY SAVER
Proms 16 & 17
(see page 164)*

WEDNESDAY 30 JULY

PROM 18

7.30pm–c10.05pm • Royal Albert Hall

PRICE BAND **A** *Seats £7.50 to £38 (plus booking fee*)*

Sir Harrison Birtwistle
Night's Black Bird   13'

Ravel
Piano Concerto for the Left Hand   18'

INTERVAL

Mahler
Symphony No. 5 in C sharp minor   73'

Alexandre Tharaud *piano*

**BBC Philharmonic
Juanjo Mena** *conductor*

The intense, contrasting moods of Mahler's
Symphony No. 5 – the bitter solemnity of its funeral
march, the violence of its second movement and the
tenderness of the famous Adagietto – make this
one of the great orchestral showpieces. In his Proms
concerto debut, French pianist Alexandre Tharaud
performs Ravel's atmospheric and virtuosic Piano
Concerto for the Left Hand, and the concert opens
with the first of several works at this year's Proms
celebrating Sir Harrison Birtwistle's 80th birthday –
an atmospheric plunge into
mossy, melancholic
darkness, lightened only
by the call of birds. *See
'Northern Knights', pages
48–51.*

BROADCAST
RADIO *Live on BBC Radio 3*
ONLINE *Listen live and
on-demand at bbc.co.uk/proms*
TV *Recorded for broadcast on
BBC Four on 8 August*

ALEXANDRE THARAUD

PROMS PLUS INTRO
5.45pm • **Royal College of Music** Louise Fryer talks to Julian
Johnson about Mahler's Fifth Symphony, with particular
focus on the heartrending Adagietto and the composer's
relationship with his wife, Alma, for whom it was written.
Edited version broadcast on BBC Radio 3 during tonight's interval

Denis Rouvre (Christie); Marco Borggreve (Tharaud)

THURSDAY 31 JULY

PROM 19
7.30pm–c10.05pm • Royal Albert Hall

PRICE BAND Ⓐ *Seats £7.50 to £38 (plus booking fee*)*

R. Strauss
Festival Prelude   *11'*
Deutsche Motette   *19'*
Four Last Songs   *24'*

INTERVAL

Elgar
Symphony No. 2 in E flat major   *57'*

Inger Dam-Jensen *soprano*

BBC Singers
Royal Liverpool
Philharmonic Orchestra
Vasily Petrenko *conductor*

Two rarely heard works continue our 150th-anniversary celebration of Richard Strauss. Scored for organ and an orchestra calling for no fewer than 10 trumpets (six offstage), the *Festival Prelude* packs symphonic weight into its brief duration. It is matched for impact by the *Deutsche Motette* – a concerto for choir by any other name: its vocal lines trace the same expansive arcs and arabesques as the composer's exquisite, autumnal *Four Last Songs*. Maintaining the mood of late-Romantic nostalgia, Elgar's Second Symphony delights in flexible chromaticism, its shifting moods coloured in delicate shades. See *'Inside the Head of Richard Strauss', pages 16–21.*

INGER DAM-JENSEN

BROADCAST
RADIO *Live on BBC Radio 3*
ONLINE *Listen live and on-demand at bbc.co.uk/proms*
TV *Recorded for broadcast on BBC Four on 3 August*

PROMS PLUS INTRO
5.45pm • Royal College of Music Graham Johnson explores Strauss's relationship with the human voice in discussion with Sara Mohr-Pietsch.
Edited version broadcast on BBC Radio 3 during tonight's interval

FRIDAY 1 AUGUST

PROM 20
7.30pm–c9.40pm • Royal Albert Hall

PRICE BAND Ⓐ *Seats £7.50 to £38 (plus booking fee*)*
WEEKEND PROMMING PASS *see page 164*

Gurney
War Elegy   *11'*

Sally Beamish
Violin Concerto   *29'*
London premiere

INTERVAL

Walton
Symphony No. 1 in B flat minor   *47'*

Anthony Marwood *violin*

BBC Symphony Orchestra
Martyn Brabbins *conductor*

Commemorating 100 years since the outbreak of the First World War, the BBC Symphony Orchestra explores English responses to conflict across three generations. Gassed while fighting in the trenches in 1917, Gurney never fully recovered. His *War Elegy* (1920) is a characteristically personal lament – heavy with bittersweet sadness and regret. Sally Beamish's 1994 Violin Concerto, written for tonight's soloist, Anthony Marwood, takes inspiration from Erich Maria Remarque's novel *All Quiet on the Western Front*. While not explicitly programmatic, the slow movement of Walton's First Symphony is among the 20th century's most poignant orchestral cries of grief – an echo, perhaps, of horrors past, and a foreshadow of horrors yet to come. See *'Lest We Forget', pages 24–29; 'Behind the Façade', pages 42–45;' New Music', pages 64–73.*

BROADCAST
RADIO *Live on BBC Radio 3*
ONLINE *Listen live and on-demand at bbc.co.uk/proms*

PROMS PLUS PORTRAIT
5.45pm • Royal College of Music Sally Beamish discusses the London premiere of her Violin Concerto in conversation with Andrew McGregor and introduces performances of her chamber works.
Broadcast on BBC Radio 3 after tonight's Prom

SATURDAY 2 AUGUST

PROMS SATURDAY MATINEE 1
3.00pm–c4.30pm • Cadogan Hall

Seats £10 / £12 (plus booking fee)*

Handel
Alessandro – overture   *6'*

Hasse
Artemisia – sinfonia   *5'*

Paisiello
Olimpiade – 'E mi lasci così?' …
'Ne' giorni tuoi felici'   *5'*

Lully
Phaeton – suite   *10'*

Vivaldi
Giustino – 'Vedrò con mio diletto'   *9'*

Gluck
Orphée et Eurydice – Dance of the
Blessed Spirits; Dance of the Furies   *10'*
Iphigénie en Aulide – 'Ma fille, Jupiter'   *4'*

Paisiello
Olimpiade – 'Sciogli, oh Dio! le
sue catene'   *7'*

Myrsini Margariti *soprano*
Irini Karaianni *mezzo-soprano*

Armonia Atenea
George Petrou *conductor*

The first Greek orchestra ever to appear at the Proms, Armonia Atenea is joined by its Artistic Director George Petrou to present a programme with an appropriately classical flavour. Greek myths form the thread through a Baroque labyrinth of arias and overtures from French, German and Italian operas, including Gluck's *Orphée*, Handel's *Arianna in Creta* and Lully's *Phaeton*. Furies rage, sons defy their fathers and heroines bewail their fate in what promises to be a concert of high drama. See *'Global Visitors', pages 32–35.*

BROADCAST
RADIO *Live on BBC Radio 3*
ONLINE *Listen live and on-demand at bbc.co.uk/proms*

SATURDAY 2 AUGUST

PROM 21
7.30pm–c10.30pm • Royal Albert Hall

PRICE BAND **D** *Seats £18 to £68 (plus booking fee*)*
WEEKEND PROMMING PASS *see page 164*

Porter
Kiss Me, Kate

John Wilson Orchestra
John Wilson *conductor*

There will be one interval

The appearances of John Wilson and his orchestra
have become one of the annual highlights of the
Proms. Following the enormous success of the
staged performance of *My Fair Lady* in 2012, John
Wilson returns to perform Cole Porter's Tony
Award-winning musical *Kiss Me, Kate* in its original
1948 arrangements. He is
joined by a cast of leading
singers in this irreverent
reworking of *The Taming of
the Shrew* – a play within a
play. See 'Brush Up Your
Shakespeare', pages 82–83.

JOHN WILSON

BROADCAST
RADIO *Live on BBC Radio 3*
ONLINE *Listen live and on-
demand at bbc.co.uk/proms*
TV *Recorded for broadcast on
BBC Two in December*

PROMS PLUS SING
2.00pm • Royal College of Music Sing excerpts from
Kiss Me, Kate, led by Anna Flannagan, with members
of the BBC Singers, and pick up some musical theatre
performance tips along the way. Suitable for ages 7-plus.
See pages 104–109 for details of how to sign up

PROMS PLUS LITERARY
5.45pm • Royal College of Music Actress and director
Janet Suzman and director Jude Kelly discuss their
approach to Shakespeare's *The Taming of the Shrew* and
how 21st-century audiences react to its sexual politics.
Edited version broadcast on BBC Radio 3 during tonight's interval

PROMS PLUS LATE
Elgar Room, Royal Albert Hall Informal post-Proms music and
poetry, featuring young talent. For details see bbc.co.uk/proms

---

SUNDAY 3 AUGUST

PROM 22
4.30pm–c6.00pm • Royal Albert Hall

PRICE BAND **C** *Seats £14 to £57 (plus booking fee*)*
WEEKEND PROMMING PASS *see page 164*

WAR HORSE PROM

Programme to include:

Bridge
Summer   11'

Elgar
Two Partsongs, Op. 26 – The Snow   5'

Holst
Ave Maria; Home they brought
her warrior dead   7'

Ravel
Le tombeau de Couperin – excerpts   10'

Adrian Sutton
War Horse Suite   25'

Life-Size War Horse Puppets by the
Handspring Puppet Company

Proms Military Wives Choir
Gareth Malone *conductor*

Cambiata North West
BBC Concert Orchestra
David Charles Abell *conductor*

A Prom inspired by the National Theatre's play
based on Michael Morpurgo's novel, featuring a new
suite created by Adrian Sutton from his score for
the original production, as well as other music from
the period with performers including the Proms
Military Wives Choir and Gareth Malone.
See 'Lest We Forget', pages 24–29.

BROADCAST
RADIO *Live on BBC Radio 3*
ONLINE *Listen live and on-demand at bbc.co.uk/proms*
TV *Recorded for broadcast on BBC Two in November*

PROMS PLUS FAMILY ORCHESTRA & CHORUS
1.30pm • Royal College of Music Join professional musicians
to create your own music inspired by this afternoon's
War Horse Prom. Suitable for all the family (ages 7-plus).
See pages 104–109 for details of how to sign up

SUNDAY 3 AUGUST

PROM 23
8.00pm–c10.15pm • Royal Albert Hall

PRICE BAND **A** *Seats £7.50 to £38 (plus booking fee*)*
WEEKEND PROMMING PASS *see page 164*

John McLeod
The Sun Dances   13'
London premiere

Beethoven
Symphony No. 4 in B flat major   35'

INTERVAL

Mozart, compl. Robert D. Levin
Requiem in D minor   50'

Carolyn Sampson *soprano*
Christine Rice *mezzo-soprano*
Jeremy Ovenden *tenor*
Neal Davies *bass*

National Youth Choir of Scotland
BBC Scottish Symphony Orchestra
Donald Runnicles *conductor*

Donald Runnicles and the BBC Scottish Symphony
Orchestra are joined by the National Youth Choir
of Scotland for Mozart's ever-popular *Requiem* –
the composer's poignant and prescient
anticipation of his own death. Scottish
composer John McLeod's *The Sun Dances* is
a glowing, iridescent work inspired by an
Easter folk legend from the West of Scotland.
At the centre of the programme is Beethoven's
Fourth Symphony, its muscular, structural elegance
wound around a boisterous scherzo. See 'Power of
Six', pages 58–61; 'New Music', pages 64–73;
'Birthday Batonists', pages 78–81.

SAME-
DAY SAVER
Proms 22 & 23
(see page 164)

BROADCAST
RADIO *Live on BBC Radio 3*
ONLINE *Listen live and on-demand at bbc.co.uk/proms*
TV *Recorded for broadcast on BBC Four on 7 August*

PROMS PLUS INTRO
6.15pm • Royal College of Music Martin Handley talks
to Roderick Swanston about Mozart's final years and
the composition of the *Requiem*.
Edited version broadcast on BBC Radio 3 during tonight's interval

MONDAY 4 AUGUST

PROMS CHAMBER MUSIC 3
1.00pm–c2.00pm • Cadogan Hall

Seats £10/£12 (plus booking fee*)

Mozart
Serenade in C minor, K388   25'

R. Strauss
Suite in B flat major for
13 wind instruments   23'

London Winds
Michael Collins *clarinet/director*

There will be no interval

Richard Strauss was just 20 when he composed his
Suite – and steeped in the conservative musical
traditions of his horn-player father, who revered
Haydn, Mozart and Beethoven above all. It's a
legacy present here in the young Strauss's music,
but developed and transformed into something
altogether more rich and strange. Clarinettist
Michael Collins and his ensemble London Winds
set Strauss and his favourite composer, Mozart,
side by side, presenting their very different takes
on the 18th-century 'Harmonie' ensemble of wind
instruments, and revealing the early seeds of
Strauss's signature lyricism that would eventually
flower in *Der Rosenkavalier*. See *'Inside the Head
of Richard Strauss', pages 16–21; 'Cadogan Hall
Complement', pages 92–93.*

BROADCAST
RADIO *Live on BBC Radio 3*
ONLINE *Listen live and on-demand at bbc.co.uk/proms*

SPOTLIGHT ON…
Michael Collins • PCM 3

This will be Michael Collins's 19th solo
appearance at the Proms since his debut in
1984, although he reminds us the total number
of performances is actually much higher, 'as I've
played with the Nash Ensemble, the London
Sinfonietta and as a member of the Philharmonia
Orchestra'. Britain's leading clarinettist may be
one of the most experienced, but retains an
infectious zest that has kept his playing youthful
in the best sense. He enjoys the Proms Chamber
Music concerts, 'in that you feel each member
of the audience is hanging on every note you
play. They're special for the intensity achieved
in a more intimate surrounding.'

His programme with London Winds
includes one of Mozart's more nocturnal
serenades: 'It's much darker than the "Gran
Partita" and feels as if the wonderful musical
line never stops. The oboes play a big role and
I love sometimes (if it's going well) to just sit
back and enjoy it!' In honour of Strauss's 150th
anniversary, he's including the composer's early
Suite in B flat major: 'Like all of Strauss's wind
music, it has this rare quality stemming from
his total understanding of all the instruments
involved. He uses the four horns to real effect.
The richness they add to the ensemble makes
one feel at times in the middle of a large
symphony orchestra, when in fact there
are only 13 instruments.'

MONDAY 4 AUGUST

PROM 24
6.30pm–c8.25pm • Royal Albert Hall

PRICE BAND A *Seats £7.50 to £38 (plus booking fee*)*

Vaughan Williams
Fantasia on a Theme by Thomas Tallis   15'

Mahler
Symphony No. 9   85'

BBC Scottish Symphony Orchestra
Donald Runnicles *conductor*

There will be no interval

In the second of his two concerts with the
BBC Scottish Symphony
Orchestra, Donald Runnicles
conducts a programme that
looks to the past – a musical
meditation on history, death
and loss that still speaks
powerfully, 100 years after the
start of the First World War.
Written at the bleakest point in
Mahler's life, following the death

DONALD RUNNICLES

of his daughter, his wife's illness
and the diagnosis of the disease
that would quickly kill him, the Ninth
Symphony gazes bitterly into the abyss,
before bidding farewell to the world in
its elegiac final movement. The ecstatic
string-writing of Vaughan Williams's
Fantasia on a Theme by Thomas Tallis looks
back to his musical forebears, reimagining an
English identity that would so soon find itself under
threat. See *'Power of Six', pages 58–61; 'Birthday
Batonists', pages 78–81.*

SAME-
DAY
SAVER
—
Proms
24 & 25
(see page
164)

BROADCAST
RADIO *Live on BBC Radio 3*
ONLINE *Listen live and on-demand at bbc.co.uk/proms*

PROMS PLUS LITERARY
4.45pm • Royal College of Music On the centenary of
Britain's entry into the First World War, Dame Shirley
Williams and Colonel Tim Collins introduce an anthology
of poetry and prose from 1914.
Edited version broadcast on BBC Radio 3 after tonight's first Prom

MONDAY 4 AUGUST

PROM 25
9.15pm–c10.30pm • Royal Albert Hall

PRICE BAND **E** *Seats £14/£18 (plus booking fee*)*

Tavener
Ikon of Light   41'
Requiem Fragments   c25'
BBC commission: world premiere

Heath Quartet
Tallis Scholars
Peter Phillips *conductor*

There will be no interval

Spiritual in a secular age, combining silence and
sound, simplicity and radiance, John Tavener
captured the public imagination like few other
composers. The other-worldly atmosphere of a
Late Night Prom frames a musical meditation by
the English composer, who would have celebrated
his 70th birthday this year, as we approach the
exact anniversary of Britain's declaration of the
First World War 100 years ago, at 11.00pm. The
Tallis Scholars and conductor Peter Phillips are
joined by the Heath Quartet to perform two
works written especially for them, including
the heartbreakingly prescient *Requiem
Fragments*, composed shortly before
Tavener's death. See *'Lest We Forget'*,
pages 24–29; *'New Music'*, pages 64–73.

SAME-DAY SAVER Proms 24 & 25 (see page 164)

BROADCAST
RADIO *Live on BBC Radio 3*
ONLINE *Listen live and on-demand at*
bbc.co.uk/proms
TV *Recorded for broadcast on BBC Four on 10 August*

TALLIS SCHOLARS

SPOTLIGHT ON...
Peter Phillips • Prom 25

'I have so many good memories of John,' says
Peter Phillips of the late John Tavener, who
passed away last year, 'but perhaps the
happiest is a holiday we shared on a Greek
island in 1980. He'd been looking for a new
direction, and had heard the Tallis Scholars
singing Taverner, from whom he'd decided he
was descended. I remember the light was so
extraordinary on this island, and we'd get up
early and talk about Renaissance polyphony.
He was working on something at the time,
and not long afterwards *Ikon of Light*
appeared. It was a new departure, a great
piece. I feel it defines his work in the early
1980s.' It wasn't easy to mould the Tallis
sound to Tavener: 'He would often ask for
these long bottom C drones, which are so
hard to sustain with two voices to a part,
so we did have to speed things up.'

Only a year ago, the composer became
fascinated by a 24-voice canon by Josquin
and wanted to see the score. Phillips took it
down to Dorset and they listened to it over
and over again. 'He absorbed its sound-world.
The *Requiem Fragments* has three choirs and
it's a canon. Tavener's wife Maryanna rang
me afterwards, saying, "You know, he's
writing this for you." It's thrilling to be
performing these two pieces, written for
us, linked across the decades.'

TUESDAY 5 AUGUST

PROM 26
7.30pm–c9.50pm • Royal Albert Hall

PRICE BAND **B** *Seats £9.50 to £46 (plus booking fee*)*

Berio
Sinfonia   33'

INTERVAL

Shostakovich
Symphony No. 4 in C minor   64'

London Voices
European Union Youth Orchestra
Semyon Bychkov *conductor*

A contemporary classic opens this concert from
the European Union Youth Orchestra and Semyon
Bychkov. Berio's *Sinfonia* is a witty, whistle-stop tour
through centuries of Western culture – a high-water
mark of 1960s
experimentalism, with
musical references
extending from Bach and
Brahms to Boulez and The
Beatles. The orchestra and
eight amplified soloists
muse their way through an
intricate and joyous web of
quotations that frustrate
interpretation even as they
invite it. Shostakovich's
embattled Fourth Symphony

SEMYON BYCHKOV

asks the same questions as Berio, trying to reconcile
the same conflicts and contradictions and finding
only Babel and madness in one of the composer's
most confrontational works.

BROADCAST
RADIO *Live on BBC Radio 3*
ONLINE *Listen live and on-demand at bbc.co.uk/proms*

PROMS PLUS LITERARY
5.45pm • **Royal College of Music** Borrowing and reshaping
existing phrases is a feature of both music and literature.
Poet and essayist Craig Raine discusses how expressions
change their meaning and why writers adopt a magpie
approach to language.
Edited version broadcast on BBC Radio 3 during tonight's interval

Eric Richmond (Tallis Scholars, Phillips); Sheila Rock (Bychkov)

WEDNESDAY 6 AUGUST

PROM 27
7.00pm–c9.25pm • Royal Albert Hall

PRICE BAND **A** *Seats £7.50 to £38 (plus booking fee*)*

Wagner
Das Liebesverbot – overture   9'

Mathias
Violin Concerto   39'
London premiere

INTERVAL

Elgar
Symphony No. 1 in A flat major   53'

Matthew Trusler violin

BBC National Orchestra of Wales
Mark Wigglesworth conductor

Exciting young British violinist Matthew Trusler
continues this season's selection of more rarely
heard violin concertos with William Mathias's
neglected 1991 work – a virtuosic celebration of
song and dance. He is joined by the BBC National
Orchestra of Wales and its former Music Director
Mark Wigglesworth (soon to take the helm at
English National Opera), who together also
perform the exuberantly rhythmic overture to
Wagner's early comedy *Das Liebesverbot* and
Elgar's richly orchestrated First Symphony –
itself a work steeped in the
Germanic tradition of
Wagner, Brahms and
Beethoven. See *'New Music',*
pages 64–73.

MATTHEW TRUSLER

BROADCAST
RADIO *Live on BBC Radio 3*
ONLINE *Listen live and on-
demand at bbc.co.uk/proms*

PROMS PLUS INTRO
5.15pm • Royal College of Music Martin Handley and Bruce
Wood delve into the history of the British symphony and its
revival with the premiere of Elgar's First Symphony in 1908.
Edited version broadcast on BBC Radio 3 during tonight's interval

SPOTLIGHT ON...
Mark Wigglesworth • Prom 27

Mark Wigglesworth has happy memories of
his time as Music Director of the BBC National
Orchestra of Wales. 'Ravel's *Daphnis and
Chloe* and Mahler's *Das Lied von der Erde*
with Waltraud Meier have stayed with me as
highlights. It will be lovely to make music with
the BBC NOW players again, and also to see
old faces and meet new ones.'

He relishes the challenge of presenting Elgar
at the Proms: 'Elgar at the Royal Albert Hall is
like Mozart in Salzburg or Mahler in Vienna:
it belongs. It's a privilege to be part of a sense of
tradition, but with that comes the responsibility
to keep it alive and fresh for contemporary
audiences. Elgar's First Symphony is the essence
of England. Nostalgic, yet never sentimental –
that's a fine line to tread.'

It seems astonishing that William Mathias's
swansong, the 1991 Violin Concerto, a heady
brew of folk song and dance, has had to wait
so long for its London premiere. 'Mathias's
music is both lyrical and dramatic,' says
Wigglesworth. 'You get both the valleys and
the mountains.' He draws a similarity between
the Proms audience and that of English
National Opera, of which he becomes Music
Director next year. 'They are knowledgeable,
but curious; passionate and articulate; diverse
across class and culture. The sense of occasion
that that generates every night is thrilling.'

THURSDAY 7 AUGUST

PROM 28
7.30pm–c9.40pm • Royal Albert Hall

PRICE BAND **A** *Seats £7.50 to £38 (plus booking fee*)*

Beethoven
Egmont – overture   9'

Luca Francesconi
Duende – The Dark Notes   25'
BBC co-commission: UK premiere

INTERVAL

Stravinksy
Oedipus rex   51'

Leila Josefowicz violin

Allan Clayton Oedipus
Hilary Summers Jocasta
Juha Uusitalo Creon
Brindley Sherratt Tiresias
Duncan Rock Messenger
Samuel Boden Shepherd

BBC Singers (men's voices)
BBC Symphony Chorus (men's voices)
BBC Symphony Orchestra
Sakari Oramo conductor

Sakari Oramo conducts one of the great 20th-
century dramatic showpieces – Stravinsky's
opera-oratorio *Oedipus rex*. Driving with powerful
inevitability to its climax, this monumental work
matches Sophocles's tragedy in its visceral horror.
In the violin concerto *Duende – The Dark Notes*,
written for tonight's soloist Leila Josefowicz,
Luca Francesconi summons the dark, magical force
believed by some to be the demon of flamenco.
See *'Power of Six', pages 58–61; 'New Music',*
pages 64–73.

BROADCAST
RADIO *Live on BBC Radio 3*
ONLINE *Listen live and on-demand at bbc.co.uk/proms*

PROMS PLUS LITERARY
5.45pm • Royal College of Music Poet and playwright
Tony Harrison talks about his passionate commitment
to the classics, poetic language and political writing.
Edited version broadcast on BBC Radio 3 during tonight's interval

Sheila Rock (Trusler), Sim Canetty-Clarke (Wigglesworth)

FRIDAY 8 AUGUST

PROM 29
6.30pm–c9.10pm • Royal Albert Hall

PRICE BAND **A** *Seats £7.50 to £38 (plus booking fee*)*
WEEKEND PROMMING PASS *see page 164*

Casella
Elegia eroica   *16'*

Chopin
Piano Concerto No. 1 in E minor   *38'*

INTERVAL

Franck
Symphonic Variations   *16'*

Saint-Saëns
Symphony No. 3 in C minor, 'Organ'   *35'*

Benjamin Grosvenor *piano*
David Goode *organ*

BBC Philharmonic
Gianandrea Noseda *conductor*

Casella's haunting 'Heroic Elegy', dedicated
to the 'unknown soldier', continues our
series of works written in the shadow of
the First World War. Former BBC Radio 3
New Generation Artist Benjamin Grosvenor,
still only 22, returns for his fourth Proms
appearance in Chopin's lyrical but virtuosic
First Piano Concerto; he is also the soloist in
Franck's *Symphonic Variations* – once a Proms
favourite (performed here on 60 occasions),
though it has been largely absent since the 1960s.
Saint-Saëns's 'Organ' Symphony continues the
French theme. 'With it I have given all I could give,'
the composer observed. 'What I did I could not
achieve again.' See 'Lest We Forget', pages 24–29.

BROADCAST
RADIO *Live on BBC Radio 3*
ONLINE *Listen live and on-demand at bbc.co.uk/proms*

PROMS PLUS INTRO
4.45pm • Royal College of Music Ian Skelly looks at the
misunderstood and unknown side of two contrasting French
composers, Saint-Saëns and Franck, with Roy Howat.
Edited version broadcast on BBC Radio 3 during tonight's interval

FRIDAY 8 AUGUST

PROM 30
10.15pm–c11.30pm • Royal Albert Hall

PRICE BAND **E** *Seats £14/£18 (plus booking fee*)*
WEEKEND PROMMING PASS *see page 164*

Battle of the Bands

Clare Teal *singer/presenter*

Count Pearson Proms Band
James Pearson *conductor*

Duke Windsor Proms Band
Grant Windsor *conductor*

Leading jazz singer Clare Teal presents a Late Night
Prom with a difference as we are transported back
to the swing era of the 1930s and 1940s with two
of the greatest bands of the day, led at the time by
Count Basie and Duke Ellington. With selections
including *Jumpin' at the Woodside* and *It Don't Mean
a Thing (If It Ain't Got That Swing)*, and culminating in
a bespoke 'Battle Royal', the roof will surely be raised
as these giants of jazz do battle for the approval of
the audience. See 'The Night Thing', pages 90–91.

BROADCAST
RADIO *Live on BBC Radio 3 and BBC Radio 2*
ONLINE *Listen live and on-demand
at bbc.co.uk/proms*
TV *Recorded for broadcast on BBC Four on 17 August*

JAMES PEARSON   GRANT WINDSOR

SAME-
DAY SAVER
Proms 29 & 30
(see page 164)

SPOTLIGHT ON...
Clare Teal • Prom 30

For her Late Night Prom, Clare Teal is taking
a step back in time to a golden age of jazz in
the 1930s and 1940s. 'It's basically going to
be a recreation of a battle of the bands,'
explains the British jazz singer. 'Two bands
would perform in the same venue and take
it in turns to play. It would build to an
absolute frenzy, with the floorboards shaking.
It was a fantastic musical event.'

Teal, who presents BBC Radio Two's
show *Big Band Special*, has always dreamt
of staging this kind of event. 'We don't do
concerts like this nowadays and we should,'
she says. 'It's about exciting an audience and
musicians raising their game to their peak.'

Of course, a certain amount of
imagination needs to be used when recreating
concerts from the past, as Teal explains:
'It's hard in some ways because the records
that were made at that time were three and
a half minutes long and were very scratchy.
But live songs could go on for 20 minutes
and just build and build until they virtually
exploded.' With some of today's top jazz
musicians set to be involved in the two
bands, it will be an exciting, theatrical event.
'It will be the "Battle Royal" with the duel-off
at the end,' says Teal. 'If you haven't heard
a big band going full throttle, the sound
is extraordinary.'

6–8 AUGUST

133

Jerry Lacey (Pearson); Tungsten (Windsor)

SATURDAY 9 AUGUST

PROMS SATURDAY MATINEE 2
3.00pm–c4.30pm • Cadogan Hall

Seats £10 / £12 (plus booking fee*)

C. P. E. Bach
Symphony in B minor, 'Hamburg'   8'

Sir Harrison Birtwistle
Endless Parade   18'

Honegger
Pastoral d'été   8'

Sir Peter Maxwell Davies
Sinfonia   20'

Sibelius
Rakastava   15'

Håkan Hardenberger *trumpet*

Lapland Chamber Orchestra
John Storgårds *conductor*

There will be no interval

John Storgårds appears later this season with the
BBC Philharmonic, but today directs his Lapland
Chamber Orchestra – the most northerly
professional orchestra in the EU – making its
Proms debut. Contemporary music forms a
key role in the ensemble's work, and here the
group celebrates the 80th birthdays of two
major British composers –
Sir Harrison Birtwistle and
Sir Peter Maxwell Davies.
Swedish trumpeter Håkan
Hardenberger is the soloist
in Birtwistle's concerto
Endless Parade, whose dark,
maze-like landscape is
matched by the languorous
vistas of Honegger. The
anniversary celebrations of
C. P. E. Bach continue with
the spiky, brooding textures
of his Symphony in B minor. See 'Northern Knights',
pages 48–51.

HÅKAN HARDENBERGER

BROADCAST
RADIO *Live on BBC Radio 3*
ONLINE *Listen live and on-demand at bbc.co.uk/proms*

SATURDAY 9 AUGUST

PROM 31
7.30pm–c9.45pm • Royal Albert Hall

PRICE BAND Ⓐ *Seats £7.50 to £38 (plus booking fee*)*
WEEKEND PROMMING PASS *see page 164*

Berlioz
Overture 'Le corsaire'   10'

Elgar
Sea Pictures   23'

INTERVAL

Helen Grime
Near Midnight   10'
London premiere

Beethoven
Symphony No. 3 in E flat major, 'Eroica'   47'

Alice Coote *mezzo-soprano*

Hallé
Sir Mark Elder *conductor*

The sea lies the centre of tonight's concert from
Sir Mark Elder and the Hallé. The sunshine glitters
on the waves of Berlioz's swashbuckling overture *Le
corsaire*, written while the composer was holidaying
in Nice. A celebrated Elgar champion, Elder is joined
by British mezzo-soprano Alice Coote for *Sea
Pictures*: Elgar's only orchestral song-cycle, which
ebbs and flows evocatively as it explores the
fascination and fear inspired by the sea. While Helen
Grime's *Near Midnight* explores a nocturnal theme,
Beethoven created a storm of human drama in his
'Eroica' Symphony – a stirring musical meditation on
heroism and valour. See 'New Music', pages 64–73.

BROADCAST
RADIO *Live on BBC Radio 3*
ONLINE *Listen live and on-demand at bbc.co.uk/proms*
TV *Recorded for broadcast on BBC Four on 15 August*

PROMS PLUS INTRO
5.45pm • Royal College of Music Tim Blanning talks to
Louise Fryer about Beethoven's 'Eroica' Symphony and
the influence of the French Revolution on its composition.
Edited version broadcast on BBC Radio 3 during tonight's interval

PROMS PLUS LATE
Elgar Room, Royal Albert Hall Informal post-Proms music and
poetry, featuring young talent. *For details see bbc.co.uk/proms*

SPOTLIGHT ON...
Alice Coote • Prom 31

Alice Coote has graced recent recordings of
The Dream of Gerontius and *The Apostles*
with Sir Mark Elder and the Hallé, and is
reunited with both conductor and orchestra at
the Proms in *Sea Pictures*. She can remember
trying out the songs 'as a teenager, in my first
singing lessons, and in competitions all over
the north of England!' In Elder she has found
a conductor in tune with her approach: 'His
interpretations are deeply honest and visceral:
the depth of his exploration is clear in the
sound the Hallé produces in response to him.'
She finds in *Sea Pictures* 'characteristically
huge, majestic and transcendental passages
but also that intimacy Elgar's works always
contain. One senses a vulnerable human soul
questing through a vast universe.'

She's particularly keen that Elgar shouldn't
be diminished by his 'Englishness': 'I feel
his great works are on a par with any of the
landmark late-Romantic European pieces.
He created music that is on such a huge scale
– spiritually and emotionally.' Coote inspires
a fervent devotion among her fans, but is
refreshingly unaware of it: 'The composer
chooses to communicate something most
intimately when writing for the voice. I feel
so lucky to be able to share in the process.
I always feel connected to the audience and
I hope they feel as connected to me.'

SUNDAY 10 AUGUST

PROM 32
4.00pm–c6.20pm • Royal Albert Hall

PRICE BAND **A** Seats £7.50 to £38 (plus booking fee*)

WEEKEND PROMMING PASS see page 164

Beethoven
Symphony No. 1 in C major   26'

Bruch
Violin Concerto No. 1 in G minor   25'

INTERVAL

Walton, arr. C. Palmer
Henry V: A Shakespeare Scenario   50'

London Philharmonic Choir
Academy of St Martin in the Fields
Joshua Bell violin/director
Sir Neville Marriner conductor

In his First Symphony Beethoven retained the 18th-century grace and wit of Haydn and Mozart, adding his own forward-looking innovations. Bruch's First Violin Concerto is pure, swooning 19th-century Romanticism, while Walton's *Henry V* recalls a golden age of 20th-century film music. Sir Neville Marriner, 90 this year, returns to conduct the arrangement of *Henry V* he himself premiered in 1988. He is joined by Joshua Bell, his successor as Artistic Director of The Academy of St Martin in the Fields, who appears as both director and soloist. *See 'Behind the Façade', pages 42–45; 'Birthday Batonists', pages 78–81.*

SIR NEVILLE MARRINER

BROADCAST
RADIO Live on BBC Radio 3
ONLINE Listen live and on-demand at bbc.co.uk/proms

PROMS PLUS FAMILY
5.45pm • Royal College of Music Join Natasha Zielazinski, Detta Danford and professional musicians for a family-friendly introduction to tonight's Prom. Bring your instrument and join in! See pages 104–109 for more details

---

SUNDAY 10 AUGUST

PROM 33
7.45pm–c10.00pm • Royal Albert Hall

PRICE BAND **A** Seats £7.50 to £38 (plus booking fee*)

WEEKEND PROMMING PASS see page 164

Stravinsky
Petrushka (1911 version)   35'

Prokofiev
Piano Concerto No. 1 in D flat major   16'

INTERVAL

Sir Harrison Birtwistle
Sonance Severance 2000   3'

Lutosławski
Concerto for Orchestra   28'

Louis Schwizgebel piano

National Youth Orchestra
of Great Britain
Edward Gardner conductor

SAME-DAY SAVER
Proms 32 & 33
(see page 164)

The National Youth Orchestra of Great Britain makes its annual visit to the Proms with a fiery and virtuosic programme of 20th-century orchestral showpieces, conducted by Proms regular Edward Gardner. A Russian first half sees BBC Radio 3 New Generation Artist Louis Schwizgebel take the lead in Prokofiev's youthful First Piano Concerto. Written while the composer was still a student, it brims with the same audacious energy that pulses through Stravinsky's great ballet *Petrushka*. Lutosławski's vivacious *Concerto for Orchestra* closes the evening with still more primary-coloured, folkloric brilliance and drama. See 'Northern Knights', pages 48–51.

BROADCAST
RADIO Live on BBC Radio 3
ONLINE Listen live and on-demand at bbc.co.uk/proms
TV Recorded for broadcast on BBC Four on 28 August

PROMS PLUS FAMILY ORCHESTRA & CHORUS
1.00pm • Royal College of Music Join Alison Walker and professional musicians and create your own music inspired by this afternoon's Matinee Prom. Suitable for all the family (open to ages 7-plus) See pages 104–109 for more details

---

SPOTLIGHT ON...

Louis Schwizgebel • Prom 33

'I like to imagine the faces of that first, serious conservatory jury when the young Prokofiev came on and played his new concerto to them,' says Swiss pianist Louis Schwizgebel, who came to prominence as a prize-winner at the 2012 Leeds International Piano Competition. 'They would have been listening to a string of Tchaikovsky concertos and Prokofiev's is so provocative and playful, full of disobedience. The way it begins with that glorious theme – everyone playing in unison as if it was some grand Romantic opening – and then suddenly we hear the pianist playing something like a study: very virtuosic, but completely unexpected. They must have been shocked but impressed.'

This will be Schwizgebel's Proms debut: 'I've watched Proms concerts so many times on TV and online – Evgeny Kissin's solo recital in 1997 was unforgettable, so inspiring. But I've never actually been to a Prom so I'm very excited. TV cameras bring extra pressure, but it's wonderful to have the experience recorded in vision as well as sound.' The opportunity to broadcast is an aspect of the BBC Radio 3 New Generation Artist scheme that he values highly: 'The amount of solo repertoire I can record and concertos I can perform with the top-quality BBC orchestras is fantastic, and a rare gift. I would never in any other circumstances be able to do that.'

MONDAY 11 AUGUST

PROMS CHAMBER MUSIC 4
1.00pm–c2.00pm • Cadogan Hall

Seats £10 / £12 (plus booking fee*)

Prokofiev
Five Melodies   13'
Sonata in C major for two violins   15'

Schubert
Fantasie in C major, D934   25'

Janine Jansen *violin*
Sakari Oramo *violin*
Itamar Golan *piano*

There will be no interval

Prior to her appearances at the Royal Albert Hall later this week and at the Last Night of the Proms, Dutch violinist Janine Jansen performs as a chamber musician alongside pianist Itamar Golan and violinist-turned-conductor Sakari Oramo. Although a familiar face on the podium, Oramo is only now making his Proms debut as a violinist. Two richly coloured works by Prokofiev contrast with the Fantasie for violin and piano in which Schubert leans towards the sublime, less than a year before his death. *See 'Cadogan Hall Complement', pages 92–93.*

ITAMAR GOLAN

BROADCAST
RADIO *Live on BBC Radio 3*
ONLINE *Listen live and on-demand at bbc.co.uk/proms*

MONDAY 11 AUGUST

PROM 34
7.30pm–c9.55pm • Royal Albert Hall

PRICE BAND Ⓐ *Seats £7.50 to £38 (plus booking fee*)*

R. Strauss
Tod und Verklärung   26'
Burleske   22'

INTERVAL

Mozart
Rondo in A major
for piano and orchestra, K386   9'

Nielsen
Symphony No. 5   36'

Francesco Piemontesi *piano*

BBC National Orchestra of Wales
Thomas Søndergård *conductor*

THOMAS SØNDERGÅRD

In the first of his two concerts with the BBC National Orchestra of Wales, Thomas Søndergård directs Nielsen's Fifth Symphony, shaped by the conflicts and oppositions of the First World War and touching on a bleak nostalgia that is also at the core of Strauss's tone-poem *Tod und Verklärung* ('Death and Transfiguration') – a musical dramatisation of the roaming thoughts of a dying artist. Profundity is balanced by virtuosity in the 'complicated nonsense' of Strauss's youthful *Burleske* and Mozart's sunny Rondo in A major, both featuring former BBC Radio 3 New Generation Artist Francesco Piemontesi. *See 'Inside the Head of Richard Strauss', pages 16–21; 'Power of Six', pages 58–61.*

BROADCAST
RADIO *Live on BBC Radio 3*
ONLINE *Listen live and on-demand at bbc.co.uk/proms*

PROMS PLUS LITERARY
5.45pm • **Royal College of Music** National Poet of Wales Gillian Clarke celebrates the centenary of the birth of Dylan Thomas.
Edited version broadcast on BBC Radio 3 during tonight's interval

---

TUESDAY 12 AUGUST

PROM 35
7.00pm–c9.20pm • Royal Albert Hall

PRICE BAND Ⓐ *Seats £7.50 to £38 (plus booking fee*)*

Sir Peter Maxwell Davies
Caroline Mathilde – suite from Act 2   22'

Walton
Violin Concerto   31'

INTERVAL

Sibelius
The Swan of Tuonela   9'
Symphony No. 5 in E flat major   32'

Mary Bevan *soprano*
Kitty Whately *mezzo-soprano*

James Ehnes *violin*

BBC National Orchestra of Wales
Thomas Søndergård *conductor*

Commissioned by Jascha Heifetz, Walton's concerto extended the possibilities of what could be achieved on the violin, while at the same time maintaining a striking intimacy and emotional directness. Søndergård and the BBC NOW open with a suite from Sir Peter Maxwell Davies's ballet *Caroline Mathilde*, in which the English princess is sent to an unhappy marriage in Denmark, and continue with two great orchestral works by Sibelius. A painting of a flight of swans hung on the wall of the composer's study, and these birds inspired both the majestic 'swan theme' apotheosis of Sibelius's Fifth Symphony and the more serene and mystical tone-poem *The Swan of Tuonela. See 'Behind the Façade', pages 42–45; 'Northern Knights', pages 48–51; 'Power of Six', pages 58–61.*

BROADCAST
RADIO *Live on BBC Radio 3*
ONLINE *Listen live and on-demand at bbc.co.uk/proms*
TV *Recorded for broadcast on BBC Four on 21 August*

PROMS PLUS INTRO
5.15pm • **Royal College of Music** Martin Handley and Daniel Grimley look at how Sibelius's love of nature and landscape permeates his compositions.
Edited version broadcast on BBC Radio 3 during tonight's interval

11–13 AUGUST

136

BOOK ONLINE AT **BBC.CO.UK/PROMS** • BY TELEPHONE **0845 401 5040*** • IN PERSON AT THE **ROYAL ALBERT HALL** • BOOKING OPENS 9.00AM ON 17 MAY

Dan Carabas (Golan), Gerant Tellem (Søndergård)

SPOTLIGHT ON...
Janine Jansen • Prom 36

In 2005 Janine Jansen appeared at the First Night of the Proms. So it's significant that, nine years later, the violinist is getting ready to perform at the Last. 'There will be nerves,' she says, 'but, while the Royal Albert Hall is huge, it feels so intimate in some ways. This is what makes the atmosphere at the Proms unique. I am honoured to be performing at the Last Night and also to be featuring in two other Proms this year.'

Earlier in the season she gives two concerts with the conductor and violinist Sakari Oramo: they form a duo for Prokofiev's Sonata for two violins at a Proms Chamber Music concert at Cadogan Hall; then Jansen performs Vaughan Williams's *The Lark Ascending* under Oramo's baton at the Royal Albert Hall. Jansen first worked with Oramo 15 years ago, when she played the Britten Violin Concerto with him in Birmingham, but they have little experience of working together as violinists. As she explains, collaborating with a musician in two such different capacities is 'something that doesn't happen that often, but it doesn't change the way we make music together'. She appreciates the 'expressivity' that characterises both Oramo's conducting and his violin-playing and values the ease with which they exchange ideas. 'It's impossible to make music together if you're not able to share thoughts,' she says, 'so it's nice to be able to be so open with each other.'

WEDNESDAY 13 AUGUST

PROM 36
6.30pm–c9.05pm • Royal Albert Hall

PRICE BAND **A** *Seats £7.50 to £38 (plus booking fee*)*

Vaughan Williams
The Wasps – overture   9'

Alwyn
Symphony No. 1   41'

Vaughan Williams
The Lark Ascending   15'

INTERVAL

Vaughan Williams
Job: A Masque for Dancing   43'

Janine Jansen *violin*

BBC Symphony Orchestra
Sakari Oramo *conductor*

Following his thrilling performance of *A Sea Symphony* at last year's First Night of the Proms, Sakari Oramo – a longtime champion of English music – returns with more Vaughan Williams. Ahead of her Last Night appearance, violinist Janine Jansen joins Oramo for that quintessentially English work *The Lark Ascending*, its dreamy pastoralism balanced by the jaunty charm and vigour of *The Wasps* overture. *Job* continues this season's thread of great 20th-century ballet scores, while William Alwyn's rarely heard First Symphony adds to the evening's nostalgia with the endless melody of its slow movement. See 'Power of Six', pages 58–61.

BROADCAST
RADIO *Live on BBC Radio 3*
ONLINE *Listen live and on-demand at bbc.co.uk/proms*

SAME-DAY SAVER
Proms 36 & 37
(see page 164)

PROMS PLUS INTRO
4.45pm • Royal College of Music Tom Service talks with Ceri Owen about Vaughan Williams and his Blake-inspired ballet *Job: A Masque for Dancing*.
Edited version broadcast on BBC Radio 3 during tonight's interval

---

WEDNESDAY 13 AUGUST

PROM 37
10.15pm–c11.30pm • Royal Albert Hall

PRICE BAND **E** *Seats £14/£18 (plus booking fee*)*

Steve Reich
It's Gonna Rain   17'
The Desert Music   48'

BBC Singers
Endymion
David Hill *conductor*

There will be no interval

The after-hours late-night atmosphere is a fitting backdrop to the pulsing rhythmic repetitions of Minimalism's founding father, Steve Reich. Relive the experimentation of *It's Gonna Rain* – the tape piece that first put Reich on the map back in 1965 – its hypnotic layers of spoken sound transforming a street preacher into a strange, disembodied instrument. *The Desert Music* twitches and throbs with life, offering a meditation on fragments of William Carlos Williams's poetry. The BBC Singers are joined by contemporary specialists the Endymion ensemble. See 'Power of Six', pages 58–61; 'The Night Thing', pages 90–91.

BROADCAST
RADIO *Live on BBC Radio 3*
ONLINE *Listen live and on-demand at bbc.co.uk/proms*

STEVE REICH

THURSDAY 14 AUGUST

PROM 38
7.30pm–c10.05pm • Royal Albert Hall

PRICE BAND Ⓐ *Seats £7.50 to £38 (plus booking fee*)*

Sibelius
Finlandia   9'

Sir Peter Maxwell Davies
Symphony No. 5   27'

Bridge
Oration   30'

INTERVAL

Sibelius
Symphony No. 2 in D major   46'

Leonard Elschenbroich *cello*

BBC Philharmonic
John Storgårds *conductor*

The chain of influence between Sibelius and
Sir Peter Maxwell Davies is a direct one. Sibelius's
seamlessly shifting structures and stirring musical
language (both showcased in his Second Symphony)
are echoed and evolved by Davies, who celebrates
his 80th birthday this year. His Fifth Symphony
shares its single-movement form with Sibelius's
Seventh and its vigorous brass writing also owes
a debt to the elder composer. Finnish conductor
John Storgårds, Principal Guest Conductor of the
BBC Philharmonic, champions his nation's musical
hero and also pays tribute to the First World War
anniversary in Bridge's haunting *Oration* –
part lament, part warning. See 'Lest We Forget',
pages 24–29; 'Northern Knights', pages 48–51.

BROADCAST
RADIO *Live on BBC Radio 3*
ONLINE *Listen live and on-demand at bbc.co.uk/proms*

PROMS PLUS PORTRAIT
5.45pm • Royal College of Music To mark his 80th birthday,
Sir Peter Maxwell Davies introduces performances of his
chamber works in conversation with Andrew McGregor.
Broadcast on BBC Radio 3 after tonight's Prom

SPOTLIGHT ON...
John Storgårds • Prom 38

There is a certain affinity between Nordic and
British composers, reckons conductor John
Storgårds. 'I think an amount of individualism
has been more possible in the North and in
Britain than it is in Central Europe, where
everything is more strictly related to traditions,'
says the Finnish conductor, who this summer
conducts the BBC Philharmonic in a Prom
featuring works by Sibelius, Bridge and Sir Peter
Maxwell Davies. It opens with *Finlandia* and
closes with the Second Symphony, two of
Sibelius's most popular works – and ones with
which the orchestra is very familiar after recently
recording all of the composer's symphonies.

Sibelius also lurks behind the Fifth
Symphony of Maxwell Davies, 80 this year.
'I can hear the influence of the Seventh
Symphony and *En Saga*,' says Storgårds.
'But also the Fourth Symphony in terms of
general atmosphere, orchestral colour and
especially in the mood of the ending. It's
serious in a special way.' That's also true
of Bridge's masterly *Oration* for cello and
orchestra, in which Leonard Elschenbroich
will be playing the solo part. 'It's dramatic,
intense and even tragic,' says Storgårds.
'Actually there's a lot of seriousness in this
programme, but there's happiness too. And
of course with Sibelius's Symphony No. 2,
it all ends very majestically.'

FRIDAY 15 AUGUST

PROM 39
7.30pm–c10.00pm • Royal Albert Hall

PRICE BAND Ⓐ *Seats £7.50 to £38 (plus booking fee*)*
WEEKEND PROMMING PASS *see page 164*

Rameau
Les Indes galantes – suite   16'

Bernard Rands
Concerto for Piano and Orchestra   25'
UK premiere

INTERVAL

Mozart
Symphony No. 1 in E flat major, K16   13'

R. Strauss
Ein Heldenleben   45'

Jonathan Biss *piano*

BBC Scottish Symphony Orchestra
Markus Stenz *conductor*

Rameau's opera *Les Indes galantes* and Strauss's
tone-poem *Ein Heldenleben* were both flops at their
premieres, yet they soon won over a public
suspicious of the new. The BBC Scottish Symphony
Orchestra tackles both works, taking us from
18th-century France to *fin-de-siècle* Germany –
with a quick stop-off in Chelsea, where the
8-year-old Mozart composed his First Symphony.
Former BBC Radio 3 New Generation Artist
Jonathan Biss gives the UK premiere of Bernard
Rands's colourful new Piano Concerto, written for
Biss himself. See 'Inside the Head of Richard Strauss',
pages 16–21; 'New Music', pages 64–73; 'L'Eau de
Rameau', pages 86–87.

BROADCAST
RADIO *Live on BBC Radio 3*
ONLINE *Listen live and on-demand at bbc.co.uk/proms*

PROMS PLUS LITERARY
5.45pm • Royal College of Music Nature writers
Horatio Clare and Miriam Darlington celebrate the
life of Gavin Maxwell, author of *Ring of Bright Water*.
Edited version broadcast on BBC Radio 3 during tonight's interval

PROMS PLUS LATE
Elgar Room, Royal Albert Hall Informal post-Proms music and
poetry, featuring young talent. For details see bbc.co.uk/proms

Marco Borggreve (Storgårds)

SPOTLIGHT ON...

Bernard Haitink • Prom 40

'The older I get, the more I love Mahler's Fourth Symphony,' says Bernard Haitink, who conducts the piece in a performance with the London Symphony Orchestra. 'It is as if, in this work, he is trying to find more in life than he can encompass.' Many listeners may recall the 2009 Proms, when the world-renowned conductor guided the same orchestra through a deeply moving rendition of Mahler's Ninth Symphony. And this performance looks set to be another memorable occasion.

For Haitink, the Fourth Symphony 'is a sort of oasis in Mahler's symphonic cycle – totally different from the Third, Fifth, Sixth and Seventh. It is a respite from the *Weltschmerz* ('world-pain') that you can find in his other works. There is a childlike quality in it; a simplicity and an innocence conveyed, for example, by all those themes from his *Das Knaben Wunderhorn* songs.'

In this respect, it pairs well with the first offering in the programme, Schubert's Fifth Symphony, a piece which Haitink describes as 'very innocent and light', and which, he believes, goes straight to the emotional nerve centre. 'Schubert knows how to touch people as nearly no other composer does,' he says. 'I really do not know anybody in my world who does not like his music.'

PROM 40
6.30pm–c8.30pm • Royal Albert Hall

PRICE BAND **B** *Seats £9.50 to £46 (plus booking fee*)*
WEEKEND PROMMING PASS *see page 164*

Schubert
Symphony No. 5 in B flat major   27'

INTERVAL

Mahler
Symphony No. 4 in G major   58'

Camilla Tilling soprano

London Symphony Orchestra
Bernard Haitink conductor

The London Symphony Orchestra returns to the Proms, joined by noted Mahlerian Bernard Haitink, for the composer's Fourth Symphony. Opening with one of Mahler's most charming melodies, lit by sleigh-bells, it closes with a song offering a child's-eye view of heaven, delivered here by soprano Camilla Tilling. Famously described as a 'pearl of great price', Schubert's Fifth Symphony presents Classical perfection on a miniature scale. This compact symphony glows with melody and is as light on its feet as anything the composer ever wrote.

BROADCAST
RADIO *Live on BBC Radio 3*
ONLINE *Listen live and on-demand at bbc.co.uk/proms*

CAMILLA TILLING

PROMS PLUS INTRO
4.45pm • Royal College of Music Harry Eyres explores Viennese culture during the lives of Schubert and Mahler, with Louise Fryer.
Edited version broadcast on BBC Radio 3 during tonight's interval

---

PROM 41
10.15pm–c11.30pm • Royal Albert Hall

PRICE BAND **E** *Seats £14/£18 (plus booking fee*)*
WEEKEND PROMMING PASS *see page 164*

Mozart
Symphony No. 40 in G minor, K550   28'

Dobrinka Tabakova
Spinning a Yarn   7'

Benedict Mason
Meld   c25'
BBC commission: world premiere

Alexandra Wood violin
Stevie Wishart hurdy-gurdy

Chantage
Aurora Orchestra
Nicholas Collon conductor

There will be no interval

SAME-DAY SAVER
Proms 40 & 41
(see page 164)

Admired by Schumann for its 'Grecian light and grace', Mozart's evergreen Symphony No. 40 combines rhythmic verve and dance-like elegance, streaked with stormy drama.

For a performance in Vienna, the composer added parts for two clarinets – an instrument at the time still largely absent from the orchestra. Bulgarian-born Dobrinka Tabakova goes one further in her recent *Spinning a Yarn*, in which the rustic hurdy-gurdy takes a solo role alongside the violin. Benedict Mason experiments with much more besides in his BBC commission, *Meld* – at once an enigma and a spectacle, that confounds what we think of as an orchestra, of a concert, and even of music itself. Prepare to be surprised …!
See 'Illusion for the Ears', pages 54–55; 'New Music', pages 64–73; 'The Night Thing', pages 90–91.

NICHOLAS COLLON

BROADCAST
RADIO *Live on BBC Radio 3*
ONLINE *Listen live and on-demand at bbc.co.uk/proms*

SUNDAY 17 AUGUST

PROM 42
7.30pm–c9.25pm • Royal Albert Hall

PRICE BAND Ⓐ Seats £7.50 to £38 (plus booking fee*)
WEEKEND PROMMING PASS see page 164

Stephan
Music for Orchestra (1912)   18'

Kelly
Elegy for strings, in memoriam
Rupert Brooke   9'

Butterworth, orch. P. Brookes
Six Songs from 'A Shropshire Lad'   12'

INTERVAL

Vaughan Williams
Pastoral Symphony (No. 3)   37'

Allan Clayton tenor
Roderick Williams baritone

BBC Scottish Symphony Orchestra
Andrew Manze conductor

Butterworth's A Shropshire Lad reflects a world on
the brink of collapse while Vaughan Williams's
Pastoral Symphony is a vision of war-ravaged France.
Like Butterworth, both Rudi Stephan and Frederick
Kelly were killed in the First World War; the latter's
exquisite Elegy for strings was performed at his own
memorial concert. Stephan's Music for Orchestra
(1912) finds a desperate intensity in its Expressionist
colours. See 'Lest We Forget', pages 24–29.

BROADCAST
RADIO Live on BBC Radio 3
ONLINE Listen live and on-demand at bbc.co.uk/proms
TV Recorded for broadcast on BBC Four on 22 August

PROMS PLUS SING
2.00pm • Royal College of Music Sing excerpts from
Britten's War Requiem (see Prom 47), led by Mary King,
with members of the BBC Singers. Suitable for ages 16-plus.
See pages 104–109 for details of how to sign up

PROMS PLUS LITERARY
5.45pm • Royal College of Music Novelist and poet
Helen Dunmore, author of several books exploring the
First World War, and writer Simon Heffer discuss the
myths and realities behind the idea of the Lost Generation.
Edited version broadcast on BBC Radio 3 during tonight's interval

MONDAY 18 AUGUST

PROMS CHAMBER MUSIC 5
1.00pm–c2.00pm • Cadogan Hall

Seats £10/£12 (plus booking fee*)

R. Strauss
Eight Poems from 'Letzte Blätter'   19'

Wolf
Mörike- and Goethe-Lieder – selection   21'

R. Strauss
Four Songs, Op. 27 – Nos. 1, 3 & 4   10'

Alice Coote mezzo-soprano
Julius Drake piano

There will be no interval

Having joined Sir Mark Elder and the Hallé earlier
this season for Elgar's Sea Pictures, mezzo-soprano
Alice Coote returns for a recital with pianist Julius
Drake. Her programme of German songs includes
Strauss's Eight Poems from 'Letzte Blätter' – some of
the very earliest and loveliest of the 200 or so songs
he composed over his lifetime. Dedicated to his wife
Pauline and a gift to her on their wedding day, the
Op. 27 Lieder are also among Strauss's most
heartfelt. For Wolf, inspiration came more from
literature: poems by the gentle pastoralist Mörike
and the philosopher of emotion Goethe inspired
him to some of his most expressive musical
extremes. See 'Inside the Head of Richard Strauss',
pages 16–21; 'Cadogan Hall
Complement', pages 92–93.

BROADCAST
RADIO Live on BBC Radio 3
ONLINE Listen live and on-
demand at bbc.co.uk/proms

JULIUS DRAKE

MONDAY 18 AUGUST

PROM 43
7.30pm–c9.40pm • Royal Albert Hall

PRICE BAND Ⓐ Seats £7.50 to £38 (plus booking fee*)

Stravinsky
Scherzo fantastique   12'

Rachmaninov
The Bells   35'

INTERVAL

Stravinsky
Violin Concerto   22'

Tchaikovsky
Overture '1812'   16'

Baiba Skride violin
Luba Orgonášová soprano
Stuart Skelton tenor
Mikhail Petrenko baritone

Crouch End Festival Chorus
BBC Symphony Chorus
BBC Symphony Orchestra
Edward Gardner conductor

Tonight's all-Russian programme opens with the
buzzing energy of Stravinsky's Scherzo fantastique
and ends in a burst of cannon-fire, bells and brass
as Tchaikovsky's '1812' Overture celebrates the
defeat of Napoleon. This musical spectacle is more
than matched by Rachmaninov's choral symphony
The Bells, chiming the journey from birth to death.
After making her Proms debut last year with
Szymanowski's Violin Concerto, young Latvian
violinist Baiba Skride returns to perform Stravinsky's
neo-Classical Violin Concerto – lively with dance
and invention.

BROADCAST
RADIO Live on BBC Radio 3
ONLINE Listen live and on-demand at bbc.co.uk/proms

PROMS PLUS INTRO
5.45pm • Royal College of Music An exploration of
Rachmaninov's symphonic setting of Edgar Allan Poe's
poem The Bells, with David Huckvale and Tom Service.
Edited version broadcast on BBC Radio 3 during tonight's interval

Marco Borggreve (Drake)

TUESDAY 19 AUGUST

PROM 44

6.30pm–c9.00pm • Royal Albert Hall

PRICE BAND **B** Seats £9.50 to £46 (plus booking fee*)

R. Strauss
Don Juan   17'

Elgar
Cello Concerto in E minor   30'

INTERVAL

Berlioz
Symphonie fantastique   54'

Truls Mørk cello

Melbourne Symphony Orchestra
Sir Andrew Davis conductor

This season's showcase of global orchestras
continues with the Proms debut of the Melbourne
Symphony Orchestra, under its new Chief
Conductor, Sir Andrew Davis. Together they
explore the musical extremes of passion, despair,
love and death. Perhaps the most powerful
artistic expression of unrequited love,
Berlioz's *Symphonie fantastique* is a dark, vivid
fantasy inspired by the woman who would
eventually become his wife. Strauss too had
just married when he composed the soaring love
theme of *Don Juan*. Elgar's last major work, the
Cello Concerto, traces more questioning shades
of emotion. There's a beautiful melancholy and
tentative yearning to this work, coloured by the First
World War: an elegy by any other name. *See 'Inside
the Head of Richard Strauss', pages 16–21; 'Global
Visitors', pages 32–35; 'Birthday Batonists', pages 78–81.*

BROADCAST
RADIO Live on BBC Radio 3
ONLINE Listen live and on-demand at bbc.co.uk/proms
TV Recorded for broadcast on BBC Four on 24 August

PROMS PLUS LITERARY
4.45pm • Royal College of Music Melbourne prides itself
on its reputation as the cultural and sporting capital of
Australia, in addition to its status as a UNESCO City
of Literature. Melbourne-born publisher Carmen Callil
and theatre producer Garry McQuinn discuss the city's
cultural heritage.
Edited version broadcast on BBC Radio 3 during tonight's interval

TUESDAY 19 AUGUST

PROM 45

10.15pm–c11.30pm • Royal Albert Hall

PRICE BAND **F** Seats £18/£24 (plus booking fee*)

LATE NIGHT WITH ...
LAURA MVULA

Songs to include:

Father, Father   5'

Flying Without You   4'

Make Me Lovely   5'

She   4'

Laura Mvula singer

Metropole Orchestra
Jules Buckley conductor

There will be no inverval

Brit Award- and Mercury Prize-nominated
singer-songwriter Laura Mvula made her Proms
debut last year in the hugely successful Urban
Classic Prom. Now the classically trained artist
returns for a Late Night Prom that showcases
her talents in a new light. This Prom includes
the public premiere of Jules Buckley's new
orchestral remix
of Mvula's album *Sing
to the Moon*, in which
the Netherlands-based
Metropole Orchestra
makes its Proms debut.
*See 'The Night Thing',
pages 90–91.*

JULES BUCKLEY

BROADCAST
RADIO Live on BBC Radio 3
and Radio 1
ONLINE Listen live and on-
demand at bbc.co.uk/proms

(circular badge) SAME-
DAY SAVER
Proms 44 & 45
(see page 164)

SPOTLIGHT ON...
Laura Mvula • Prom 45

Laura Mvula made her auspicious debut at last
year's Proms with artists such as Jacob Banks,
Fazer, Lady Leshurr, Maverick Sabre and
Wretch 32. The invitation came out of the
blue for her: 'It had only been five months
since I released an album, so I never expected
to find myself at the Royal Albert Hall
performing at the Proms – it was incredible!
It was special to be part of the Urban Classic
Prom, in particular, as I think making
classical music accessible to a new generation
is really important.'

With a background in directing and singing
in gospel choirs, and a degree in composition
from the Birmingham Conservatoire, Mvula
is thoroughly at home in the concert hall.
Her dream was to expand the canvas of her
album *Sing to the Moon* into something
grander and deeper. Enter composer-arranger
Jules Buckley – who played a key role in the
Urban Classic Prom, not least as conductor –
and his Metropole Orchestra: 'Jules somehow
managed to get into my head with his
arrangements; he's such an incredible talent.'

She won't give away the programme:
'I want people to be surprised, but I hope
there'll be something for everyone! Being
able to bring my music to life as I imagined
it is such a privilege; I'm putting everything
into it.'

WEDNESDAY 20 AUGUST

PROM 46
7.30pm–c9.45pm • Royal Albert Hall

PRICE BAND **D** *Seats £18 to £68 (plus booking fee*)*

Mozart
The Marriage of Figaro – overture   5'

Kareem Roustom
Ramal   12'
UK premiere

Ayal Adler
Resonating Sounds   12'
UK premiere

INTERVAL

Ravel
Rapsodie espagnole   17'
Alborada del gracioso   7'
Pavane pour une infante défunte   8'
Boléro   16'

West–Eastern Divan Orchestra
Daniel Barenboim *conductor*

The West–Eastern Divan Orchestra and Daniel
Barenboim return for a colourful Spanish-flavoured
evening. We begin just outside Seville in Mozart's
vivacious *Figaro* overture, before drifting into the
dreamy Spanish nights of Ravel's *Rapsodie espagnole*.
Dreams give way to convulsing, urgent dance as we
reach the *Rapsodie*'s latter movements – a preview
of the rhythmic intensity of the composer's *Boléro*.
Also featuring here are two works newly composed
for the orchestra – both exploring the musical
junctions of East and West. *See 'Global Visitors',
pages 32–35; 'New Music', pages 64–73.*

BROADCAST
RADIO *Live on BBC Radio 3*
ONLINE *Listen live and on-demand at bbc.co.uk/proms*
TV *Recorded for broadcast on BBC Four on 29 August*

PROMS PLUS INSPIRE
5.00pm • **Royal College of Music** The Aurora Orchestra,
under Nicholas Collon, performs the winning entries
from this year's BBC Proms Inspire Young Composers'
Competition.
Broadcast on BBC Radio 3 after Prom 52 on 25 August

THURSDAY 21 AUGUST

PROM 47
7.30pm–c9.15pm • Royal Albert Hall

PRICE BAND **A** *Seats £7.50 to £38 (plus booking fee*)*

Britten
War Requiem   95'

Susan Gritton *soprano*
Toby Spence *tenor*
Hanno Müller-Brachmann *baritone*

BBC Proms Youth Choir
City of Birmingham
Symphony Orchestra
Andris Nelsons *conductor*

There will be no interval

'My subject is War, and the pity of War.' Wilfred
Owen's shattering verse sits at the heart
of Britten's *War Requiem* – that
great pacifist outpouring of
horror and sorrow. To mark
100 years since the start of the
1914–18 conflict, the *War
Requiem* is performed here by
the same orchestra that
premiered it in 1962. The CBSO
and Music Director Andris
Nelsons are joined by the BBC
Proms Youth Choir in its third
great English choral work, following powerful
performances of Tippett's *A Child of Our Time* (2012)
and Vaughan Williams's *A Sea Symphony* (2013).
See 'Lest We Forget', pages 24–29.

SUSAN GRITTON

BROADCAST
RADIO *Live on BBC Radio 3*
ONLINE *Listen live and on-demand at bbc.co.uk/proms*

PROMS PLUS LITERARY
5.45pm • **Royal College of Music** Wilfred Owen is
considered to be one of the greatest voices of the First
World War. The poets Michael Longley and Fred D'Aguiar
discuss Owen's work, which inspired Britten's *War Requiem*.
Edited version broadcast on BBC Radio 3 after tonight's Prom

SPOTLIGHT ON...
Andris Nelsons • Prom 47

Britten's *War Requiem*, written for the
consecration of the new Coventry Cathedral
in 1962, is one of the great choral masterpieces
of the 20th century. Setting parts of the Latin
Requiem alongside the First World War poetry
of Wilfred Owen, it's a distinctive work, strongly
pacifist in sentiment. The CBSO premiered
the piece, and in 2012 gave a performance
at Coventry Cathedral to mark its 50th
anniversary. At the helm was Andris Nelsons.
'It was a very emotional experience,' he recalls.
'We did it in Coventry, but also in Dresden,
Hanover and Birmingham. Everywhere we
performed, there was the same reaction – nobody
spoke for a long time. It's such deep music that
you can't immediately applaud or react.'

Nelsons will be bringing his Birmingham
forces to the Proms this year, with a different
line-up of soloists, and expects it to be a
memorable occasion. 'There's always such a
magic, extraordinary atmosphere at the Proms
that, whether a piece is small or huge, it works
there,' he says. 'In the *War Requiem*, there's such
a range of emotion and dynamic, from *fortissimos*
to the softest, most intimate whisperings.' It is,
says Nelsons, 'universal music'. 'It talks about
things we're all worried about – death and what
happens after death. The connection with the
war adds an extra layer of emotion. The war
poems are profound and intimate.'

FRIDAY 22 AUGUST

PROM 48
7.30pm–c10.00pm • Royal Albert Hall

PRICE BAND **A** *Seats £7.50 to £38 (plus booking fee*)*
WEEKEND PROMMING PASS *see page 164*

Haukur Tómasson
Magma 16'
UK premiere

Schumann
Piano Concerto in A minor 31'

INTERVAL

Leifs
Geysir 10'

Beethoven
Symphony No. 5 in C minor 33'

Jonathan Biss *piano*

Iceland Symphony Orchestra
Ilan Volkov *conductor*

Ilan Volkov directs the Iceland Symphony Orchestra
(of which he is Music Director) in the ensemble's
Proms debut. Together they bring works from two
major Icelandic composers, both inspired by the
power and drama of their native country's geology.
There's a slow-growing, primal force to Leifs's
Geysir that balances the shifting tectonics of
Tómasson's *Magma*. Jonathan Biss makes his second
appearance this season with Schumann's Piano
Concerto, written for the composer's wife
Clara, and the concert closes with Beethoven's
Fifth Symphony, whose darkness-to-light scenario
culminates in a blaze of glory. *See 'Global Visitors',*
pages 32–35; 'New Music', pages 64–73.

BROADCAST
RADIO *Live on BBC Radio 3*
ONLINE *Listen live and on-demand at bbc.co.uk/proms*

PROMS PLUS LITERARY
5.45pm • Royal College of Music To mark the Iceland
Symphony Orchestra's first appearance at the Proms,
Radio 3's New Generation Thinker and expert on the
Norse sagas Eleanor Rosamund Barraclough joins novelist
Joanna Kavenna to discuss Icelandic culture.
Edited version broadcast on BBC Radio 3 during tonight's interval

SPOTLIGHT ON...
Jonathan Biss • Prom 49

'Every time I've played it, I've found it to be a
heartwarming experience,' says Jonathan Biss of
the Schumann Piano Concerto. 'It combines the
poetry you find in all of his music with a more
public, generous quality which you don't always
feel in the solo or chamber works.' Schumann's
1845 masterpiece didn't immediately win over
the audience at its premiere, but it has since
become a concert-hall favourite. Yet despite
its familiarity, does it still pose challenges for
soloists today? 'I don't think it is an obvious
piece. It has a lot of big gestures in it, but like
most of Schumann's music it lives or dies on
how the detail is managed,' reflects Biss. 'There's
an exquisite chamber-music quality that needs
to be just so. With the possible exception of the
Mozart concertos there is no work I play where
I feel the piano is so interwoven into the
orchestral writing.'

Doing the honours in this Prom – a week,
incidentally, after Biss's Proms debut in Bernard
Rands's Piano Concerto – will be the Iceland
Symphony Orchestra and conductor Ilan
Volkov. 'I recently went to Iceland for the first
time,' says the American pianist. 'It is an
incredibly beautiful place, with a wonderful set
of people. There's this fantastic goodwill from
the musicians, and with the Schumann
Concerto it makes an enormous difference
to have that collaborative spirit.'

SATURDAY 23 AUGUST

PROM 49
7.30pm–c10.00pm • Royal Albert Hall

PRICE BAND **A** *Seats £7.50 to £38 (plus booking fee*)*
WEEKEND PROMMING PASS *see page 164*

Ravel
Mother Goose – ballet 29'

Szymanowski
Songs of a Fairy Princess 20'
with three additional songs orchestrated
by Sakari Oramo: UK premiere

INTERVAL

Jukka Tiensuu
Voice verser 17'
UK premiere

Rimsky-Korsakov
Scheherazade 42'

Anu Komsi *soprano*

BBC Symphony Orchestra
Sakari Oramo *conductor*

Sakari Oramo returns together with his wife,
soprano Anu Komsi, to perform Szymanowski's
atmospheric *Songs of a Fairy Princess*. Rimsky-
Korsakov's *Scheherazade* sees the orchestra
turn storyteller and the curtain rises with Ravel's
deftly coloured fairy-tale ballet. *See 'Power of Six',*
pages 58–61; 'New Music', pages 64–73.

BROADCAST
RADIO *Live on BBC Radio 3*
ONLINE *Listen live and on-demand at bbc.co.uk/proms*

PROMS PLUS FAMILY ORCHESTRA & CHORUS
2.00pm • Royal College of Music Join Lincoln Abbotts and
professional musicians to create your own music inspired
by some of the highlights of the season. Suitable for ages
7-plus). *See pages 104–109 for details of how to sign up*

PROMS PLUS FAMILY
5.30pm • Royal College of Music Join Rachel Leach and
professional musicians for a family-friendly introduction
to tonight's Prom. Bring your instrument and join in!
See pages 104–109 for more details

PROMS PLUS LATE
Elgar Room, Royal Albert Hall Informal post-Proms music and
poetry, featuring young talent. *For details see bbc.co.uk/proms*

SUNDAY 24 AUGUST

PROM 50
7.30pm–c9.50pm • Royal Albert Hall

PRICE BAND **B** *Seats £9.50 to £46 (plus booking fee*)*
WEEKEND PROMMING PASS *see page 164*

Janáček, arr. F. Jílek
From the House of the Dead – overture 7'

Dvořák
Cello Concerto in B minor 39'

INTERVAL

Beethoven
Symphony No. 7 in A major 42'

Alisa Weilerstein *cello*

Czech Philharmonic Orchestra
Jiří Bělohlávek *conductor*

Recent recordings of the Elgar and Dvořák cello concertos have propelled young American cellist Alisa Weilerstein into a fully fledged musical star. She makes her second visit to the Proms with the Dvořák – one of the great Romantic concertos. The composer sets his soloist against an unusually prominent orchestra, here the forces of the Czech Philharmonic, returning under Chief Conductor Jiří Bělohlávek. After the interval Bělohlávek directs Beethoven's 'apotheosis of the dance' – Wagner's expression referring to the rhythmic verve of the Seventh Symphony. The evening opens with the authentic Czech soundscape of Janáček, in the overture from his final opera *From the House of the Dead*.

JIŘÍ BĚLOHLÁVEK

BROADCAST
RADIO *Live on BBC Radio 3*
ONLINE *Listen live and on-demand at bbc.co.uk/proms*

PROMS PLUS INTRO
5.45pm • Royal College of Music Continuing our focus on global orchestras, we look at the cultural situation and the importance of classical music in the Czech Republic. Petroc Trelawny presents.
Edited version broadcast on BBC Radio 3 during tonight's interval

---

SPOTLIGHT ON...
Alisa Weilerstein • Prom 50

The last two years have been something of a whirlwind for American cellist Alisa Weilerstein – although she is an experienced performer, having made her debut with the Cleveland Orchestra at 13. Last year she toured with and recorded the Elgar and Carter cello concertos with Daniel Barenboim, a release which went on to win the 2014 *BBC Music Magazine* Concerto Award, as well as Disc of the Year. She then recorded a disc of music by Dvořák, featuring the Cello Concerto with the Czech Philharmonic Orchestra, with which she collaborates for this Prom. 'I continue to be inspired by this incredible music every time I return to it. During the recording I focused on many structural details and the piece's lyrical sweep. The atmosphere and excitement at the Proms is unique, so I cannot wait to share this concerto with that very special audience.'

The piece has woven its way into her life in another significant way: she met Venezuelan conductor Rafael Payare at a rehearsal for the Dvořák Concerto with the Simón Bolívar Symphony Orchestra, and they married last August: 'It's appropriate that we met through the Dvořák! It's one of the most Romantic, epic stories ever composed, and has been inside me for as long as I can remember.'

MONDAY 25 AUGUST

PROMS CHAMBER MUSIC 6
1.00pm–c2.00pm • Cadogan Hall

Seats £10 / £12 (plus booking fee*)

Mozart
Piano Sonata in D major, K311 15'

Mahler
Piano Quartet in A minor 11'

R. Strauss, arr. R. Leopold
Metamorphosen (version for septet) 26'

Louis Schwizgebel *piano*
Katarzyna Budnik-Gałązka *viola*
Marcin Zdunik *cello*
Tomasz Januchta *double bass*
Royal String Quartet

There will be no interval

BBC Radio 3 New Generation Artist Louis Schwizgebel made his concerto debut at the Proms earlier this season and now returns for a programme of chamber music. He is joined by the Royal String Quartet for a concert that concludes with Richard Strauss's

LOUIS SCHWIZGEBEL

extraordinary *Metamorphosen* – heard here in the string septet form in which Strauss originally drafted it, before he expanded it for an ensemble of 23 solo strings. Alongside it is a rarely heard curiosity – Mahler's contemplative Piano Quartet movement, the tantalising torso of a work never completed. *See 'Inside the Head of Richard Strauss', pages 16–21; 'Cadogan Hall Complement', pages 92–93.*

BROADCAST
RADIO *Live on BBC Radio 3*
ONLINE *Listen live and on-demand at bbc.co.uk/proms*

MONDAY 25 AUGUST

PROM 51
3.00pm–c5.15pm • Royal Albert Hall

FREE PROM: tickets available from 4 July

Dvořák
Slavonic Dance in C major, Op. 46/1	*5'*
Slavonic Dance in E minor, Op. 72/2	*6'*
Slavonic Dance in G minor, Op. 46/8	*5'*

Grieg
Piano Concerto in A minor	*28'*

INTERVAL

Bax
Roscatha	*11'*

Bill Whelan
Riverdance: A Symphonic Suite	*25'*

UK premiere

Zhang Zuo *piano*

Ulster Orchestra
Jac van Steen *conductor*

This year's Free Prom is a Bank Holiday matinee bursting with dance rhythms and colour – the perfect chance to experience the Proms for the first time. A trio of Dvořák's colourful, folk-inspired *Slavonic Dances* opens the concert and Grieg's Piano Concerto, with its lively dance-themed finale and Norwegian folk echoes, continues the mood; the soloist is BBC Radio 3 New Generation Artist Zhang Zuo, making her Proms debut. The concert ends in the Ulster Orchestra's Irish musical heartland with Bax's tone-poem *Roscatha* and Bill Whelan's new *Riverdance* suite – adapted from his music for the ever-popular stage show. See 'New Music', pages 64–73; 'A World of Wonder', pages 104–109.

BROADCAST
RADIO *Live on BBC Radio 3*
ONLINE *Listen live and on-demand at bbc.co.uk/proms*

PROMS PLUS FAMILY ORCHESTRA & CHORUS
11.30am • **Royal College of Music** Join Lincoln Abbotts and professional musicians to create your own music inspired by some of the highlights of the season. Suitable for ages 7-plus. See pages 104–109 for details of how to sign up

---

MONDAY 25 AUGUST

PROM 52
7.30pm–c9.35pm • Royal Albert Hall

PRICE BAND **B** *Seats £9.50 to £46 (plus booking fee*)*

Brahms, orch. I. Fischer
Hungarian Dance No. 14 in D minor	*3'*
Hungarian Dance No. 7 in A major	*2'*
Hungarian Dance No. 6 in D major	*3'*

Mozart
March in D major, K335/1	*4'*

Schubert
Symphony No. 8 in B minor, 'Unfinished'	*30'*

INTERVAL

Josef Strauss
Sphären-Klänge – waltz	*8'*

Johann Strauss II
Vergnügüngszug – polka	*3'*

Dvořák
Legend in B flat minor, Op. 59/10	*4'*

Kodály
Dances of Galánta	*16'*

Budapest Festival Orchestra
Iván Fischer *conductor*

A programme of orchestral showpieces as we welcome back the Budapest Festival Orchestra. Sparkling Strauss dances are matched by a selection of Brahms's colourful *Hungarian Dances*, and Kodály's sweeping *Dances of Galánta* are balanced by the crisp Classical textures of Mozart's March in D major. At the centre is Schubert's 'Unfinished' Symphony, with its mood-swings and elusive harmonies.

SAME-DAY SAVER Proms 51 & 52 *(see page 164)*

BROADCAST
RADIO *Live on BBC Radio 3*
ONLINE *Listen live and on-demand at bbc.co.uk/proms*

PROMS PLUS INTRO
5.45pm • **Royal College of Music** Continuing our focus on global orchestras, we explore the cultural situation in Hungary. Petroc Trelawny presents.
Edited version broadcast on BBC Radio 3 during tonight's interval

---

SPOTLIGHT ON...
Iván Fischer • Prom 52

For the first of their two Proms this year, Iván Fischer and the Budapest Festival Orchestra are performing a rich programme featuring seven different composers. 'You could call it a Viennese programme because it is music of the Austro-Hungarian Empire,' explains Fischer, 'Exactly 100 years ago this empire exploded, but before that it had a rich culture. Dvořák, Mahler, Bartók, Kodály and Bruckner lived in the same country.' So, if the idea of a Viennese programme brings to mind the world of the New Year's Concerts, think again. 'They give us only half of its music – the Viennese half. The other half was in Bohemia, Hungary or in a Balkan pub played by Gypsy musicians.'

This year's programme includes Schubert's 'Unfinished' Symphony – 'I love Schubert,' says Fischer. 'Without his songs the world would be a much poorer place' – alongside Kodály's *Dances of Galánta* and short works by Brahms, Strauss brothers Johann II and Josef, Mozart and Dvořák. In many ways, it sums up the spirit of this exuberant orchestra, formed in 1983 and renowned for its interpretations of the Central European composers. The BFO feels at home at the Proms: 'Something clicks for us,' says Fischer. 'It's the combination of the festival feel, the joyous character and the openness to innovation of both this orchestra and this audience.'

Marco Borggreve

TUESDAY 26 AUGUST

PROM 53
7.00pm–*c*9.05pm • Royal Albert Hall

PRICE BAND **B** *Seats £9.50 to £46 (plus booking fee*)*

Brahms
Symphony No. 3 in F major   38'

INTERVAL

Brahms
Symphony No. 4 in E minor   40'

Budapest Festival Orchestra
Iván Fischer *conductor*

The second of two concerts by Iván Fischer and the
Budapest Festival Orchestra launches our series of
Brahms's symphonies. While the intimate, autumnal
Third was inspired by a visit to the Rhine in 1883,
the noble stature of the Fourth was dismissed by
the composer as 'a few entr'actes and polkas
which I happened to have lying about', despite
it containing one of the most richly lyrical
slow movements Brahms ever wrote.

BROADCAST
RADIO *Live on BBC Radio 3*
ONLINE *Listen live and on-demand at bbc.co.uk/proms*

SAME-DAY SAVER
Proms 53 & 54
(see page 164)

TUESDAY 26 AUGUST

PROM 54
10.15pm–*c*11.30pm • Royal Albert Hall

PRICE BAND **F** *Seats £18/£24 (plus booking fee*)*

Beethoven
Missa solemnis   72'

Lucy Crowe *soprano*
Jennifer Johnston *mezzo-soprano*
Michael Spyres *tenor*
Matthew Rose *bass*

Monteverdi Choir
English Baroque Soloists
Sir John Eliot Gardiner *conductor*

There will be no interval

Celebrating its 50th anniversary this year, the
Monteverdi Choir returns
to the Proms with its
founder-conductor Sir
John Eliot Gardiner
for one of the
greatest of all choral
works – Beethoven's
mighty setting of the Mass.
It's a work the choir has
performed throughout its
history, most recently in a
second acclaimed recording.
The unique atmosphere of a Late Night Prom is the
perfect setting for this tumultuous spiritual journey,
in which we acknowledge doubt and search for
redemption. *See 'The Night Thing', pages 90–91.*

SIR JOHN ELIOT GARDINER

BROADCAST
RADIO *Live on BBC Radio 3*
ONLINE *Listen live and on-demand at bbc.co.uk/proms*
TV *Recorded for broadcast on BBC Four on 5 September*

WEDNESDAY 27 AUGUST

PROM 55
7.30pm–*c*9.50pm • Royal Albert Hall

PRICE BAND **A** *Seats £7.50 to £38 (plus booking fee*)*

Debussy
La mer   25'

Unsuk Chin
Šu   19'

INTERVAL

Tchaikovsky
Symphony No. 6 in B minor, 'Pathétique'   47'

Wu Wei *sheng*

Seoul Philharmonic Orchestra
Myung-Whun Chung *conductor*

Myung-Whun Chung makes
his first Proms appearance
as Music Director of the
Seoul Philharmonic
Orchestra, which makes its
own Proms debut as one of
our series of global
orchestras. They bring with
them the sounds of South
Korea in a concerto for
sheng (traditional reed
mouth organ) and orchestra written by their
compatriot Unsuk Chin – a sonic game between
soloist and orchestra. Chin's evocative textures
are framed by the sensuous richness of Debussy's
La mer, capturing the sea in all its moods, and
Tchaikovsky's final symphony, with its elusive but
turbulent narrative. *See 'Global Visitors', pages 32–35.*

MYUNG-WHUN CHUNG

BROADCAST
RADIO *Live on BBC Radio 3*
ONLINE *Listen live and on-demand at bbc.co.uk/proms*

PROMS PLUS INTRO
5.15pm • Royal College of Music Laura Tunbridge and
Nicholas Baragwanath examine Brahms's place in the great
tradition of German composers and discuss how he learnt
his trade, with Ian Skelly.
Edited version broadcast on BBC Radio 3 during tonight's interval

PROMS PLUS INTRO
5.45pm • Royal College of Music Continuing our focus
on global orchestras, we look at the cultural situation
in South Korea. Petroc Trelawny presents.
Edited version broadcast on BBC Radio 3 during tonight's interval

Chris Christodoulou (Gardiner) Ricardo Musacchio (Chung)

SPOTLIGHT ON...
Wu Wei • Prom 55

Wu Wei is one of the world's top sheng players. 'The sheng is the grandfather of European instruments such as the accordion and the harmonica,' he explains. 'What I play is a development of the traditional sheng. The original has 17 pipes but mine has 37 – it's something like a flute in terms of pitch range – and it can play more than 10 notes together.'

The instrument may extend back over 3,000 years, but much of the classical music Wu Wei plays is contemporary – he's commissioned over 200 pieces. In 2009 he gave the world premiere of Unsuk Chin's concerto Šu in Tokyo, and he brings it here for his Proms debut. 'Unsuk Chin is such a great composer. The Violin Concerto was the first piece I heard, and I was immediately an absolute fan,' says Wu Wei. 'She liked my playing and decided to write a piece for me. That was a dream.'

How would he describe the character of the music, whose title comes from the Egyptian for 'air'? 'It begins very poetically and then it becomes more powerful – there's a strong energy in this piece,' he says. 'Air and breathing go together and the sheng is special as I can play by both inhaling and exhaling. This piece is like a big breath in, beginning very softly and building.'

THURSDAY 28 AUGUST

PROM 56
7.30pm–c9.35pm • Royal Albert Hall

PRICE BAND **A** *Seats £7.50 to £38 (plus booking fee*)*

Holst
The Planets   50'

INTERVAL

Schoenberg
Five Orchestral Pieces, Op. 16   16'

Scriabin
Prometheus: The Poem of Fire   20'

Alexander Toradze *piano*

London Philharmonic Choir
London Philharmonic Orchestra
Vladimir Jurowski *conductor*

20th-century music takes three contrasting paths here in masterpieces by Holst, Schoenberg and Scriabin. Tuneful good humour and vivid characterisation see the century at its most approachable in Holst's well-loved *The Planets*. Scriabin's *Prometheus* is more eccentric – scored for piano, 'colour organ' and orchestra. This performance of it includes the optional part for choir and responds to the composer's imaginative ideas on colour. Premiered at the Proms in 1912, Schoenberg's *Five Orchestral Pieces* take tonality to the limit, anticipating the composer's later development of serialism.

BROADCAST
RADIO *Live on BBC Radio 3*
ONLINE *Listen live and on-demand at bbc.co.uk/proms*

VLADIMIR JUROWSKI

FRIDAY 29 AUGUST

PROM 57
7.30pm–c9.10pm • Royal Albert Hall

PRICE BAND **B** *Seats £9.50 to £46 (plus booking fee*)*
WEEKEND PROMMING PASS *see page 164*

Mahler
Symphony No. 2 in C minor,
'Resurrection'   85'

Kate Royal *soprano*
Christianne Stotijn *mezzo-soprano*

Swedish Radio Choir
Philharmonia Chorus
Swedish Radio Symphony Orchestra
Daniel Harding *conductor*

There will be no interval

In a symphony that took over six years to complete, Mahler wrestles with the essential questions of all humanity. Birth, death and the fragile stages in between are the subject of this grand musical exploration that culminates in a glowing, transcendent choral finale. At the head of tonight's huge musical forces is Daniel Harding. Following his two Proms performances last year, he appears for the first time as Music Director of the Swedish Radio Symphony Orchestra. He is joined by soloists Christianne Stotijn and Kate Royal, who also sang the role of the Marschallin in Strauss's *Der Rosenkavalier* earlier in this Proms festival.

BROADCAST
RADIO *Live on BBC Radio 3*
ONLINE *Listen live and on-demand at bbc.co.uk/proms*

DANIEL HARDING

PROMS PLUS FAMILY
5.30pm • Royal College of Music Join Rachel Leach and professional musicians for a family-friendly introduction to tonight's Prom. Bring your instrument and join in! See pages 104–109 for more details

PROMS PLUS LITERARY
5.45pm • Royal College of Music Novelist Martin Amis discusses *The Zone of Interest*, his 13th novel, in which he revisits the Holocaust for the first time since his controversial book *Time's Arrow*.
Edited version broadcast on BBC Radio 3 after tonight's Prom

Elsa Thorpe (Wu), Chris Christodoulou (Jurowski), Harald Hoffmann/DG (Harding)

SATURDAY 30 AUGUST

PROMS SATURDAY MATINEE 3
3.00pm–c4.30pm • Cadogan Hall

Seats £10/£12 (plus booking fee*)

Sir Peter Maxwell Davies

Linguae ignis	27'
Revelation and Fall	26'
A Mirror of Whitening Light	21'

Timothy Gill cello
Rebecca Bottone soprano

London Sinfonietta
Sian Edwards conductor

Celebrating his 80th birthday this year and the subject of one of this season's Proms Plus Composer Portraits, Sir Peter Maxwell Davies is one of the greats of contemporary British music. This programme chosen by the composer himself explores his wide-ranging sound-worlds, from the sleek and glittering chamber textures of *A Mirror of Whitening Light* (completed in 1977, shortly after his move to Orkney) to the confrontational music drama of *Revelation and Fall*. London Sinfonietta Principal Cellist Timothy Gill is the soloist in *Linguae ignis*'s writhing plainchant melodies, and Sian Edwards returns to conduct, following her Proms Saturday Matinee appearance last year. *See 'Northern Knights', pages 48–51; 'Cadogan Hall Complement', pages 92–93.*

BROADCAST
RADIO *Live on BBC Radio 3*
ONLINE *Listen live and on-demand at bbc.co.uk/proms*

SIAN EDWARDS

SATURDAY 30 AUGUST

PROM 58
7.30pm–c9.35pm • Royal Albert Hall

PRICE BAND C Seats £14 to £57 (plus booking fee*)
WEEKEND PROMMING PASS see page 164

R. Strauss

Salome	109'
(sung in German)	

Burkhard Ulrich *Herod*
Ildikó Komlósi *Herodias*
Nina Stemme *Salome*
Samuel Youn *Jokanaan*
Thomas Blondelle *Narraboth*
Ronnita Miller *Herodias's Page*
Paul Kaufmann *1st Jew*
Gideon Poppe *2nd Jew*
Jörg Schörner *3rd Jew*
Clemens Bieber *4th Jew*
Andrew Harris *5th Jew*
Noel Bouley *1st Nazarene*
Carlton Ford *2nd Nazarene*
Ante Jerkunica *1st Soldier*
Tobias Kehrer *2nd Soldier*
Seth Carico *Cappadocian*

Deutsche Oper Berlin
Donald Runnicles conductor

There will be no interval

In Richard Strauss's 150th-anniversary year the Proms presents his two great psychological dramas on consecutive nights. Donald Runnicles brings his Deutsche Oper forces to the Proms for *Salome*, with a cast led by star soprano Nina Stemme. *See 'Inside the Head of Richard Strauss', pages 16–21; 'Birthday Batonists', pages 78–81.*

BROADCAST
RADIO *Live on BBC Radio 3*
ONLINE *Listen live and on-demand at bbc.co.uk/proms*

PROMS PLUS INTRO
5.45pm • Royal College of Music Sara Mohr-Pietsch is joined by Hugo Shirley for an introduction to Strauss's *Salome*. *Edited version broadcast on BBC Radio 3 before tonight's Prom*

PROMS PLUS LATE
Elgar Room, Royal Albert Hall Informal post-Proms music and poetry, featuring young talent. *For details see bbc.co.uk/proms*

SUNDAY 31 AUGUST

PROM 59
7.30pm–c9.25pm • Royal Albert Hall

PRICE BAND B Seats £9.50 to £46 (plus booking fee*)
WEEKEND PROMMING PASS see page 164

R. Strauss

Elektra	100'
(sung in German)	

Christine Goerke *Electra*
Gun-Brit Barkmin *Chrysothemis*
Dame Felicity Palmer *Clytemnestra*
Robert Künzli *Aegisthus*
Johan Reuter *Orestes*
Katarina Bradić *1st Maid*
Zoryana Kushpler *2nd Maid*
Hanna Hipp *3rd Maid*
Marie-Eve Munger *4th Maid*
Iris Kupke *5th Maid*
Miranda Keys *Overseer*
Ivan Turšić *Young Servant*
Jongmin Park *Orestes' Tutor*

BBC Singers
BBC Symphony Orchestra
Semyon Bychkov conductor

There will be no interval

Strauss's brutal and ferociously powerful retelling of the Greek revenge myth is brought to life by Semyon Bychkov, a long-time champion of his music. The international cast is led by American soprano Christine Goerke, who recently dazzled in the title-role at the Royal Opera House, with Danish baritone Johan Reuter as her beloved brother Orestes. *See 'Inside the Head of Richard Strauss', pages 16–21.*

BROADCAST
RADIO *Live on Radio 3*
ONLINE *Listen live and on-demand at bbc.co.uk/proms*

PROMS PLUS INTRO
5.45pm • Royal College of Music Hugo Shirley completes his survey of this season's Strauss operas with an introduction to *Elektra*, with Sara Mohr-Pietsch. *Edited version broadcast on BBC Radio 3 before tonight's Prom*

MONDAY 1 SEPTEMBER

PROMS CHAMBER MUSIC 7
1.00pm–c2.00pm • Cadogan Hall

Seats £10 / £12 (plus booking fee*)

Chopin
Ballade No. 1 in G minor   9'

Mompou
Paisajes   11'

Ravel
Valses nobles et sentimentales   14'

Judith Weir
Day Break Shadows Flee   c12'
BBC commission: world premiere

Gounod, arr. Liszt
Waltz from 'Faust'   10'

Benjamin Grosvenor *piano*

There will be no interval

He may only just have turned 22, but pianist
Benjamin Grosvenor is already a Proms regular.
The precocious British pianist returns for his first
Proms Chamber Music concert, performing a mixed
programme with a dance theme pulsing through it.
He explores the waltz from the contrasting
perspectives of Ravel and
Liszt, exchanging bladed
impressionism for dizzying
virtuosity, while Mompou's
Paisajes transports us to
Barcelona, offering an
evocative vision of a city
from which the composer
had been distanced for
many years. The contrast of
nocturnal scurrying and
warm radiance suggested
the title for Judith Weir's

BENJAMIN GROSVENOR

new commission, written specially for Grosvenor.
See 'New Music', pages 64–73; 'Cadogan Hall
Complement', pages 92–93.

See 'New Music', pages 64–73; 'Cadogan Hall
Complement', pages 92–93.

BROADCAST
RADIO *Live on BBC Radio 3*
ONLINE *Listen live and on-demand at bbc.co.uk/proms*

MONDAY 1 SEPTEMBER

PROM 60
7.30pm–c9.45pm • Royal Albert Hall

PRICE BAND B *Seats £9.50 to £46 (plus booking fee*)*

Berlioz
Overture 'Le carnaval romain'   9'

Walton
Sinfonia concertante (original version)   19'

INTERVAL

Respighi
Roman Festivals   25'
Fountains of Rome   15'
Pines of Rome   20'

Danny Driver *piano*

Royal Philharmonic Orchestra
Charles Dutoit *conductor*

Veteran conductor Charles Dutoit takes up an
Italian theme with Berlioz's intoxicating *Roman
Carnival* overture and Respighi's Roman trilogy.
Rarely heard in full, this triptych of flamboyant
orchestral showpieces paints a vivid picture of life
in the 'Eternal City'. Respighi takes us down into
the catacombs where plainchant fills the air, through
the streets where children
play, and we watch as the
sun rises and sets over the
city's seven hills. Danny
Driver joins the Royal
Philharmonic Orchestra as
soloist in Walton's early
Sinfonia concertante – a
piano concerto in all but
name. See 'Behind the
Façade', pages 42–45.

CHARLES DUTOIT

See 'Behind the
Façade', pages 42–45.

BROADCAST
RADIO *Live on BBC Radio 3*
ONLINE *Listen live and on-demand at bbc.co.uk/proms*

PROMS PLUS INTRO
5.45pm • **Royal College of Music** Benjamin Earle examines
Respighi's three symphonic poems, in conversation with
Ian Skelly.
Edited version broadcast on BBC Radio 3 during tonight's interval

---

TUESDAY 2 SEPTEMBER

PROM 61
7.30pm–c9.50pm • Royal Albert Hall

PRICE BAND A *Seats £7.50 to £38 (plus booking fee*)*

Glinka
Ruslan and Lyudmila – overture   6'

Zhou Long
Postures   20'
European premiere

INTERVAL

Rachmaninov
Symphony No. 2 in E minor   60'

Andreas Haefliger *piano*

Singapore Symphony Orchestra
Lan Shui *conductor*

Continuing the World Orchestras strand this year,
the Singapore Symphony Orchestra makes its
Proms debut under Music Director Lan Shui,
bringing with it the European premiere of Pulitzer
Prize-winning Chinese composer Zhou Long's Piano
Concerto – a fusion of Western forms and Eastern
memories. The concert opens with the overture to
Glinka's fairy-tale opera *Ruslan and Lyudmila*, which
weaves three melodies together with intricate skill.
We end with Rachmaninov's
Second Symphony, in which
the composer overcame his
early artistic doubts to
produce an expansive work
with a brilliant, vivacious
scherzo and one of his very
loveliest slow movements.
See 'Global Visitors', pages
32–35; 'New Music', pages
64–73.

LAN SHUI

See 'Global Visitors', pages
32–35; 'New Music', pages
64–73.

BROADCAST
RADIO *Live on BBC Radio 3*
ONLINE *Listen live and on-demand at bbc.co.uk/proms*

PROMS PLUS INTRO
5.45pm • **Royal College of Music** Continuing our focus on
global orchestras, Petroc Trelawny looks at the cultural
situation in Singapore with Simon Calder.
Edited version broadcast on BBC Radio 3 during tonight's interval

WEDNESDAY 3 SEPTEMBER

PROM 62

7.30pm–c9.35pm • Royal Albert Hall

PRICE BAND **B** Seats £9.50 to £46 (plus booking fee*)

Beethoven
Symphony No. 8 in F major   24'

Berlioz
Romeo and Juliet – Romeo Alone   12'

INTERVAL

Dvořák
Symphony No. 9 in E minor,
'From the New World'   43'

**Stuttgart Radio Symphony Orchestra
(SWR)**
Sir Roger Norrington conductor

Following his *St John Passion* earlier in the season, Roger Norrington returns here as Honorary Conductor of the Stuttgart Radio Symphony Orchestra. Symphonies from Beethoven and Dvořák bookend a programme of big musical emotions that has at its core the wistful romance of the Romeo Alone section of Berlioz's sprawling choral symphony. Beethoven's 'little symphony in F' brings joy and wit to the mix, belying the composer's troubled personal life with its sunny good humour. By contrast, biography is woven tightly into the melodies and rhythms of Dvořák's final symphony – the elegiac testimony to his love of his Bohemian homeland and his new-found fascination for the stories and traditions of America. See 'Birthday Batonists', pages 78–81.

BROADCAST
RADIO *Live on BBC Radio 3*
ONLINE *Listen live and on-demand at bbc.co.uk/proms*

SIR ROGER NORRINGTON

PROMS PLUS INTRO
5.45pm • Royal College of Music Marking Sir Roger Norrington's 80th-birthday year, Tom Service speaks with the eminent conductor about his life and career. *Edited version broadcast on BBC Radio 3 during tonight's interval*

THURSDAY 4 SEPTEMBER

PROM 63

7.30pm–c9.45pm • Royal Albert Hall

PRICE BAND **A** Seats £7.50 to £38 (plus booking fee*)

John Adams
Short Ride in a Fast Machine   5'

Saxophone Concerto   30'
UK premiere

INTERVAL

Mahler
Symphony No. 1 in D major   55'

Timothy McAllister alto saxophone

BBC Symphony Orchestra
Marin Alsop conductor

Marin Alsop makes a welcome return following her triumph at last year's Last Night, to conduct the BBC Symphony Orchestra in Mahler's First Symphony. Originally designated a 'symphonic poem', the work retains all the programmatic colour this suggests. A young hero travels through life, marvelling at nature and growing to maturity, but encountering the sorrows and conflicts of Fate at every turn. Mahler's long-limbed lyricism meets its match in the muscular drive of John Adams's Saxophone Concerto, written for virtuoso soloist Timothy McAllister, and his iconic orchestral miniature *Short Ride in a Fast Machine*, which pulses with anarchic life. See 'New Music', pages 64–73.

MARIN ALSOP

BROADCAST
RADIO *Live on BBC Radio 3*
ONLINE *Listen live and on-demand at bbc.co.uk/proms*
TV *Broadcast on BBC Four this evening*

PROMS PLUS INTRO
5.45pm • Royal College of Music Andrew McGregor talks with tonight's soloist Timothy McAllister about the saxophone and its creator, Adolphe Sax, born 200 years ago. *Edited version broadcast on BBC Radio 3 during tonight's interval*

FRIDAY 5 SEPTEMBER

PROM 64

6.30pm–c8.35pm • Royal Albert Hall

PRICE BAND **D** Seats £18 to £68 (plus booking fee*)
WEEKEND PROMMING PASS see page 164

Rachmaninov
Symphonic Dances   36'

INTERVAL

Stravinsky
The Firebird   46'

Berliner Philharmoniker
Sir Simon Rattle conductor

Heard most recently at the Proms in 2012, Sir Simon Rattle and the Berliner Philharmoniker return for the first of their two concerts this summer. An all-Russian programme inspired by dance opens with Rachmaninov's *Symphonic Dances* – the composer's blazing 'final spark' and, for many, his finest orchestral work. Embracing jazz, plainchant and the waltz, this mercurial piece is a showcase of dramatic skill. After the interval we enter the Russian fairy-tale world of Stravinsky's *The Firebird*, the vivid, folk-infused ballet score for Diaghilev's Ballet Russes that established the young composer as a rising star.

SIR SIMON RATTLE

BROADCAST
RADIO *Live on BBC Radio 3*
ONLINE *Listen live and on-demand at bbc.co.uk/proms*

SAME-DAY SAVER
Proms 64 & 65
(see page 164)

PROMS PLUS LITERARY
4.45pm • Royal College of Music Poets Andrew Motion and Kate Clanchy discuss Philip Larkin and his collection *The Whitsun Weddings*, which was first published 50 years ago in 1964. *Edited version broadcast on BBC Radio 3 during tonight's interval*

| 3–6 SEPTEMBER

150

BOOK ONLINE AT BBC.CO.UK/PROMS • BY TELEPHONE 0845 401 5040* • IN PERSON AT THE ROYAL ALBERT HALL • BOOKING OPENS 9.00AM ON 17 MAY

Chris Christodoulou (Norrington, Grant Leighton (Alsop), Stephen Rabin/Berliner Philharmoniker (Rattle)

FRIDAY 5 SEPTEMBER

PROM 65
10.15pm–c11.30pm • Royal Albert Hall

PRICE BAND F Seats £18/£24 (plus booking fee*)
WEEKEND PROMMING PASS see page 164

LATE NIGHT WITH ... PALOMA FAITH

Songs to include:

Paloma Faith, arr. G. Barker
Picking Up the Pieces   4'
Can't Rely on You   4'
Only Love Can Hurt Like This   6'
Upside Down   3'

Paloma Faith singer

Urban Voices Collective
Guy Barker Orchestra
Guy Barker conductor

There will be no interval

Stay on after the Berliner Philharmoniker's evening concert for a special Late Night Prom by Brit Award-nominated artist Paloma Faith, fêted for her sleek vocals and retro style. This Prom sees the British singer-songwriter joined by a 42-piece jazz orchestra and the elite Urban Voices Collective for a performance that includes new arrangements of songs from her first two, double-platinum-selling albums, as well as from her most recent release, *A Perfect Contradiction*. A one-off performance striking an intimate mood in the Royal Albert Hall. See *'The Night Thing'*, pages 90–91.

SAME-DAY SAVER Proms 64 & 65 (see page 164)

PALOMA FAITH

SATURDAY 6 SEPTEMBER

PROMS SATURDAY MATINEE 4
3.00pm–c4.30pm • Cadogan Hall

Seats £10/£12 (plus booking fee*)

Sir Harrison Birtwistle
Verses for Ensembles   26'
Dinah and Nick's Love Song   6'
Meridian   27'

Christine Rice mezzo-soprano

Exaudi
Birmingham Contemporary Music Group
Oliver Knussen conductor

There will be no interval

Along with fellow Lancastrian composer Sir Peter Maxwell Davies, Sir Harrison Birtwistle celebrates his 80th birthday this year. The Proms marks the occasion with a concert from one of the UK's leading new music ensembles, the Birmingham Contemporary Music Group. The group's relationship with Birtwistle's music is a long one, and here it performs three of the composer's classic early works. Each explores the spatial dramatisation of music, playing aural games with the audience and exposing them to intriguing and unfamiliar textures, while never neglecting the ever-unfolding melody that is at the core of all Birtwistle's music. See *'Northern Knights'*, pages 48–51.

OLIVER KNUSSEN

SATURDAY 6 SEPTEMBER

PROM 66
7.00pm–c10.45pm • Royal Albert Hall

PRICE BAND D Seats £18 to £68 (plus booking fee*)
WEEKEND PROMMING PASS see page 164

J. S. Bach
St Matthew Passion
(staging by Peter Sellars; sung in German) 187'

Mark Padmore Evangelist
Christian Gerhaher Christus
Camilla Tilling soprano
Magdalena Kožená mezzo-soprano
Topi Lehtipuu tenor
Eric Owens tenor

Berlin Radio Choir
Berliner Philharmoniker
Sir Simon Rattle conductor

There will be one interval

Sir Simon Rattle conducts Peter Sellars's innovative staging of Bach's *St Matthew Passion*. While the dramatic *St John Passion* (heard earlier this season) is all musical action and reaction, the *St Matthew* is altogether more contemplative – confronting suffering and torture as well as salvation and redemption in some of Bach's most moving music. A starry line-up of soloists is led by Mark Padmore's Evangelist, and includes celebrated German baritone Christian Gerhaher singing the words of Christ. See *'Resurrecting the Passion'*, pages 84–85.

PROMS PLUS SING
1.30pm • Royal College of Music Sing excerpts from Bach's *St Matthew Passion*, led by Adey Grummet with members of the BBC Singers. Suitable for ages 16-plus. See pages 104–109 for details of how to sign up

PROMS PLUS INTRO
5.15pm • Royal College of Music Peter Sellars offers an insight into his semi-staged production of Bach's *St Matthew Passion*, in conversation with Louise Fryer. Edited version broadcast on BBC Radio 3 during tonight's interval

PROMS PLUS LATE
Elgar Room, Royal Albert Hall Informal post-Proms music and poetry, featuring young talent. For details see bbc.co.uk/proms

Alice Hawkins (Faith); Mark Allan/BBC (Knussen)

Han-Na Chang • Prom 67

Young South-Korean Han-Na Chang is no stranger to the Proms, but it's as a virtuoso cellist that she has so far taken the stage. This year marks her Proms debut as a conductor, and she brings with her the Qatar Philharmonic Orchestra, of which she became Music Director last year. 'Conducting', she says, 'offers me a vast repertoire, endless possibilities of sound and a depth of collaboration that I find very rewarding.'

The orchestra, formed in 2007 by the Qatar Foundation, is a cosmopolitan group: 'We have about 10 musicians from the region, specifically Egypt, Lebanon and Syria; in total there are 101 musicians from 29 countries.' Chang relishes the challenge of moulding this new ensemble: 'It's a young orchestra, so with all the individual talent here, we're working to mature as a group. I'm searching for a unique sound, a collective heartbeat and the flexibility to perform diverse repertoire. We have a special role to play in the community as the only orchestra in Qatar.' The ensemble also gives a platform to new works by Arabic composers, including Marcel and Rami Khalifé, Houtaf Khoury and Abdalla El-Masri. Chang's Tchaikovsky concerts have been a big hit: 'I love Tchaikovsky's honesty, dedication, passion and dignity. His Fifth Symphony is his diary; one sees and feels his emotions in every note, yet how masterfully he balances the personal with the universal symphonic form.'

SUNDAY 7 SEPTEMBER

PROM 67
3.30pm–c5.50pm • Royal Albert Hall

PRICE BAND A Seats £7.50 to £38 (plus booking fee*)
WEEKEND PROMMING PASS see page 164

Behzad Ranjbaran
Seemorgh – The Sunrise   8'
European premiere

Rachmaninov
Piano Concerto No. 2 in C minor   34'

INTERVAL

Tchaikovsky
Symphony No. 5 in E minor   45'

Denis Matsuev *piano*

Qatar Philharmonic Orchestra
Han-Na Chang *conductor*

Cellist and conductor Han-Na Chang makes her Proms conducting debut as Music Director of the Qatar Philharmonic Orchestra – one of this year's global orchestras, also making its debut. Their concert culminates in Tchaikovsky's Symphony No. 5, haunted by its recurring 'Fate' theme. Vivid with contrasts and surging climaxes, the symphony is matched for drama by Rachmaninov's Second Piano Concerto, a Proms favourite whose slow movement burns with restrained passion. Behzad Ranjbaran's *Seemorgh* is inspired by the mythical Persian bird of its title. See *'Global Visitors'*, pages 32–35; *'New Music'*, pages 64–73.

DENIS MATSUEV

BROADCAST
RADIO Live on BBC Radio 3
ONLINE Listen live and on-demand at bbc.co.uk/proms
TV Recorded for broadcast on BBC Four on 12 September

SUNDAY 7 SEPTEMBER

PROM 68
7.30pm–c9.35pm • Royal Albert Hall

PRICE BAND C Seats £14 to £57 (plus booking fee*)
WEEKEND PROMMING PASS see page 164

Brahms
Academic Festival Overture   10'

Jörg Widmann
Flûte en suite   21'
UK premiere

INTERVAL

Brahms
Symphony No. 1 in C minor   41'

Joshua Smith *flute*

Cleveland Orchestra
Franz Welser-Möst *conductor*

SAME-DAY SAVER
Proms 67 & 68
(see page 164)

The Cleveland Orchestra is one of America's great ensembles. After an absence of almost a decade it returns to the Proms under Music Director Franz Welser-Möst for the first of two concerts. If Brahms's stormy and intricately structured First Symphony sees the composer at his most serious and structurally ambitious, his *Academic Festival Overture* is a rare example of his levity – an elegantly constructed musical thank-you-letter to Breslau University, taking its themes from boisterous student songs. At the centre of the programme is a concerto commissioned by the Cleveland Orchestra for its principal flautist Joshua Smith. Rejecting anything too grandiose, young German composer Jörg Widmann has opted for a suite of dance movements – playful, referential and imaginatively disorienting. See *'New Music'*, pages 64–73.

BROADCAST
RADIO Live on BBC Radio 3
ONLINE Listen live and on-demand at bbc.co.uk/proms
TV Broadcast on BBC Four this evening

PROMS PLUS INTRO
5.45pm • Royal College of Music Tom Service talks with tonight's soloist, Joshua Smith, about the life and work of the Cleveland Orchestra.
Edited version broadcast on BBC Radio 3 during tonight's interval

MONDAY 8 SEPTEMBER

PROMS CHAMBER MUSIC 8
1.00pm–c2.00pm • Cadogan Hall

Seats £10 / £12 (plus booking fee*)

Shostakovich, arr. L. Atovmyan
Four Waltzes   10'

Walton
Façade   40'

Ian Bostridge reciter
Dame Felicity Palmer reciter

Nash Ensemble
John Wilson conductor

There will be no interval

This year's focus on William Walton wouldn't be complete without his witty, genre-bending 'entertainment' *Façade*. Walton's first big success, the work sets poems by his friend and patron Edith Sitwell to create a sequence of colourful, whimsical and piquant numbers for chamber ensemble and reciters. The whimsical side of Shostakovich is also represented, in his Four Waltzes. Arranged from the composer's earlier film scores, they range from the good-humoured 'Spring Waltz', the *faux naïf* 'Waltz-Scherzo' and the charmingly kitsch 'Barrel Organ Waltz'. See *'Behind the Façade'*, pages 42–45; *'Cadogan Hall Complement'*, pages 92–93.

BROADCAST
RADIO Live on BBC Radio 3
ONLINE Listen live and on-demand at bbc.co.uk/proms

DAME FELICITY PALMER

MONDAY 8 SEPTEMBER

PROM 69
7.00pm–c9.10pm • Royal Albert Hall

PRICE BAND **C** Seats £14 to £57 (plus booking fee*)

Brahms
Tragic Overture   14'

Jörg Widmann
Teufel Amor   30'
UK premiere

INTERVAL

Brahms
Symphony No. 2 in D major   40'

Cleveland Orchestra
Franz Welser-Möst conductor

Completing this year's cycle of Brahms symphonies, the Cleveland Orchestra returns to perform the sunny Second. The composer was in unusually high spirits while composing it, joking with his publisher, 'I have never written anything so sad'. The result, in fact, sets aside Brahms's habitual seriousness and dramatic tensions in an open-hearted score of great warmth and appeal. By contrast, Brahms's *Tragic Overture* lives up to its name with turbulent intensity, and the concert is completed by Jörg Widmann's *Teufel Amor* – a musical account of the contradictions, tensions and resolutions of love, inspired by Schiller's lost poem. See *'New Music'*, pages 64–73.

BROADCAST
RADIO Live on BBC Radio 3
ONLINE Listen live and on-demand at bbc.co.uk/proms

FRANZ WELSER-MÖST

PROMS PLUS LITERARY
5.15pm • Royal College of Music In 1914 American poet Robert Frost published *North of Boston*, hailed by the Anglo-Welsh poet Edward Thomas as 'one of the most revolutionary books of modern times'. Matthew Hollis, who has written about the Frost–Thomas friendship, is joined by Frost's biographer Jay Parini to discuss Frost's work. *Edited version broadcast on BBC Radio 3 during tonight's interval*

MONDAY 8 SEPTEMBER

PROM 70
10.15pm–c11.30pm • Royal Albert Hall

PRICE BAND **E** Seats £14/£18 (plus booking fee*)

Sir Peter Maxwell Davies
Concert Overture 'Ebb of Winter'   18'
London premiere
Strathclyde Concerto No. 4   27'
An Orkney Wedding, with Sunrise   14'

Dimitri Ashkenazy clarinet

Scottish Chamber Orchestra
Ben Gernon conductor

There will be no interval

On Sir Peter Maxwell Davies's 80th birthday the Proms pays tribute to this leading figure in contemporary British music with a late-night programme of works selected by the composer. The tone-poem *Ebb of Winter*, commissioned by the Scottish Chamber Orchestra as part of its 40th-anniversary celebrations, captures the rugged, rough-hewn beauty of Davies's Orkney home. We see a different side of island life in the joyous ebullience of the much-loved *An Orkney Wedding, with Sunrise*. The fourth Strathclyde Concerto, for clarinet and orchestra, completes the concert – a thrilling tour de force, demanding equal virtuosity from soloist and ensemble. See *'Northern Knights'*, pages 48–51; *'New Music'*, pages 64–73; *'The Night Thing'*, pages 90–91.

BROADCAST
RADIO Live on BBC Radio 3
ONLINE Listen live and on-demand at bbc.co.uk/proms
TV Recorded for broadcast on BBC Four on 11 September

BEN GERNON

SAME-DAY SAVER
Proms 69 & 70
(see page 164)

*SEE PAGE 160 FOR BOOKING FEES • †SEE PAGE 163 FOR CALL-COST INFORMATION   PROM ON THE DAY FOR £5.00 (SEE PAGE 158)

TUESDAY 9 SEPTEMBER

PROM 71
7.30pm–c9.40pm • Royal Albert Hall

PRICE BAND B *Seats £9.50 to £46 (plus booking fee*)*

Copland
Appalachian Spring – suite	23'
Quiet City	10'
Rodeo – Four Dance Episodes	18'

INTERVAL

Brubeck, arr. C. Brubeck
Blue Rondo à la Turk	5'

UK premiere

Chris Brubeck
Travels in Time for Three	26'

UK premiere

Time for Three
BBC Concert Orchestra
Keith Lockhart *conductor*

It's American Night at the Proms, courtesy of the BBC Concert Orchestra and its New York State-born Principal Conductor Keith Lockhart. Toes will be tapping in a concert that starts with folk songs and dances – joyously orchestrated and reworked by Aaron Copland – and ends in Chris Brubeck's distinctive blend of classical, jazz, blues and country music. Take an exhilarating musical journey with the UK premiere of his *Travels in Time for Three* – a thrill-ride concerto composed for virtuoso string trio and orchestra. See 'Power of Six', pages 58–61; 'New Music', pages 64–73.

KEITH LOCKHART

BROADCAST
RADIO Live on BBC Radio 3
ONLINE Listen live and on-demand at bbc.co.uk/proms

PROMS PLUS FAMILY
5.30pm • Royal College of Music Join Rachel Leach and professional musicians for a family-friendly introduction to tonight's Prom. Bring your instrument and join in! See pages 104–109 for details of how to sign up

---

WEDNESDAY 10 SEPTEMBER

PROM 72
7.30pm–c9.55pm • Royal Albert Hall

PRICE BAND A *Seats £7.50 to £38 (plus booking fee*)*

Vaughan Williams
Fantasia on 'Greensleeves'	5'

Sir Harrison Birtwistle
Exody	31'

INTERVAL

Walton
Viola Concerto	24'

Vaughan Williams
Symphony No. 4 in F minor	35'

Lise Berthaud *viola*

BBC Symphony Orchestra
Andrew Litton *conductor*

Andrew Litton joins the BBC Symphony Orchestra for an evening of 20th-century British music that looks beyond the pastoral stereotypes. The idyll of Vaughan Williams's *Fantasia on 'Greensleeves'* is soon abandoned in the composer's dark and questioning Symphony No. 4 and Birtwistle's *Exody*, an overwhelming musical labyrinth of sound. This year's composer focus on William Walton continues with his much-loved Viola Concerto – a work that had its premiere at the Proms, conducted by the composer and featuring composer and violist Paul Hindemith as soloist. See 'Behind the Façade', pages 42–45; 'Northern Knights', pages 48–51.

LISE BERTHAUD

BROADCAST
RADIO Live on BBC Radio 3
ONLINE Listen live and on-demand at bbc.co.uk/proms

PROMS PLUS PORTRAIT
5.45pm • Royal College of Music In celebration of his 80th birthday, Sir Harrison Birtwistle introduces performances of some of his chamber works, in conversation with Andrew McGregor.
Broadcast on BBC Radio 3 after tonight's Prom

SPOTLIGHT ON...
Andrew Litton • Prom 72

'There are some unexpected links in this all-English programme,' explains the exuberant Andrew Litton, whose first Prom was in 1983 with the BBC Concert Orchestra. 'We started with the idea of celebrating Sir Harrison Birtwistle's 80th birthday, so we chose *Exody*. It's a complex, demanding work, but the BBC Symphony Orchestra is so familiar with his language. For contrast, we looked to a composer whose music Birtwistle admires, Vaughan Williams, and his severe Fourth Symphony. Of all Vaughan Williams's symphonies, the Fourth has been recorded by more American conductors than any other. I think it's the rhythmic, jazzy dynamism of it that fires their imagination, the "take it or leave it" quality, which it shares with Birtwistle's *Exody*. Walton particularly admired it and said it was "the greatest symphony since Beethoven". I think its visceral energy contrasts well with his own Viola Concerto, which is essentially lyrical and tender, for all its liveliness.'

Litton has often worked with the BBC SO, but this is their first Prom together: 'The prospect of playing this programme with the "mothership" to a vast audience is really exciting. These musicians have a lovely attitude to all music, treating it with the same level of seriousness and fascination, whether it's Beethoven or Birtwistle; that's a rare phenomenon.'

PROM 73
7.00pm–c8.50pm • Royal Albert Hall

PRICE BAND D *Seats £18 to £68 (plus booking fee*)*

Mahler
Symphony No. 3 in D minor   *100'*

Gerhild Romberger *mezzo-soprano*

Leipzig Opera and Gewandhaus Choir
(women's voices)
Leipzig Gewandhaus Children's Choir
Leipzig Gewandhaus Orchestra
Riccardo Chailly *conductor*

There will be no interval

'The world will never have heard the likes of my symphony!' A bold claim by any composer, but one more than justified by Mahler's Third Symphony. This epic, unorthodox work unfolds over six movements, painting a musical portrait of nature's very essence. Pagan gods and Christian saints, flower meadows and silent forests, instruments and voices all come together in a work that moves beyond the confines of programme music. Celebrated Italian conductor Riccardo Chailly returns to conduct this masterpiece in the first of his two Proms with the Leipzig Gewandhaus Orchestra.

BROADCAST
RADIO *Live on BBC Radio 3*
ONLINE *Listen live and on-demand at bbc.co.uk/proms*

GERHILD ROMBERGER

PROMS PLUS INTRO
5.15pm • Royal College of Music Join Proms Director Roger Wright and Chris Cotton, Chief Executive of the Royal Albert Hall, as they look back over the 2014 season with Petroc Trelawny.

PROM 74
10.15pm–c11.30pm • Royal Albert Hall

PRICE BAND F *Seats £18/£24 (plus booking fee*)*

LATE NIGHT WITH ...
RUFUS WAINWRIGHT

Songs to include:

Poses	5'
Going to a Town	4'
Cigarettes and Chocolate Milk	5'
Over the Rainbow	5'
Dinner at Eight	5'
Me and Liza	3'

Rufus Wainwright *singer*

Britten Sinfonia
Johannes Debus *conductor*

There will be no interval

He has already taken over the Royal Opera House and staged his first opera; now charismatic singer-songwriter Rufus Wainwright comes to the Proms. Joined by the instrumentalists of the Britten Sinfonia, the Canadian-American Grammy nominee performs a spectacular set, filling the Royal Albert Hall with his own brand of 'baroque pop' that references everything from opera to ragtime, Lieder to jazz. Wainwright returns on Saturday to close the festival at Proms in the Park. See "The Night Thing', pages 90–91.

SAME-DAY SAVER
Proms 73 & 74
(see page 164)

BROADCAST
RADIO *Live on BBC Radio 3*
ONLINE *Listen live and on-demand at bbc.co.uk/proms*

SPOTLIGHT ON...
Rufus Wainwright • Prom 74

For Rufus Wainwright's Late Night Prom, he'll be offering songs from all parts of his varied career. 'I'm going on tour to coincide with the release of my "best of" album,' he explains. 'This Prom is the only concert where I get to present very dramatically my songs from across the years with an orchestra in such a great venue. Lots of the songs I will do have never been performed live with an orchestra.'

The American-Canadian singer-songwriter has plenty of material to draw on, from the pop songs of his seven acclaimed studio albums to extracts from his 2009 opera *Prima Donna*. 'As a pop performer who loves opera and classical music, I've always heavily leant on my sensibilities from that world,' says Wainwright. 'It's nice to bring these two elements together with the wonderful Britten Sinfonia. And, at the end of the day, what makes my career interesting and viable is that I've never drawn too many borders between forms of music – I just make sure it's good.'

It's not the first time that Wainwright has worked with the enterprising Britten Sinfonia: back in 2011 they shared the stage during a five-day residency at the Royal Opera House. 'I was struck by how exuberant, positive and unhardened the players were about music,' recalls Wainwright. 'And it's a tremendous gift to be joined by them at the Proms.'

FRIDAY 12 SEPTEMBER

PROM 75
7.30pm–c8.55pm • Royal Albert Hall

PRICE BAND **D** *Seats £18 to £68 (plus booking fee*)*

Friedrich Cerha
Paraphrase on the Opening of
Beethoven's Symphony No. 9   *10'*

Beethoven
Symphony No. 9 in D minor, 'Choral'   *63'*

Christina Landshamer *soprano*
Gerhild Romberger *mezzo-soprano*
Steve Davislim *tenor*
Dmitry Belosselskiy *bass*

**Members of the Leipzig
Opera Chorus**
Leipzig Gewandhaus Choir
Leipzig Gewandhaus Children's Choir
London Symphony Chorus
Leipzig Gewandhaus Orchestra
Riccardo Chailly *conductor*

There will be no interval

A highlight of every season in recent Proms history,
Beethoven's Symphony No. 9 this year returns to its
once-traditional slot on the penultimate night – a
symphonic finale before the musical party that is
the Last Night. Giving their second performance
this summer, the Leipzig Gewandhaus Orchestra
and conductor Riccardo Chailly are joined by an
international cast of soloists for this audacious
musical testament of faith and unity across all
nations and creeds. When Mahler later said that
a symphony should 'embrace the whole universe',
it's hard to imagine he wasn't thinking of Beethoven's
mighty 'Choral' Symphony.

BROADCAST
RADIO *Live on BBC Radio 3*
ONLINE *Listen live and on-demand at bbc.co.uk/proms*

PROMS PLUS POETRY COMPETITION
5.45pm • Royal College of Music Poet Daljit Nagra and
poet and broadcaster Ian McMillan introduce the winning
entries in this year's Proms Poetry Competition, and
welcome some of the winners on stage to read them.
In association with the Poetry Society.
Edited version broadcast on BBC Radio 3 after tonight's Prom

SATURDAY 13 SEPTEMBER

PROM 76
7.30pm–c10.30pm • Royal Albert Hall

PRICE BAND **G** *Seats £27 to £95 (plus booking fee*)*

THE LAST NIGHT OF THE PROMS 2014

Gavin Higgins
Velocity   *c3'*
BBC commission: world premiere

Arnold
Overture 'Peterloo'   *9'*
*new choral version with lyrics
by Sir Tim Rice: world premiere*

Walton
Façade – Popular Song   *3'*

Chausson
Poème   *16'*

Tavener
Song for Athene   *7'*

R. Strauss
Taillefer   *18'*

INTERVAL

Khachaturian
Gayane – Sabre Dance   *3'*

Ravel
Tzigane   *9'*

Kern, arr. R. Williams
Show Boat – 'Ol' Man River'   *2'*

Trad., arr. Williams
Joshua Fit the Battle of Jericho   *3'*

Richard M. &
Robert B. Sherman
Mary Poppins – medley   *11'*

Ansell
Plymouth Hoe   *8'*

Arne, arr. Sargent
Rule, Britannia!   *7'*

Elgar
Pomp and Circumstance March No. 1
in D major ('Land of Hope and Glory')   *6'*

Parry, orch. Elgar
Jerusalem   *4'*

The National Anthem (arr. Britten)

Janine Jansen *violin*
Elizabeth Watts *soprano*
John Daszak *tenor*
Roderick Williams *baritone*

BBC Singers
BBC Symphony Chorus
BBC Symphony Orchestra
Sakari Oramo *conductor*

Sakari Oramo directs his first Last Night, joined by
star Dutch violinist Janine Jansen. We pay tribute
to the late John Tavener with his touching *Song for
Athene*, and mark the 50th anniversary of the film
Mary Poppins with a singalong medley. Arnold's
Peterloo overture receives its first performance in
a new choral version with lyrics by Sir Tim Rice,
while our Strauss-anniversary celebrations conclude
with the Proms premiere of the composer's massive
cantata *Taillefer*. The nautical flavour of Ansell's
Plymouth Hoe (and its brief quotation of *Rule,
Britannia!*) forms an upbeat to the traditional Last
Night favourites, led by baritone Roderick Williams.
*See 'Inside the Head of Richard Strauss', pages 16–21;
'Behind the Façade', pages 42–45; 'Power of Six',
pages 58–61; 'New Music', pages 64–73.*

BROADCAST
RADIO *Live on BBC Radio 3*
ONLINE *Listen live and on-demand at bbc.co.uk/proms*
TV *First half live on BBC Two, second half live on BBC One*

PROMS PLUS SING
5.00pm • Royal College of Music Prepare for the Last Night
of the Proms singalong with Mary King and members of
the BBC Singers. Suitable for ages 7-plus. *See pages
104–109 for details of how to sign up*

BBC Proms
IN THE PARK

SATURDAY 13 SEPTEMBER
HYDE PARK, LONDON

TICKETS £38 (under-3s free)

PUMEZA MATSHIKIZA *soprano*
RUFUS WAINWRIGHT
EARTH, WIND & FIRE
BBC CONCERT ORCHESTRA
ROYAL CHORAL SOCIETY
RICHARD BALCOMBE *conductor*
SIR TERRY WOGAN *presenter*

Join in the Last Night of the Proms celebrations in Hyde Park, hosted by Proms in the Park stalwart **Sir Terry Wogan**. The open-air concert features a host of musical stars, including Proms in the Park favourites the **BBC Concert Orchestra** under the baton of **Richard Balcombe**, and special guests **Pumeza Matshikiza**, **Rufus Wainwright** and **Earth, Wind & Fire**.

Presenter **Tony Blackburn** joins us again to get this year's party under way, introducing a range of artists, including the **Dhol Foundation** and the cast of **20th Century Boy**.

Gates open: 3.00pm
Entertainment from: 5.15pm

For details of how to order a picnic hamper for collection on the day, or to find out about VIP packages and corporate hospitality, visit bbc.co.uk/promsinthepark.

Tickets £38 (booking fees apply)

ONLINE bbc.co.uk/promsinthepark

BY PHONE from **SEE Tickets** on **0844 209 7353*** (a transaction fee of £2.00, plus a booking fee of £1.35 per ticket applies); from the **Royal Albert Hall** on **0845 401 5040**† (a booking fee of 2% of the total value plus £1.50 per ticket up to a maximum of £20.00 applies for telephone bookings)

IN PERSON at the Royal Albert Hall Box Office (a booking fee of 2% of the total value applies to in-person bookings for more than two tickets, if paying by credit/debit card)

BY POST see page 162

PLEASE NOTE: in the interest of safety, please do not bring glass items (including bottles), barbeques or flaming torches to the event

* Calls cost 6p/min plus standard network charges.
† Calls cost up to 5p/min from most landlines (an additional connection fee may also apply). Calls from mobiles may be considerably more. (All calls to the Royal Albert Hall Box Office will be recorded and may be monitored for quality-control purposes.)

with thanks to

THE ROYAL PARKS

EXPERIENCE THE LAST NIGHT MAGIC, LIVE IN THE OPEN AIR!

The BBC Proms in the Park event offers a live, open-air concert featuring high-profile artists and well-loved presenters, culminating in a fireworks finale and a BBC Big Screen link-up to the Royal Albert Hall. So gather your friends and your Last Night spirit for an unforgettable evening.

Last Night celebrations will be taking place around the UK

HYDE PARK, LONDON · WALES · NORTHERN IRELAND · SCOTLAND

Keep checking bbc.co.uk/promsinthepark for venue information.

Highlights of the Last Night celebrations around the UK will be included as part of the live coverage of the last Night on BBC One and BBC Two. Digital viewers can also access Proms in the Park content via the red button.

BROADCAST
RADIO Live on BBC Radio 2
ONLINE Listen live and on-demand at **bbc.co.uk/proms**
TV Watch highlights from all of the Proms in the Park concerts live on the red button
Highlights of all of the Proms in the Park concerts will be recorded for broadcast later this year on BBC Four

---

BBC Radio 2 Live in Hyde Park
A festival in a day

Sunday 14 September 2014
Tickets on sale Friday 13 June
£38 plus booking fee
Child tickets £10
bbc.co.uk/radio2

BBC RADIO 2

HOW TO PROM

WHAT IS PROMMING?

The popular tradition of Promming (standing in the Arena or Gallery areas of the Royal Albert Hall) is central to the unique and informal atmosphere of the BBC Proms.

Up to 1,400 standing places are available for each Proms concert at the Royal Albert Hall – just turn up and, if you are in doubt about where to go, Royal Albert Hall stewards will point you in the right direction. The traditionally low prices allow you to enjoy world-class performances for just £5.00 each (or even less with a Season Ticket or Weekend Promming Pass). There are two standing areas: the Arena, located directly in front of the stage, and the Gallery, running round the top of the Hall. All spaces are unreserved.

DAY PROMMERS

Over 500 Arena and Gallery tickets (priced £5.00) are available for every Prom. These tickets are available on the day and cannot be booked in advance, so even if all seats have been sold, you always have a good chance of getting in (although early queuing is advisable for the more popular concerts). You must buy your ticket in person and must pay by cash.

A limited number of Arena tickets will usually be sold to the Day Queue from two and a half hours before each performance (one and a quarter hours before morning Proms). The remaining Day Promming tickets will then be sold from Door 11 (Arena) and Door 10 (Gallery) from 45 minutes before the performance to those queuing. Tickets for Late Night Proms are available only on the doors, from 30 minutes before the performance. Arena and Gallery tickets are available only at Door 11 and Door 10, not at the Box Office.

PROMMING FOR DISABLED CONCERT-GOERS

The Gallery can accommodate up to four wheelchair users and ambulant disabled Prommers (disabled concert-goers who do not use a wheelchair) can access both the Arena and the Gallery. Please see page 168 for detailed information, including new queue arrangements on a trial basis for 2014.

PROMMING SEASON TICKETS AND WEEKEND PROMMING PASSES

Frequent Prommers can save money by purchasing a Season Ticket covering the whole Proms season (including the Last Night), or only the first or second half (ie Proms 1–38 or Proms 39–75, excluding the Last Night), or a Weekend Promming Pass. These allow access to either the Arena or Gallery.

Season Ticket- and Promming Pass-holders benefit from:

- guaranteed entrance (until 20 minutes before each concert)
- great savings – prices can work out at less than £2.65 per concert

Important information: Season Ticket- and Promming Pass-holders arriving at the Hall less than 20 minutes before a concert are not guaranteed entry and should join the back of the Day Queue.

For further details and prices of Season Tickets and Weekend Promming Passes, see page 164.

QUEUING

Prommers should join the relevant Arena or Gallery Day or Season queue, as shown on the map below. Stewards will be on hand to assist Prommers from 9.00am, for anyone wishing to make an early start.

PROMS AT CADOGAN HALL

For Cadogan Hall Day Seats (priced £5.00) and Proms Chamber Music Series Passes, see pages 160 and 164 respectively.

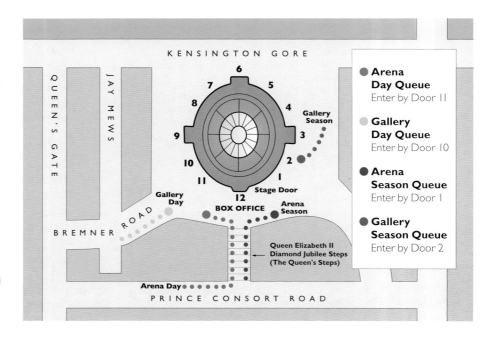

THE LAST NIGHT OF THE PROMS

The majority of tickets for the Last Night of the Proms will be allocated by ballot to customers who have bought tickets to at least five other Proms concerts at the Royal Albert Hall. A further 200 tickets will be allocated by the Open Ballot (see far right).

The Five-Concert Ballot To be eligible to enter the Five-Concert Ballot, you must book tickets for at least five other concerts. (The Free Prom [Bank Holiday Matinee, Prom 51], concerts at Cadogan Hall and Proms in the Park do not count towards the Five-Concert Ballot.) You can apply to buy a maximum of two tickets for the Last Night. If you are successful in the Ballot, you will not be obliged to buy Last Night tickets should your preferred seating area not be available.

Please note: you must tick the Ballot opt-in box when booking online, or inform the Box Office that you wish to enter this Ballot when booking by telephone, in person or by post.

If you require a wheelchair space for the Last Night of the Proms, you will still need to book for five other concerts but you must phone the Access Information Line (020 7070 4410) by Thursday 29 May and ask to be entered into the separate Ballot for wheelchair spaces. This Ballot cannot be entered online.

The Five-Concert Ballot closes on Thursday 29 May and you will be informed by Friday 6 June whether or not you have been successful. If you are successful, **please note that your Last Night Tickets will not be issued until Friday 5 September.** We regret that, if you are unsuccessful in the Five-Concert Ballot, no refunds for other tickets purchased will be payable.

GENERAL AVAILABILITY FOR THE LAST NIGHT

Any tickets not allocated by the Five-Concert Ballot or the Open Ballot will go on sale on Friday 11 July. There is exceptionally high demand for Last Night tickets, but returns occasionally become available, so it is always worth checking with the Box Office.

Please note: for all Last Night bookings, only one application (for a maximum of two tickets) can be made per household.

PROMMING AT THE LAST NIGHT

Day Prommers and Weekend Promming Pass-holders who have attended five or more concerts (in either the Arena or the Gallery) are eligible to purchase one ticket each for the Last Night (priced £5.00) on presentation of their used tickets (which will be retained) at the Box Office. A number of tickets will go on sale on Tuesday 22 July; a further allocation will be released on Tuesday 19 August; and a final, smaller allocation on Friday 5 September.

Season Ticket-Holders Whole Season Tickets include admission to the Last Night. A limited allocation of Last Night tickets (priced £5.00) is also reserved for Half Season Ticket-holders, and will be available to buy from the Box Office from Tuesday 22 July (for First Half Season Ticket-holders) and Tuesday 19 August (for both First and Second Half Season Ticket-holders). A final, smaller allocation available for both will go on sale on Friday 5 September.

Queuing All Prommers (Day or Season) with Last Night tickets should queue on The Queen's Steps (formerly the South Steps), west side (Arena), or the top of Bremner Road, south side (Gallery). Whole Season Ticket-holders are guaranteed entrance until 20 minutes before the concert. Whole Season Ticket-holders who arrive less than 20 minutes before the concert should join the back of the Day Queue on The Queen's Steps, east side (Arena), or the top of Bremner Road, north side (Gallery).

Sleeping Out Please note it is not necessary for Prommers with Last Night tickets to camp out overnight to secure their preferred standing place inside the Hall. Ticket-holders may add their name to a list which will be held at the Stage Door at the Royal Albert Hall from 4.00pm on Friday 12 September. They then need to return to the queue in list order by 10.00am on Saturday 13 September.

On the Night A limited number of standing tickets are available on the Last Night itself (priced £5.00, one per person). No previous ticket purchases are necessary. Just join the queue on The Queen's Steps, east side (Arena), or the top of Bremner Road, north side (Gallery), and you may well be lucky.

LAST NIGHT OF THE PROMS
2014 Open Ballot Form

One hundred Centre Stalls seats (priced £87.50* each) and 100 Front Circle seats (priced £57.00* each) for the Last Night of the Proms at the Royal Albert Hall will be allocated by Open Ballot. The Five-Concert Ballot rule does not apply: no other ticket purchases are necessary. Only one application (for a maximum of two tickets) may be made per household. *Booking fees apply (see overleaf)

If you would like to apply for tickets by Open Ballot, please complete the official Open Ballot Form on the back of this slip and send it by post only – to arrive no later than Thursday 3 July – to:

BBC Proms Open Ballot
Box Office
Royal Albert Hall
London SW7 2AP

Note that the Open Ballot application is completely separate from other Proms booking procedures. Envelopes should be clearly addressed to 'BBC Proms Open Ballot' and should contain only this official Open Ballot Form. The Open Ballot takes place on Friday 4 July and successful applicants will be contacted by Thursday 10 July.

This form is also available to download from bbc.co.uk/proms; or call 020 7765 2044 to receive a copy by post.

Please note: if you are successful in the Five-Concert Ballot, you will not be eligible for Last Night tickets via the Open Ballot.

Chris Christodoulou/BBC

LAST NIGHT OF THE PROMS
2014 Open Ballot Form

Title _____ Initial(s) _____

Surname _____

Address _____

_____

_____

_____

Postcode _____

Country _____

Daytime tel. _____

Evening tel. _____

Mobile tel. _____

Email _____

_____

_____

Please indicate your preferred seating option ‡ (Booking fees apply, see box right)

☐ I wish to apply for one Centre Stalls ticket (£87.50)

☐ I wish to apply for two Centre Stalls tickets (£175.00)

☐ I wish to apply for one Front Circle ticket (£57.00)

☐ I wish to apply for two Front Circle tickets (£114.00)

‡ *We cannot guarantee that you will be offered tickets in your preferred seating section. You will not be obliged to buy tickets outside your preference, but we regret we cannot offer alternatives.*

The personal information given on this form will not be used for any purpose by the BBC or the Royal Albert Hall other than this Ballot.

TICKET PRICES

ROYAL ALBERT HALL

Concerts fall into one of eight price bands, indicated below each concert listing on pages 118–156.

	A	B	C	D	E	F	G	H
Grand Tier Boxes 12 seats, price per seat	£38.00	£46.00	£57.00	£68.00	£18.00	£24.00	£95.00	(As most grand tier boxes are privately owned, availability is limited)
Loggia Boxes 8 seats, price per seat	£34.00	£42.00	£52.00	£62.00	£18.00	£24.00	£90.00	
2nd Tier Boxes 5 seats, price per seat	£30.00	£38.00	£48.00	£58.00	£18.00	£24.00	£86.00	
Centre Stalls	£30.00	£38.00	£48.00	£58.00	£18.00	£24.00	£87.50	
Side Stalls	£26.00	£34.00	£44.00	£54.00	£18.00	£24.00	£85.00	
Mid Choir	£18.00	£22.00	£32.00	£42.00	£18.00	£18.00	£65.00	
Upper Choir	£16.00	£20.00	£27.00	£35.00	£14.00	£18.00	£62.00	
Front Circle	£15.00	£19.00	£23.00	£27.00	£14.00	£18.00	£57.00	
Rear Circle	£12.00	£15.00	£19.00	£24.00	£14.00	£18.00	£47.00	
Restricted View Circle	£7.50	£9.50	£14.00	£18.00	N/A	N/A	£27.00	

ALL SEATS £12.00 (UNDER-18s £6.00)

Please note: a booking fee of 2% of the total value (plus £1.50 per ticket up to a maximum of £20.00) applies to all bookings (including Season Tickets and Weekend Promming Passes), other than those made in person at the Royal Albert Hall.

PROMMING **Standing places are available in the Arena and Gallery on the day for £5.00** *(see page 158).* Save by buying a Weekend Promming Pass, or a Whole- or Half-Season Ticket, available from 9.00am on Friday 16 May (see page 164 for details).

CADOGAN HALL (PROMS CHAMBER MUSIC AND PROMS SATURDAY MATINEES)
Stalls: £12.00, Centre Gallery: £10.00, Day Seats: £5.00 (Booking fees apply)
Cadogan Hall tickets are available to book from 9.00am on Saturday 17 May and may be included in the Proms Planner (see page 162). From Saturday 24 May Cadogan Hall tickets can also be bought from Cadogan Hall (020 7730 4500) as well as from the Royal Albert Hall Box Office. All online and telephone bookings made through the Cadogan Hall Box Office are subject to a fee of £2.50 per transaction.
On the day of the concert, tickets can be bought at Cadogan Hall only – from 10.00am. At least 150 Day Seats (Side Gallery bench seats) are available from 10.00am on the day of the concert. They must be purchased in person, with cash only, and are limited to two tickets per transaction.
Save by buying a Proms Chamber Music Series Pass, available from 9.00am on Friday 16 May (see page 164 for details).
Unwanted tickets for all Royal Albert Hall and Cadogan Hall Proms may be exchanged for tickets to other Proms concerts (subject to availability). A fee of £1.00 per ticket will be charged for this service. Call the Royal Albert Hall Box Office (0845 401 5040) for further details.*

BBC PROMS IN THE PARK, HYDE PARK, LONDON, SATURDAY 7 SEPTEMBER
All tickets £38.00 *(under-3s free) A booking fee of 2% of the total value (plus £1.50 per ticket up to a maximum of £20.00) applies, unless booking in person at the Royal Albert Hall and paying by cash or cheque. A booking fee of 2% of the total value applies to in-person bookings for more than two tickets, if paying by credit/ debit card. (The maximum charge of £20.00 can apply to Proms and Proms in the Park bookings combined.) See page 157 for details on how to book and booking fee information for SEE Tickets.*

Chris Christodoulou/BBC

CHOOSE YOUR SEAT

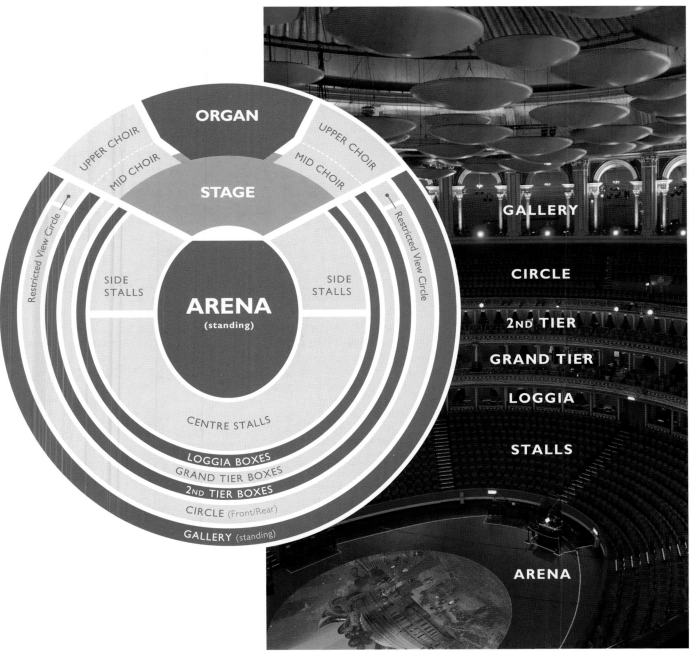

ORGAN

UPPER CHOIR

MID CHOIR

STAGE

Restricted View Circle

SIDE STALLS

ARENA (standing)

SIDE STALLS

Restricted View Circle

CENTRE STALLS

LOGGIA BOXES

GRAND TIER BOXES

2ND TIER BOXES

CIRCLE (Front/Rear)

GALLERY (standing)

GALLERY

CIRCLE

2ND TIER

GRAND TIER

LOGGIA

STALLS

ARENA

BOOK ONLINE AT **BBC.CO.UK/PROMS** • BY TELEPHONE **0845 401 5040*** • IN PERSON AT THE **ROYAL ALBERT HALL** • BOOKING OPENS 9.00AM ON 17 MAY

HOW TO BOOK

Booking opens on Saturday 17 May at 9.00am – online, by telephone and in person. Tickets may also be requested by post.

Promming Season Tickets and Weekend Promming Passes are available to purchase online, by phone and in person from 9.00am on Friday 16 May.

For **Promming** (standing) tickets in the Arena and Gallery, priced £5.00, see page 158.

Owing to high demand, special booking arrangements apply to **Last Night of the Proms** tickets: see page 159.

For **Proms in the Park** tickets, see page 157.

Tickets for the **Free Prom** (Prom 51) are available from Friday 4 July. Please note there is a limit of four tickets per booking.

ONLINE

Thursday 24 April (2.00pm) to Friday 16 May (midnight)

Use the **Proms Planner**, accessible via bbc.co.uk/proms (see instructions below), to create your personal Proms Plan. Once completed, this is ready for you to submit as soon as booking opens at 9.00am on Saturday 17 May. The Proms Planner allows you to create and amend your personal Proms Plan at your leisure before tickets go on sale, at any time from 2.00pm on Thursday 24 April until midnight on Friday 16 May. Submitting your Proms Plan as soon as booking opens speeds up the booking process and means that you may be more successful in securing your preferred tickets for concerts in high demand.

Promming Season Tickets and Weekend Promming Passes are not included in the Proms Planner and will be available to purchase online, by phone and in person from 9.00am on Friday 16 May.

Should you not wish to use the Proms Planner, you can visit www.royalalberthall.com from 9.00am on Saturday 17 May to book your tickets online. Please note that the website will experience very high demand for tickets that day, so you will be placed in a queue.

A continuous connection between your computer and the Royal Albert Hall's website is required to maintain your place in the queue. We suggest that you use a computer rather than a mobile device or tablet while queuing.

How to use the Proms Planner

- From 2.00pm on Thursday 24 April select 'Plan Your Proms Tickets' at bbc.co.uk/proms. (You will be redirected to www.royalalberthall.com.)

- Select 'Create My Proms Plan'. Then create an account (or log in if you are an existing user) and start choosing the concerts you would like to attend, along with the number of tickets and preferred seating area. You can amend your Proms Plan at any time until midnight on Friday 16 May.

  Please note: this is a request system and there is no guarantee that the tickets you select in your Proms Plan will be available once booking has opened.

- From 9.00am on Saturday 17 May visit www.royalalberthall.com and log in to your Proms Plan in order to submit it. We expect exceptionally high demand, so you will be held in an online waiting room before you are able to log in: you will be informed how many people precede you in the queue (you do not need to refresh the page). **You must submit your Proms Plan in order to make a booking.**

- Your Proms Plan will now have been updated to reflect live ticket availability and you will be given the chance to cancel tickets or choose alternatives should your selected tickets or seating areas have become unavailable.

- Confirm your online booking by submitting your Proms Plan and entering your payment details.

- Your booking will be confirmed by email.

Please note: it is not possible to book entire boxes online. If you would like to book a full box, call the Box Office on 0845 401 5040* from 9.00am on Saturday 17 May.

The 'Select Your Own Seat' option is not available via the Proms Planner or during the first few days that Proms tickets are on sale. You will be allocated the best available places within your chosen seating area. This is to allow as many customers as possible to book as efficiently as possible and to speed up the queue during the period of high demand.

If you have any queries about how to use the Proms Planner, call the Royal Albert Hall Box Office on **0845 401 5040***.

From 9.00am on Saturday 17 May

From 9.00am on Saturday 17 May you can book online at **www.royalalberthall.com**. If you already have a Proms Plan, you can redeem your plan and process your booking. If you do not have a Proms Plan, you can just book online. You will not be able to create a Proms Plan at this time.

A booking fee of 2% of the total value (plus £1.50 per ticket up to a maximum of £20.00 per booking) applies. (For Proms in the Park booking fee information, see page 157.)

BY TELEPHONE

From 9.00am on Saturday 17 May, call the Royal Albert Hall Box Office on **0845 401 5040*** (open 9.00am–9.00pm daily). From outside the UK, please call +44 20 7589 8212.

A booking fee of 2% of the total value (plus £1.50 per ticket up to a maximum of £20.00 per booking) applies. (For Proms in the Park booking fee information, see page 157.)

IN PERSON

From 9.00am on Saturday 17 May, visit the Royal Albert Hall Box Office at Door 12. (The Box Office is open 9.00am–9.00pm daily.)

No fees apply to tickets bought in person. (For Proms in the Park booking fee information, see page 157.)

BY POST

Please write to BBC Proms, Box Office, Royal Albert Hall, London SW7 2AP with the following details:

- your name, address, telephone number(s) and email address (if applicable)
- the concerts you wish to attend
- number of tickets required

*SEE PAGE 163 FOR CALL-COST INFORMATION

HOW TO BOOK

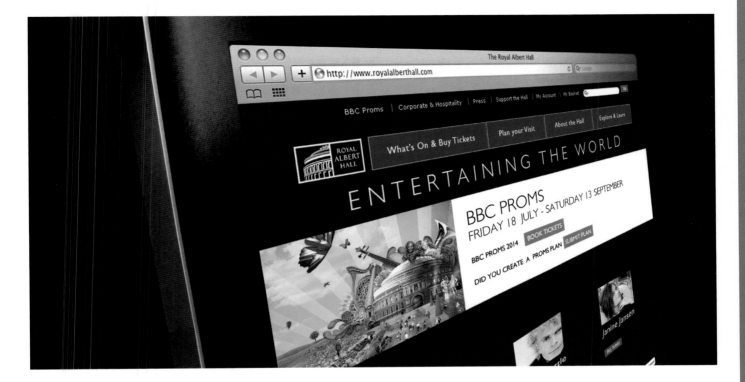

- preferred seating section, preferably with alternatives (see ticket prices on page 160 and seating plan on page 161)
- applicable discounts (see pages 164 & 168)
- a cheque, payable to 'Royal Albert Hall' and made out for the maximum amount (including booking fees); or your credit card details, including type of card, name on the card, card number, issue number (Maestro only), start date, expiry date and security code (last three digits on back of Visa/Mastercard or last four digits on front of American Express).

Your details will be held securely. Postal bookings will start to be processed from 9.00am on Saturday 17 May, when booking opens, in random order (not the order in which they were received).

Postal bookings for Season Tickets and Weekend Promming Passes must be made separately to other booking requests. Please mark your envelope 'Proms Season Ticket/Weekend Pass' and these bookings will be processed from 9.00am on Friday 16 May in random order.

A booking fee of 2% of the total value (plus £1.50 per ticket up to a maximum of £20.00 per booking) applies. (For Proms in the Park booking-fee information, see page 157.)

*Calls cost up to 5p/min from most landlines (an additional connection fee may also apply). Calls from mobiles may cost considerably more. All calls will be recorded and may be monitored for training and quality-control purposes.

TICKETS SOLD OUT? DON'T GIVE UP!

If you are unable to get tickets for a popular Prom, **keep trying** at bbc.co.uk/proms or the Royal Albert Hall Box Office, as returns often become available. In addition, many boxes and some seats at the Royal Albert Hall are privately owned, and these seats may be returned for general sale in the period leading up to the concert. The Royal Albert Hall does not operate a waiting list.

If you can't sit, stand
Up to 1,400 Promming (standing) places are available in the Arena and Gallery on the day for every Prom at the Royal Albert Hall. If you arrive early enough on the day of the concert, you have a very good chance of getting in. For more details, see page 158.

SPECIAL OFFERS

SAME-DAY SAVERS

Book seats for more than one concert on the same day, and save up to £4.00 per ticket for the later concert. This discount is available through all booking methods, including online and via the Proms Planner. When booking online, it will be applied automatically at the checkout stage.

This offer applies to performances at the Royal Albert Hall only, excluding the Arena and Gallery standing areas and the Restricted View Circle seating area. Please note that Prom 51 (the Free Prom) is excluded from this offer. *See page 160 for ticket prices.*

SAME-DAY SAVER

UNDER-18s GO HALF-PRICE

The Proms are a great way to discover live music and we encourage anyone over 5 years old to attend. Tickets for persons aged 18 and under can be purchased at half price in any seating area for all Proms except the Last Night (Prom 76). This discount is available through all booking methods, including online and via the Proms Planner.

GREAT SAVINGS FOR GROUPS

Groups of 10 or more can claim a 10% discount (5% for C-band and D-band concerts) on the price of Centre/Side Stalls or Front/Rear Circle tickets (excluding the Last Night), subject to availability. See page 160 for ticket prices.

Please note: group bookings can only be made by phone or in person at the Royal Albert Hall.
To make a group booking, or for more information, call the Group Booking Information Line on 020 7070 4408 (from 9.00am on Saturday 17 May).

PROMMING SEASON TICKETS AND WEEKEND PROMMING PASSES

With the Arena or Gallery Promming Season Tickets and Arena or Gallery Weekend Promming Passes you can save money and get guaranteed entrance up to 20 minutes before the start-time.

Season Tickets and Weekend Promming Passes can be purchased online, by phone, by post or in person at the Royal Albert Hall Box Office from 9.00am on Friday 16 May. These tickets cannot be planned online via the Proms Planner.

Season Tickets are non-transferable and two passport-sized photographs must be provided before tickets can be issued.

Whole-Season Tickets include admission to the Last Night and Half-Season Ticket-holders have special access to a reserved allocation of Last Night Tickets (see page 159).

Weekend Promming Passes must be purchased a minimum of two hours before the start of the first concert covered. Prices vary for each weekend depending on the number of concerts covered – see box right.

Please note: you may purchase a maximum of four passes per weekend.

Passes are non-transferable and ID may be requested upon entry.

There is no Weekend Promming Pass covering Proms 75 and 76. Weekend Promming Passes are not valid for concerts at Cadogan Hall.

Purchase of a Weekend Promming Pass does not guarantee entry to the Last Night, but tickets may be counted towards the Five-Concert Ballot (see page 159) in conjunction with further Passes or Day Ticket stubs.

Please note: holders of Season Tickets and Weekend Promming Passes arriving at the Hall less than 20 minutes before a concert are not guaranteed entry and should join the back of the Day Queue.

All Promming Season Tickets and Weekend Promming Passes are subject to availability.

Promming Season Tickets	Arena	Gallery
Whole Season Proms 1–76 18 July – 13 September	£200.00	£200.00
First Half Proms 1–38 18 July – 14 August	£120.00	£120.00
Second Half Proms 39–75 15 August – 12 September	£120.00	£120.00
Booking fees apply (see page 160)		

Weekend Promming Pass prices		
Weekend 1	Proms 1–4	£18.00
Weekend 2	Proms 10–14 *(not including Proms 11 & 13, CBeebies Proms)*	£13.50
Weekend 3	Proms 20–23	£18.00
Weekend 4	Proms 29–33	£22.50
Weekend 5	Proms 39–42	£18.00
Weekend 6	Proms 48–50	£13.50
Weekend 7	Proms 57–59	£13.50
Weekend 8	Proms 64–68	£22.50
Booking fees apply (see page 160)		

PROMS CHAMBER MUSIC SERIES PASS (CADOGAN HALL)

Hear all eight Monday-lunchtime Proms Chamber Music concerts for just £30.00 (plus booking fee, see page 160), with guaranteed entrance to the Side Gallery until 12.50pm (after which Proms Chamber Music Series Pass-holders may be asked to join the Day Queue). Passes can be purchased from 9.00am on Friday 16 May online, by phone or in person at the Royal Albert Hall. Two passport-sized photographs must be provided.

Please note: Proms Chamber Music Series Passes cannot be purchased from Cadogan Hall. Proms Chamber Music Series Passes are not valid for Proms Saturday Matinee concerts at Cadogan Hall and are subject to availability.

164 | BOOKING INFORMATION

BOOK ONLINE AT BBC.CO.UK/PROMS • BY TELEPHONE 0845 401 5040* • IN PERSON AT THE ROYAL ALBERT HALL • BOOKING OPENS 9.00AM ON 17 MAY

ROYAL ALBERT HALL   Kensington Gore, London SW7 2AP *(see map overleaf)* www.royalalberthall.com

FOOD AND DRINK AT THE ROYAL ALBERT HALL

With six restaurants, 14 bars and box catering, there is a wide range of food and drink to enjoy at the Royal Albert Hall, from two and a half hours before each concert.

The Hall's new Italian restaurant, Verdi, is open for lunch and dinner, offering stone-baked pizza and traditional pasta dishes. (Café Consort has been refurbished as Verdi.)

Booking in advance is recommended. Visit www.royalalberthall.com or call the Box Office on 0845 401 5040* to make your reservation.

BARS are located throughout the building, and open two and a half hours before each concert.

INTERVAL ORDERS made in a bar before the concert receive a 10% discount.

RESTAURANTS

Verdi – Italian Kitchen offers casual dining and authentic Italian dishes. (First Floor, Door 12, access from Ground level)

The Elgar Bar & Grill is relaxed and stylish, offering fantastic flavours from the Josper Grill. (Circle level, Door 9)

The Elgar Room will stay open late on 19 & 26 July, 2, 9, 15, 23 & 30 August and 6 September for the informal Proms Plus Late events – see bbc.co.uk/proms for more information.

Coda Restaurant offers food and fine wine in a classic ambience. Choose from a two-course set menu, or French-influenced à la carte dishes. (Circle level, Door 3)

Cloudy Bay Wine Bar is the perfect place to enjoy light seafood and fish dishes alongside complementary wines. (Second Tier, Door 3)

Berry Bros. & Rudd No. 3 Bar serves a selection of seasonal British dishes, sharing plates, wine and cocktails. (Basement level, Door 1)

Café Bar serves food and drink all day, including cakes, pastries, salads and sandwiches. The bar is open until 11.00pm. (Ground Floor, Door 12)

GRAND TIER, SECOND TIER AND LOGGIA BOX SEATS

If you have seats in one of the Royal Albert Hall's boxes, you can pre-order food and drinks to be served upon arrival or at the interval. The selection ranges from sandwiches and smoked salmon blinis to hot pies. Visit boxcatering.royalalberthall.com and please order at least 48 hours before the concert that you are attending.

Please note: the consumption of your own food and drink in the Hall is not permitted. In the interests of health and safety, drinks may only be taken into the auditorium in plastic containers and only cold drinks are allowed in the Promming (standing) areas. Glasses and bottles are permitted in boxes, as part of box catering ordered through "rhubarb".

CAR PARKING A limited number of parking spaces, priced £10.20 each (including a 20p card handling fee), are available from 6.00pm (or two hours before weekend matinee concerts) in the Imperial College car park. Entrances are located on Prince Consort Road (open daily until 7.00pm) and Exhibition Road. Vouchers are only valid until 45 minutes after the end of the concert. These can be booked online, by phone or in person at the Royal Albert Hall from 9.00am on Saturday 17 May, and planned online via the Proms Planner from 2.00pm on Thursday 24 April. Please note that, if you are attending both early-evening and late-night concerts on the same day, only one parking fee is payable.

DOORS OPEN 45 minutes before the start of each concert (two and a half hours for restaurant and bar access) and 30 minutes before each late-night concert. Tickets will be scanned upon entry. Please have them ready, one per person.

LATECOMERS will not be admitted into the auditorium unless or until there is a suitable break in the performance.

BAGS AND COATS may be left in the cloakrooms at Door 9 (ground level) and at basement level beneath Door 6. A charge of £1.00 per item applies (cloakroom season tickets priced £20.40, including a 40p card handling fee, are also available). Conditions apply – see www.royalalberthall.com. For reasons of safety and comfort, only small bags are permitted in the Arena. If you bring multiple bags, you may only be allowed to take one bag into the Arena for busy concerts.

SECURITY In the interests of safety, bags may be searched upon entry.

CHILDREN UNDER 5 are not allowed in the auditorium out of consideration for both audience and artists, with the exception of the CBeebies Proms (Proms 11 & 13).

DRESS CODE Come as you are: there is no dress code at the Proms.

MOBILE PHONES and other electronic devices are distracting to other audience members. Please ensure they are switched off.

THE USE OF CAMERAS, video cameras and recording equipment is strictly forbidden.

HISTORY OF THE PROMS TOURS OF THE ROYAL ALBERT HALL To learn more about the fascinating history of the Proms at the Royal Albert Hall, join a bespoke seasonal tour. For bookings, availability and further information, including the Royal Albert Hall's regular Grand Tours, call 0845 401 5045* or visit www.royalalberthall.com. For group bookings of 15 people or more, call 020 7959 0558.

A selection of **PROMS AND ROYAL ALBERT HALL GIFTS AND MERCHANDISE** is available inside the porches at Doors 6 and 12 and on the Circle level at Doors 4 and 8.

Royal Albert Hall

GETTING THERE
Royal Albert Hall & Royal College of Music

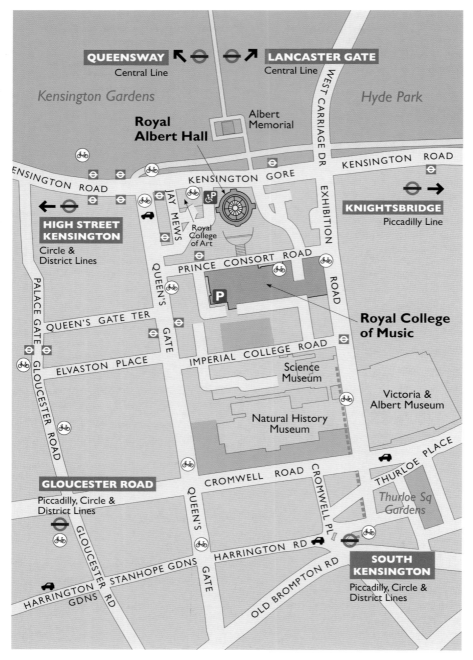

QUEENSWAY
Central Line

LANCASTER GATE
Central Line

Kensington Gardens

Hyde Park

Albert Memorial

Royal Albert Hall

KENSINGTON GORE

KENSINGTON ROAD

KENSINGTON ROAD

WEST CARRIAGE DR

HIGH STREET KENSINGTON
Circle & District Lines

KNIGHTSBRIDGE
Piccadilly Line

JAY MEWS

Royal College of Art

EXHIBITION ROAD

PRINCE CONSORT ROAD

QUEEN'S GATE

Royal College of Music

PALACE GATE

QUEEN'S GATE TER

ELVASTON PLACE

IMPERIAL COLLEGE ROAD

Science Museum

GLOUCESTER ROAD

Natural History Museum

Victoria & Albert Museum

GLOUCESTER ROAD
Piccadilly, Circle & District Lines

CROMWELL ROAD

CROMWELL PL

THURLOE PLACE

Thurloe Sq Gardens

QUEEN'S GATE

HARRINGTON RD

SOUTH KENSINGTON
Piccadilly, Circle & District Lines

GLOUCESTER RD

HARRINGTON GDNS

STANHOPE GDNS

OLD BROMPTON RD

KEY
- ⊖ Tube station
- Ⓔ Bus stop
- 🚖 Taxi rank
- 🚲 Barclays Cycle Hire
- --- Foot tunnel

The nearest Tube stations are High Street Kensington (Circle & District Lines) and South Kensington (Piccadilly, Circle & District Lines). These are all a 10- to 15-minute walk from the Hall.

The following buses serve the Royal Albert Hall and Royal College of Music (via Kensington Gore, Queen's Gate, Palace Gate and/or Prince Consort Road): 9/N9, 10 (24-hour service), 49, 52/N52, 70, 360 & 452. Coaches 701 and 702 also serve this area.

Bicycle racks are near Door 11 of the Royal Albert Hall. (Neither the Hall nor the BBC can accept responsibility for items lost or stolen from these racks.) The Royal Albert Hall has limited cloakroom space and may not be able to accept folding bicycles. Barclays Cycle Hire racks are positioned outside the Royal College of Art, the Royal College of Music and in Cadogan Place.

Please note: the Royal Albert Hall is not within the Congestion Charge zone.

For car parking at the Royal Albert Hall, see page 165.

CADOGAN HALL

5 Sloane Terrace,
London
SW1X 9DQ
www.cadoganhall.com

DOORS OPEN at 11.00am for Proms Chamber Music concerts (entrance to the auditorium from 12.30pm); and at 1.00pm for Proms Saturday Matinees (entrance to the auditorium from 2.30pm).

LATECOMERS will not be admitted unless or until there is a suitable break in the music.

BAGS AND COATS may be left in the cloakroom on the lower ground level.

CHILDREN UNDER 5 are not admitted to Cadogan Hall out of consideration for both audience and artists.

DRESS CODE Come as you are: there is no dress code at the Proms.

MOBILE PHONES and other electronic devices are distracting to other audience members. Please ensure they are switched off.

THE USE OF CAMERAS, video cameras and recording equipment is strictly forbidden.

GETTING THERE The following buses serve Cadogan Hall (via Sloane Street and/or Sloane Square): 11, 19, 22, 137, 170, 211, 319, 360, 452 & C1.

FOOD AND DRINK AT CADOGAN HALL

A selection of savouries, sandwiches and cakes are available from the Oakley Bar and Café. The café and bar will be open at 11.00am for Proms Chamber Music Concerts and at 1.00pm before Proms Saturday Matinees.

Cadogan Hall's bars offer a large selection of champagne, wines, spirits, beer, soft drinks and tea and coffee.

CAR PARKING

Please check street signs for details. Discounted car parking for Cadogan Hall performers and customers is available at the NCP Car Park, Cadogan Place, just 10 minutes' walk from Cadogan Hall. Parking vouchers are available on request from the Box Office.

ROYAL COLLEGE OF MUSIC

Prince Consort Road, London SW7 2BS
(see map, page 166) www.rcm.ac.uk

PROMS PLUS

Proms Plus pre-concert events will be held in the Amaryllis Fleming Concert Hall at the Royal College of Music.

Proms Plus events are free of charge and unticketed (seating is unreserved), with the exception of the First Night live *In Tune* event on Friday 18 July, for which free tickets will be available from BBC Studio Audiences (bbc.co.uk/tickets or 0370 901 1227†). Places must be reserved in advance for all Proms Plus Family Orchestra & Chorus events and most Proms Plus Sing events (visit bbc.co.uk/proms or call 020 7765 0557).

Please note: all Proms Plus events are subject to capacity and we advise arriving early for the more popular events. Latecomers will be admitted but, as many of these events are being recorded for broadcast, you may have to wait until a suitable break. The event stewards will guide you.

Prommers who join the Royal Albert Hall queue before the Proms Plus event should make sure they take a numbered slip from one of the Royal Albert Hall stewards to secure their place back in the queue.

If you have special access requirements, see the Royal College of Music information on page 169.

†*Standard geographic charges from landlines and mobiles will apply.*

ACCESS AT THE PROMS

PROMS ACCESS INFORMATION LINE:

020 7070 4410 (9.00am–9.00pm daily)

To download an Access Guide, visit www.royalalberthall.com/visit/accessibility/default.aspx

ACCESSIBLE PRINT MATERIALS

- Audio CD and Braille versions of this Guide are available in two parts, 'Articles' and 'Concert Listings/Booking Information', priced £3.00 each. For more information and to order, call the RNIB Helpline on 0303 123 9999.

- A text-only large-print version of the Proms Guide is available, priced £6.50.

- Large-print concert programmes can be made available on the night (at the same price as the standard programme) if ordered not less than five working days in advance.

- Complimentary large-print texts and opera librettos (where applicable) can also be made available on the night if ordered in advance.

To order any large-print BBC Proms Guide, programmes or texts, please call 020 7765 3246. The programmes and texts will be left for collection at the Door 6 Information Desk 45 minutes before the start of the concert.

TICKETS AND DISCOUNTS FOR DISABLED CONCERT-GOERS

All disabled concert-goers (and one companion) receive a 50% discount on all ticket prices (except Arena and Gallery areas) for concerts at the Royal Albert Hall and Cadogan Hall. To claim this discount, call the Access Information Line (from Saturday 17 May) if booking by phone. Note that discounts for disabled concert-goers cannot be combined with other ticket offers.

Tickets can also be purchased in person from 9.00am on Saturday 17 May at the Royal Albert Hall. The Box Office has ramped access, an induction loop and drop-down counters. Please note that there is no loop

system in the auditorium.

Ambulant disabled concert-goers can also book tickets online from 9.00am on Saturday 17 May and use the online Proms Planner from 2.00pm on Thursday 24 April. Please note that the 'Select Your Own Seat' facility will not be available to customers booking online at this time – customers will be offered 'best available' seats within the chosen section. Wheelchair spaces cannot be booked online or via the Proms Planner.

PROMMING TICKETS FOR AMBULANT DISABLED CONCERT-GOERS

Up to 20 seats in both the Arena and Gallery will be available for reservation each day by ambulant disabled concert-goers (disabled concert-goers who do not use a wheelchair) who wish to Prom. On arrival at the Royal Albert Hall, ask a steward (on duty from 9.00am) for a **Seat Reservation Card**, along with your queue number. You can then leave the queue, returning in time for doors opening, at which point all Prommers will enter in queue order. If you secure entry with a Seat Reservation Card, a seat will have been reserved for you. These arrangements (a trial for 2014) will apply to ambulant disabled concert-goers in both the Season and Day queues for the Arena and Gallery. Please note, a Seat Reservation Card does not guarantee entry.

PROMMING TICKETS FOR WHEELCHAIR USERS

The Gallery can accomodate up to four wheelchair users. On arrival at the Royal Albert Hall, ask a steward for assistance. Wheelchair users will be issued a queue number and, as above, can leave and return in time for doors opening, at which point all Prommers will enter in queue order. Please note the Arena is not accessible to wheelchair users.

ROYAL ALBERT HALL

The Royal Albert Hall has a silver-level award from the Attitude is Everything Charter of Best Practice. Full information on the facilities offered to disabled concert-goers (including car parking) is available online at www.royalalberthall.com. Information is also available through the Access Information Line.

Provision for disabled concert-goers includes:

- 20 spaces bookable for wheelchair-users with adjacent companion spaces. For more details and to book call the Access Information Line.

- Six additional Side Stalls wheelchair spaces available for Proms 58–76.

- Ramped access, located at Doors 1, 3, 8, 9 and 12. For arrival by car, taxi, minibus or Dial-a-Ride, the most convenient set-down point is at Door 1, which is at the rear of the building and has ramped access.

- A small car park for disabled concert-goers adjacent to the Royal Albert Hall

- Public lifts located at Doors 1 and 8 with automatic doors, Braille, tactile numbering and voice announcements.

- Accessibility for wheelchair-users to all bars and restaurants.

Wheelchair spaces and car parking can be booked by calling the Access Information Line or in person at the Royal Albert Hall Box Office. For information on wheelchair spaces available for the Last Night of the Proms via the Five-Concert Ballot, see page 159.

ACCESS AT THE PROMS

Other services available on request are as follows:

- The Royal Albert Hall auditorium has an infra-red system with a number of personal headsets for use with or without hearing aids. Headsets can be collected on arrival from the Information Desk at Door 6.
- If you have a guide or hearing dog, the best place to sit in the Royal Albert Hall is in a box, where your dog may stay with you. If you prefer to sit elsewhere, stewards will happy to look after your dog while you enjoy the concert.
- Transfer wheelchairs are available for customer use.
- A Royal Albert Hall steward will be happy to read your concert programme to you.

To request any of the above services, please call the Box Office Access line or complete an accessibility request form online at www.royalalberthall.com 48 hours before you attend. Alternatively you can make a request upon arrival at the Information Desk at Door 6 on the Ground Floor, subject to availability.

CADOGAN HALL

Cadogan Hall has a range of services to assist disabled customers, including:

- Three wheelchair spaces in the Stalls available for advance booking and one space reserved for sale as a day ticket from 10.00am on the day of the concert. Please note, there is no lift access to the Gallery.
- Box Office counter fitted with a loop system
- An infra-red amplification system in the auditorium. This is not the same as a loop system, so switching your hearing aid to 'T' is not sufficient. You will need to use an amplification aid.

Guide dogs are welcome to access the Hall and auditorium but please contact Cadogan Hall prior to arrival, so that any special arrangements can be made if necessary.

For further information, call 020 7730 4500.

ROYAL COLLEGE OF MUSIC

The Royal College of Music has a range of services to assist disabled customers, including:

- Six spaces for wheelchair-users in the Amaryllis Fleming Concert Hall
- An induction loop installed in the Amaryllis Fleming Concert Hall
- Step-free access from Prince Consort Road, located to the left of the main entrance.

If you require further assistance for your visit, contact the Facilities Team on 020 7591 4322 or email facilitiesstaff@rcm.ac.uk.

For further information, call the Royal College of Music on 020 7591 4314.

INDEX OF ARTISTS

Bold italic figures refer to Prom numbers
PCM indicates Proms Chamber Music concerts at Cadogan Hall
PSM indicates Proms Saturday Matinee concerts at Cadogan Hall
*first appearance at a BBC Henry Wood Promenade Concert
‡current / ‡former member of BBC Radio 3's New Generation Artists scheme

INDEX OF WORKS

Bold italic figures refer to Prom numbers
PCM indicates Proms Chamber Music concerts at Cadogan Hall
PSM indicates Proms Saturday Matinee concerts at Cadogan Hall
*first performance at a BBC Henry Wood Promenade Concert

INDEX OF WORKS

BBC Proms 2014

Director Roger Wright, Controller BBC Radio 3 and Director BBC Proms

Personal Assistant Yvette Pusey
Editor, BBC Radio 3 and BBC Proms Edward Blakeman
Concerts and Events Manager, BBC Radio 3 and BBC Proms Helen Heslop
Events Co-ordinators, BBC Proms and BBC Radio 3 Tammy Daly, Helen White
Concerts and Events Assistants Lucy Barrie, Julia Vivian
Concerts and Learning Administrator Ayesha Labrom
Concerts Assistant Katharine Plows
Concerts Department Assistant Elinor Camlin

Head of Marketing, Publications and Learning Kate Finch

Communications Manager Camilla Dervan
Assistant Publicist Victoria Taylor
Publicity Assistant Hannah Doughty

Marketing Manager Emily Caket
Marketing Assistant Sarah Byrne

Senior Learning Manager Ellara Wakely
Learning Co-ordinators Rebecca Burns, Lauren Creed, Becky Dixon
Learning Administrator Rebecca Hill

Business Co-ordinator Tricia Twigg

Head of Music Television (London) Mark Cooper
Executive Producer, Music Television Francesca Kemp
Series Production Manager Michael Ledger

Business Affairs Executives Sarah Bredl-Jones, Penelope Davies, Hilary Dodds, John Hunter, Anne-Marie Kelly, Pamela Wise

Editor, BBC Proms, Performing Groups and Radio 3 Multiplatform Steve Bowbrick
Editorial Lead, BBC Proms Multiplatform Andrew Downs

BBC PROMS GUIDE 2014

Publications Editor Laura Davis
Editor Edward Bhesania
Sub-Editor Úna-Frances Clarke
Publications Designers Christie Brewster, Nick Edwards
Publications Assistant Francesca Geach

Published by BBC Proms Publications
Room 1045, Broadcasting House, London W1A 1AA

Cover illustration Justin Krietermeyer/Premm Design/Red Bee Media/
RAH photography by Simon Keats

Distributed by BBC Books, an imprint of Ebury Publishing, a Random House Group Company, 20 Vauxhall Bridge Road, London SW1V 2SA
Advertising Cabbell Publishing Ltd, London (020 3603 7930)
Printed by APS Group. APS Group holds ISO 14001 environmental management, FSC and PEFC accreditations

© BBC 2014. All details were correct at time of going to press
ISBN 978-1-849-90810-8